ISBN 0-87666-735-3

© 1981 by T.F.H. Publications, Inc. Ltd.

Distributed in the U.S. by T.F.H. Publications, Inc., 211 West Sylvania
Avenue, PO Box 427, Neptune, NJ 07753; in England by T.F.H. (Gt. Britain)
Ltd., 13 Nutley Lane, Reigate, Surrey; in Canada to the pet trade by Rolf C.
Hagen Ltd., 3225 Sartelon Street, Montreal 382, Quebec; in Canada to the
book trade by H & L Pet Supplies, Inc., 27 Kingston Crescent, Kitchener,
Ontario N28 2T6; in Southeast Asia by Y.W. Ong, 9 Lorong 36 Geylang,
Singapore 14; in Australia and the South Pacific by Pet Imports Pty. Ltd.,
P.O. Box 149, Brookvale 2100, N.S.W. Australia; in South Africa by Valid
Agencies, P.O. Box 51901, Randburg 2125 South Africa. Published by T.F.H.
Publications, Inc., Ltd., the British Crown Colony of Hong Kong.

THE BOOK
OF THE
ROTTWEILER

by Anna Katherine Nicholas

The late Winifred Heckmann smiles admiringly at Ch. Srigo's Zinger having just placed this lovely puppy Winners Bitch. Felicia Luburich proudly handling.

Opposite:
All the nobility of his breed is extremely obvious in this handsome front view of Ch. Graudstark's Luger depicted so well through the camera of famed dog photographer Alton Anderson. Luger belongs to the Mark Schwartzes of West Nyack, NY.

Dedicated To
All those Rottweiler fanciers who
have supported this venture with
information and photographs. And
to this wonderful breed which I so
sincerely and enthusiastically admire
With my affection and esteem.

WINNERS
BUCKS COUNTY
KENNEL CLUB, INC.
MAY 5 1979

Ch. Windmaker's Arno der Gremlin is owned by James R. and Wanda White, Hickory, NC. Although an active Basset breeder and popular judge of hounds, Mr. White is also a great fancier of Rottweilers. Arlo finished in seven shows with three majors, and as a special has accounted for 19 Best of Breed wins, a Working Group first, and a Working Group second. Shown sparingly and always owner-handled by Wanda White, he is by Ch. Lyn-Mar Acres Arras v Kinta ex Plaisance Irmo; bred by Ron Gibson.

Opposite:
Ch. Radio Ranch's X-per-tease pictured at nine months taking a five point major from the puppy class. This excellent dog became one of the Top Ten Rottweilers for 1980. Shown here with Tom Sallen, co-owner with Radio Ranch.

Front cover: Ch. Radio Ranch's Axel v Notara, Top Winner and Top Producer. Sire of 27 champions including three Specialty winners and three Top Winners. Best of Breed at Westminster Kennel Club show 1976. Owner, Pamela Weller, Radio Ranch Rottweilers. Photographer, Fred Habit, Chesapeake, VA.

Back cover: Rottweiler, bred and owned by Ron Gibson, Tinton Falls, New Jersey. Photographer, Ronald Reagan, Asbury Park, NJ.

Front endpaper: A family portrait from Bethel Farms Rottweilers (from left): Ch. Bethel Farms Annon v Max, Ch. Bethel Farms Apollo, Ch. Graudstark's Irma La Deuce, Ch. Graudstarks' Adra v Bethel, Ch. Bethel Farms Ali, Ch. Bethel Farms Angela. Bethel Farm owners are Bob and Lavinia Bolden. Photo by William Gilbert.

Back endpaper: Ch. Graudstark's Irma La Deuce, CD, RO 753 (left) winning the Brood Bitch class over 11 entries at the Colonial Rottweiler Club's 1979 Specialty. Five champions at the Specialty were her get. Pictured with her are two Group placing progeny, Ch. Bethel Farms Ali and Ch. Bethel Farms Apollo (far right). Photo by William Gilbert.

Inside photographs by: Lloyd Olson, Martin Booth, John Ashbey, William Gilbert, Don Petrulis, J.D. Van Sickle, Evelyn Shafer, Glen T. Correia, Rich Bergman, Fred Habit, Earl Graham, Cammar, Cott/Francis, Stephen Klein, Clark, Jack Ritter. All other photos courtesy of private contributors.

Contents

A stunning Best of Breed winner, Ch. Srigo's Front Runner.

Opposite:
Canadian Ch. Kyladie's Avitar the Wiz, CD, at nine
months. Mr. Aime and Mrs. Adele Brosseau, owners.

Catherine M. Thompson with her first prize-winning brace, Von Gailingen's Dark Delight, CD (left), and Ch. Von Gailingen's Dassie Did It (Winners bitch and Best of Winners from the Bred-by Exhibitor Class) at the Colonial Rottweiler Club Specialty, Trenton Kennel Club, 1980.

Opposite:
Am., Can. Ch. Greta vom Hohenreissach, CD, is co-owned by Kristin M. Rugg and Judith Ann Coen. She finished her championship during National Capital week end in 1975 going Best of Opposite Sex in keen competition, and completed her obedience title when seven years old.

In
Appreciation

A number of people are responsible for the contents of this book and have contributed inestimably towards its authenticity and success.

Dr. Joseph P. Sayres, D.V.M., merits our thanks for what we consider to be an especially outstanding section, *The Veterinarian's Corner*. In addition to being a highly respected and well accredited veterinarian, Dr. Sayres is particularly well versed in the point of view of dog breeders and owners, since he is also a breeder of Irish Terriers as well as a judge. He is a member of a famous and distinguished family of dog authorities. His father, Edwin A. Sayres, Sr. and his two brothers, Henry and Edwin, Jr., all earned positions of respect in the Fancy. Dr. Sayres truly is a dog fancier who grew up knowing, studying and understanding these animals. His knowledge, experience and expertise are clearly evident as one reads the pages he has written.

To Norma and James Harwood, our gratitude for "The Early History of the Rottweiler in Germany", plus several fascinating and valuable charts on famous bloodlines, and at least several dozen of our pictures of "pillars of the breed". The time and effort they have contributed has added immensely to the importance of this book.

Dr. Evelyn Ellman has done translations for us, gathered information here and in Europe, put us in touch with numerous people who own and love the breed. Quite literally, it would have been difficult to manage without her counsel and assistance!

Barbara Hoard Dillon has discussed "The Rottweiler Standard As Applied To The Show Ring" knowledgeably and well. A very noted authority on this breed, she put in long hours with the committee from the American Rottweiler Club that worked on the revision of the Standard. Who could be better qualified to discuss and explain it? Our heartfelt thanks to her.

Dorothea Gruenerwald has supported this venture with helpful facts and information in general, as well as specifics regarding her own dogs.

Dorit Rogers, too, deserves our appreciation for background information on early Rottweiler breeders, and for having loaned us some practically unavailable photographs of important dogs.

Clara Hurley is another source of help to whom we are grateful, and to Jan Marshall for her advice and counsel.

Arthur and Ruth Twiss did the excellent chapter, "Tracking With Your Rottweiler" and supplied the pictures illustrating it along with others. They too played a part in briefing us on historical information from the New England area.

And Cathy Thompson is a lady without whom it would have been far more difficult to gather important facts. Our gratitude goes to her for suggestions, some stunning photography and a good deal of obedience information and statistical facts.

The American Rottweiler Club and its individual members have assisted in so very many ways. Our particular thanks to the Top Ten Committee, of which Kathy Evans is Chairman.

Marcia Foy has contributed much time and effort here at home helping to gather facts for this book. We are grateful.

It is difficult to express the depth of our appreciation to every single Rottweiler Club, Rottweiler breeder or owner or exhibitor, and Rottweiler handler who loaned photos and contributed information about the dogs with which they are, or have been associated. We couldn't have done this book without you, and we treasure the friends we've made along the way.

Thank you all!

Anna Katherine Nicholas

Gurley's Wildwood Bruiser, is pictured winning a four point major for owners Delores and Dale Gurley, Eufaula, AL. Handled by Millie Daughtry.

Opposite:
Above: Nello von Stolzenfels, or "Moosey" is pictured at seven months. Bred by the Ellmans, owned by John Wahl. **Below:** A puppy of great promise, Thor von Germelshausen, (by Ch. Ero von der Mauth ex Ch. Shana Tova von Paulus, CD) bred and owned by Mrs. Betty Bilsky. Thor is pictured at eight weeks of age.

23

About the Author

From early childhood, Anna Katherine Nicholas has been involved with dogs. Her first pets were a Boston Terrier, an Airedale and a German Shepherd. Then in 1925 came the first Pekingese, a gift from a friend who raised the breed. Now her home is shared with a Miniature Poodle and a dozen or so Beagles including her noted Best in Show dog and National Specialty winner, Champion Rockaplenty's Wild Oats. He is one of the breed's truly great sires having been Top Beagle in the nation in 1973. She also owns Champion Foyscroft True Blue Lou, Foyscroft Aces Are Wild, and, in co-ownership with Marcia Foy who lives with her, Champion Foyscroft Triple Mitey Migit.

Miss Nicholas is best known to the Dog Fancy as a writer and as a judge. Her first published magazine article, a column about Pekingese in *Dog News* around 1930. This was followed by the widely acclaimed breed column, *"Peeking at the Pekingese"* which appeared for at least two decades in *Dogdom* and, when that magazine ceased to exist, in *Popular Dogs*. During the 1940s she was Boxer columnist for *The American Kennel Gazette*, and for *Boxer Briefs*. More recently many of her articles of general interest to the Fancy appeared in *Popular Dogs* and *The American Kennel Gazette.* Presently she is a featured regular columnist for *Kennel Review, Dog World* and *The Canine Chronicle* in the United States and for *The Canadian Dog Fancier* in that country. She also has written for *The World of the Working Dog* magazine, and has published occasional articles in Dogs in Canada.

It was during the late 1930s that Miss Nicholas' first book *The Pekingese* appeared, published by the Judy Publishing Company. This book completely sold out and is now a collector's item, as is her *The Skye Terrier Book* which was published through the Skye Terrier Club of America during the early 1960s.

In 1970 Miss Nicholas won the Dog Writers Association of America Award for the Best Technical Dog Book with her *Nicholas Guide to Dog Judging,* published by Howell Book House. In 1979, the revision of this book again won the Dog Writers Association of America Best Technical Book Award, the first time ever that a *Revision* has been so honored by this Association.

In the early 1970s Miss Nicholas co-authored, with Joan Brearley, five breed books which were published by T.F.H. Publications, Inc. These are *This is the Bichon Frise, The Wonderful World of Beagles and Beagling, The Book of the Pekingese, This is the Skye Terrier,* and *The Book of the Boxer. The Wonderful World of Beagles and Beagling* won a Dog Writers Association Honorable Mention Award the year it was published.

Soon to be released is another book she has written for T.F.H., *Successful Dog Show Exhibiting,* which the Fancy eagerly awaits.

Miss Nicholas has been awarded *Kennel Review* "winkies" awards as Dog Writer of the Year. And, in 1977, she was winner of the Gaines "Fido" as Journalist of the Year in Dogs.

She officiated as a judge, at her first dog show when she judged a record Pekingese entry at the First Company Governors Foot Guard, Hartford, Connecticut, in 1934. She presently is approved to judge all Hounds, Terriers, Toys,

This lovely bitch is Ch. Srigo's Madchen v Kurtz, making one of her numerous Best of Breed wins. Handled by Felicia Luburich, breeder, for owners Lucille and Donald Kurtz.

Opposite:
Am., Bda. Ch. Adler von Andan in Bermuda pictured with his breeder-owner, Mrs. Benjamin C. Tilghman, when he was the first, and only, Rottweiler to go Best in Show there, which he did in November 1975 at one of the Bermuda Kennel Club all breed events.

Anna Katherine Nicholas

Non Sporting, Pointers, English and Gordon Setters, Vizslas, Weimaraners, Wire-haired Pointing Griffons, Boxers and Doberman Pinschers. In 1970 she became the third woman in history to judge Best in Show at the prestigious Westminster Kennel Club Dog Show where she has officiated on some sixteen other occasions over the years. She has judged in almost every one of the mainland United States, in four Canadian Provinces, and her services are constantly sought in other countries. In addition to her many Westminster assignments, Miss Nicholas has officiated at such prestigious events as Santa Barbara, Trenton, Chicago International, the Sportsmans in Canada, the Metropolitan in Canada, and Specialty events in several dozen breeds both here and in Canada.

Through the years, Miss Nicholas has held important offices in a great many all-breed and Specialty Clubs: she still remains an Honorary Member of several of them.

BEST OF
OPPOSITE
EASTERN
DOG CLUB
DECEMBER 1979
ASHBEY

A consistent winner in eastern Rottweiler rings is Ch. Graudstark's Luger owned by Mark and Pat Schwartz of West Nyack, NY. In very limited showing Luger has accumulated more than 25 Best of Breed wins, plus a Working Group III. He finished his championship in less than three months in keenest competition. Photo by Alton Anderson.

Opposite:
Mary Levin is owner of Ch. Sigmund's Gretel, here handled by Alan Levine to Best of Opposite Sex at the Eastern Dog Club Show, December 1979.

PROLOGUE

The layman is inclined to believe, owing to its name, that the Rottweiler originated in Germany and there are those who will try to tell you that it is descended from the Doberman Pinscher. Neither of these theories is fact. History tells us that, although the Rottweiler as we know the breed today is a product of Germany, the origin of the breed actually was in the Ancient Roman Empire.

Behind our modern Rottweiler stands a type of short coated or bristle coated herding dog one of several different types of working dogs known in Ancient Rome. Today's Rottweiler bears a strong resemblance to this early ancestor; the dogs, through the ages have shown only moderate changes in general appearance. The progenitors of the Rottweiler were reliable drover dogs, sometimes used as war dogs in battle, and we have read that the Emperor Nero always kept a number of them around his palace to discourage intruders.

The drover dogs behind the Rottweiler breed served an important function in accompanying Roman troops during their invasions of other European countries. First of all, they were needed for their proficiency at herding, for how else but "on the hoof" could food be transported for the troops in those pre-refrigeration and pre-food preservative days? A large herd for extended invasions was essential, and to guard the herd and prevent loss, so was the drover dog. These dogs probably performed other useful duties, too, on their travels across the European continent. Undoubtedly their s was a role of major importance in the success of these forays, due to their intelligence, stamina and powerful strength.

Through the St. Gothard Pass over the Alps and into Southern Germany came the invaders with their dogs, into the Wurttemberg area where Rottweil is located. The city itself is the seat of the district bearing this same name; it stands on a hill on the left bank of the Neckar River, centrally located in this lush agricultural area. It is said that Rottweil was was so named around the period of 700 A.D., at the time that a Christian Church was erected where formerly had been Roman baths. During the excavation, red tiles of an earlier Roman villa were unearthed, and soon the area became known as "das Rote Wil" or "the red tile."

Some of the drover dogs and their offspring remained in this area when the troops moved on. Owing to its central location, Rottweil became an important trading center and marketplace to which farmers and cattlemen brought produce for sale. Here again, strong intelligent working dogs of stamina and good "lasting ability" were needed not only to transport the cattle, which sometimes travelled considerable distances, but for the protection of the traders themselves. On the return journey, their money-bags were far safer tied to the collar of a formidable dog than in their own hands should thieves be encountered on these lonely trails.

The butchers, farmers and cattle dealers came in steadily increasing numbers to the Rottweil area as its popularity as a trading center flourished and cultural interests increased. Visitors, as well as those native to the area, noticed the merits of the "butcher dogs" and the practice began to purposely breed them to improve and increase their type.

Soon a brisk trade developed with people anxious to purchase these fine animals to take home. In respect for their superiority over other types of local dogs, the Roman drover dogs were given the name "Rottweiler," to associate them forever with the area in which they had been so well accepted and appreciated. Thus it is that the descendants of the original Roman drover dogs, as the Germans bred and developed them, we now know as the Rottweiler.

Very quickly a competitive spirit was aroused among owners of these Rottweilers as to who might possess the best and finest dogs, and even as to-day an especially outstanding one in looks, temperament and working ability could bring a sizeable price. One of their attributes as herding dogs has always been their ability to work calmly and without excitement, avoiding any disturbance of the cattle or disquieting behavior as they firmly keep the herd moving along together.

Another job the breed handled well was pulling a cart. Despite all their attributes, however, a time came when the new railroads and resulting regulations resulted in a different form of cattle transportation, and the job of pulling milk carts was switched to donkeys instead of the dogs, therely depriving the Rottweiler dogs of their two principal forms of usefulness. Happily there were some loyal owners who retained their dogs as guards for their homes and property.

A great surge of renewed interest in the breed began in Northern Germany rather than in their original "home area" (we understand that in 1905 there was only one Rottweiler bitch to be found in all of Rottweil). This took place early in the twentieth century because the breed at that time had been "discovered" for police work. The amusing story we have heard of how this began has to do with a brawl one night in a waterfront saloon in Hamburg. Fourteen very drunken sailors were carrying on a dispute over the favors of a member of the opposite sex. A passing policeman who was a Rottweiler owner was out walking with his dog, came upon the scene and felt that he should take some action. Of course he immediately became the target of the mob, and the Rottweiler was the hero of the situation; in almost no time at all several of the sailors were thrown to the ground and the others were beating a hasty retreat.

It is interesting to find descriptions of the early Rottweilers as they developed in Germany prior to the twentieth century. In general conformation and head shape there is said to have been little change: the massive substance, aura of power, and assured self-confidence has been present right along. A working man rather than a dandy! Two separate strains were being developed in those days, we gather from our research: the bigger, more muscular dogs for work with the carts; the smaller, more agile and less bulky were deemed more suitable for herding. This difference was due to three considerations: the largest dogs were perhaps too heavily built for lasting stamina on the road; their extra weight might cause accidents in jumping; and their additional height could cause a tendency to nip the cattle in the shoulder or buttocks rather than on the hock as they herded resulting in damaged stock which would bring down its value.

The two size categories were bred as separate strains. Performance alone was sought in the smaller dogs with little concern about their looks. In fact it was in this strain that the "off" coloring by present Standards existed, dogs with white collars, white chests, white spots or feet, or even red dogs with black stripes down their back, or light colored markings were known and accepted, while the larger strain was always scrupulously correct in color as we know it to-day.

CHAPTER 1

The Rottweiler in Germany: Early History

By James and Norma Harwood

To appreciate the breed, you need to know something of its origin. As with most breeds of today, it was created in the nineteenth century and the Stud Book begins in the early twentieth century. However, you cannot say that a breed begins only with a Stud Book. It starts far earlier as an idea in the mind's eye: a set of needs, work to be done, selection for characteristics in the animal which will solve these problems.

The history of the town of Rottweil and the hypothesis of the Rottweiler's origins have been mentioned in the preface, so they will not be repeated here. We will begin this chapter with the fact that a large black and brown dog was known as the "Rottweil metzgerhund."

To understand the Rottweiler, you should look at a map of Germany to see where the dog came from, the general circumstances which encouraged his form as he was seen then and as we see him now. Many publications written by Germans about the Rottweiler will use the term "Swabia" to refer to the original home of the breed. This is the historical name for the southwesternmost part of the old German kingdom or Reich, comprising in twentieth century terms not only the southern part of the German Federal Republic's Baden-Wurttemberg area, together with the southwestern part of Bavaria, but also eastern Switzerland and Alsace.

The town of Rottweil is located on a tributary of the Rhine, the

There are few dogs of any breed which we have heard more highly praised than this one. Sieger Hackel v Kohlerwald, 15691, a pillar of the Rottweiler breed's early German history.
Opposite:
"von Rennplatz"

River Neckar, and within the boundaries of the old German kingdom of Wurttemberg. The new name of the old subdivision of the German empire is Baden-Wurttemberg, an enlarged state or Land in the Bundes Republic of Deutschland (BRD). The town of Rottweil is in the far southwestern corner of Germany, say thirty miles north of Switzerland and Lake Constance. The area immediately to the west is the Schwartzwald, or Black Forest of legend and romance, which separates old Swabia from France. Stuttgart, the capital of the old kingdom, lies to the northeast about fifty miles. The headquarters of the breed has been there since the formation of the Allgemeinen Deutscher Rottweiler Klub (ADRK) in 1921. The area has been a producer of grain and cattle for centuries and is even now largely agricultural although increasingly industrialized. The forest areas have been famous hunting grounds for large game such as boars and bears. It is said that early dogs of the area were used for hunts and some animals in paintings and books bear some resemblance to the Rottweiler.

Emphasis on the use of the dogs in this area appears to have been of a practical nature. Early railroad construction in the old German empire was largely completed in the years 1890-1900. The railroads were controlled by the government and a law was passed requiring that cattle be shipped by rail rather than moved by foot to market along the highways. Two of the major functions of a number of breeds of dogs, including the Rottweiler, were passing from the scene, the herding and guarding of domestic animals, duties which in the past they had performed so well.

Keep in mind that dogs such as these were bred and owned by the working classes who could not afford to have useless mouths to feed. If the dogs could not be used to help produce a livelihood, it was unlikely that a large dog would be kept as a pet.

Fortunately, prior to the widespread introduction of the gasoline engine, and the resulting high use of cars and trucks, the Rottweiler could be used as a carting dog. Indeed, he was first known as the Rottweil Butcher's Dog, which was later shortened to Rottweiler. Its use as a draft animal also began to wane in the early twentieth century. About this time, several working dog breeds were judged to be especially useful for police and self-defense work.

The Rottweiler was deemed suitable for these tasks because of his temperament, structure and size. Early breeders felt that working qualities for Rottweilers would take care of themselves,

Above: Anni v Fuchseck, 2173. Owner, C. Jetter, Stuttgart. **Below:** Typical European bull with Rottweiler herding. Photo courtesy, Willie Faussner, Munich.

Cilly v Filstal, 1274. C. Jetter. Stuttgart. **Below:** A famous early German Rottweiler, Doldi von der Melenenhohe. Photo courtesy, Marianne Bruns and Dr. Evelyn Ellman.

Ch. Pondutt Von Schweitzer, C.D., practices running on a ramp for police dogs. Linda Griswold, owner.

as the breed has a lot of natural sharpness. Thus, his future was assured. New tasks showed what he was capable of doing, thanks to his intelligence and the qualities of physique and character with which he was endowed. When, in 1901, the first moves took place to use dogs in the service of the police, attention soon turned to the Rottweiler, the breed possessing all that could be required of such a dog as a natural inheritance from his ancestors. He had never been other than the most faithful companion and helper. His character was formed and ennobled by work. He was ir-reproachably loyal and devoted, industrious, intelligent, courageous in the face of danger, hardy and undemanding.

One kennel, which would be unusual for the United States, was noted in the 1924 Zuchtbuch, with three litters entered as Polizeidirektion Muchen. Thus the police department was listed as kennel and owner, using its own dogs and, from the low registration numbers of its dogs, had been doing so from early in the breed's history. Another example of institutional breeding, also in Munich, was the Polizei-Hundeschule, Bayerischen-Landespolizei. They did not turn out a great number of litters, but they did have a program.

Argo v Monrepos, 972,
born July 29, 1922.
Breeder-owner, Chair-
man Kleinmann,
Niederbieber.

Below: Cora v
Grobenzell, 1489.

The above photo depicts Hackel von Kohlerwald, 15691, SchH II, and two other Rottweilers; it was used as the heading on Certificates for Working Titles in Germany. The author is indebted for use of this photo to Willi Faussner, Munich, reproduced from *Der Rottweiler* by the late Hans Korn.

The senior officials of the Rottweiler fancy in Germany tend to be persons of experience in all aspects of the sport, including administration, training, breeding and judging. It is not unusual for them to judge breed and obedience, officiate at initial surveys for breeding prospects, and render opinions as breed wardens. One family from the Munich area, Willi Faussner, Senior and Junior, gave us an example of continuity from the beginning of the ADRK to the present day: over 60 years of consistent, valued judgment applied to the problems of the breed. Americans cannot offer this accumulation of time, and none have been on the firing line being tested for even a substantial fraction of it.

Some feel that the Americans are too superficial in the evaluation of a dog: too quick to value beauty of form than to hold it in higher regard than proper character. Quite the opposite is true of the German fancier, as beauty of form and correct character are inseparable in his eyes. Frequently both are judged at the same event, with equal importance being attached to them, such as at surveys for breeding suitability, because character is so important in the German System for the survival of the breed.

In the early years there was no question of regulated breeding in the modern sense. Pedigree information was completely lacking or had not been centrally organized. The first Rottweiler exhibited, at a show in Heilbornn in 1882, bore little comparison with

Above: Argo v Monrepos, 972. A side view of this important dog that was owned by Chairman Kleinmann. **Below:** Sieger Hackel von Kohlerwald, 15691, SchH II. Photo reproduced from *Der Rottweiler* by Hans Korn. Courtesy, Willi Faussner, Munich.

Head study of Arno
v Mullerstadel, 7712.
A Muller, owner.
Below: Arno v
Mullerstadel, 7712,
born July 21, 1921.
By Bar v.d. Harden,
3557 ex Sieglinde
v.d. Steinlach, 4104.
Breeder, A. Muller.

our present requirements. But, with the emergence of modern breeding, associations were established to cater to individual breeds. Things which had previously been left more or less to chance or to nature were now clearly regulated, and it became a matter of the highest obligation to preserve the inheritance from the past and take sensible steps to improve on it.

It was mere chance that called the Rottweiler from the shadows and led to the establishment of a society to look after him. On the occasion of the Heidelberg Kennel Club's show held in 1905, then-chairmen Karl Knauf and Albert Graf, after consultation with the well known breeder Boppel, looked around for "a fine dog of unusual breed and irreproachable character" for the Honorary President of the show. Their choice fell on a Rottweiler. The difficulty of obtaining any data about the early history of the Rottweiler as a recognized breed is shown by the complete absence of information in the two-volume work by Ludwig Beckmann published in 1894. So we may regard Heidelberg as the true birthplace of the Rottweiler of today as it was in Heidelberg that breeding on modern lines originated. The German Rottweiler Club (DRK) was founded in Heidelberg on January 13th 1907.

It was of the utmost importance for the progress of the Rottweiler that Hamburg police officers, as practical men, very quickly recognized the great value of a Rottweiler for police work and recruited several dogs. The first two dogs, Max von der Strahlenberg (breed book number 48) and Flock von Hamburg, number 49, did so well that the breed was officially recognized in 1910 by the German Police Dog Association as the fourth police dog breed. The German Rottweiler Club became affiliated with this association. But even in the early period of existence of the DRK, the expulsion of a member, because of gross infringement of the principles of genuine sport, led to the establishment of a new club, the South German Rottweiler Club, in Heidelberg on April 26th 1907. Personal factors therefore sowed the seeds of dissension in the Rottweiler movement, and also stood in the way of the unification of the two clubs. They were followed shortly afterwards by a third one, the International Rottweiler Club (IRK), which soon absorbed the remnants of the South German Rottweiler Club.

In recognition of the fact that a new breed cannot tolerate division, the negotiations to unite the two clubs, which had proved abortive in 1913, were resumed in 1920. Negotiations took place at

Above: Lump v Lonsingen, 8493, dog, born April 1922. By Stumper v Gomadingen ex Stumperin v Longingen, 5616. Owner, J. Kopf, Stuttgart. Breeder, W. Bauder. **Below:** Kastor v Hummelheim, 3988, born June 18, 1921. Sire, Sieg v Pegnitzal, 1353. Dam, Fricka v Friedberg, 1095. Breeder, Fr. Hummel. Owner, A. Muller, Mullerstadel.

Above: Dutt v.d. Melenenhohe, 7011, born March 18, 1923. By Sieger Arco Torfwerk 955 ex Trudel v Freihof, 775 (DRK Stud Book). Breeder-owner, A. Christiani. **Below:** Bar v.d. Harden, 3557, born June 26, 1921. Sire, Arco Torfwerk, 955, dam, Arca v.d. Harden, 1868. Owner, Fr. Butz, New Ulm. Breeder, Fr. Bauer, Immenhausen.

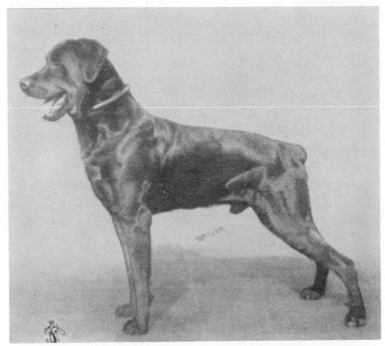

Arno v Felsengarten, 4508, by Sieger Arco Torfwerk, 955 from Anna v d Enz, 1481, dog, born February 28, 1922. Owner, Burkhardt, Stuttgart.

Gassel on July 3rd 1921 between representatives of the DRK and IRK and were ratified at a general meeting in Wurzberg on August 14th 1921, resulting in the establishment of the General German Rottweiler Club (ADRK). Since then the breed has had the advantage of a single club to represent its interests.

While the DRK published only one volume of its Stud Book, containing 286 dogs and 214 bitches, there are two volumes from the IRK with a total of 2340 entries. The second volume of the IRK Stud Book also contains 770 DRK entries. From the entries of early Stud Books of both clubs, we can see that there were basic differences in the foundation stock. In the IRK it did not take long for the Teck blood to become dominant, while the breed in the DRK was built on Sieger Ralf vom Neckar (2) and Strahlenburg blood. One must admit that DRK was placing more emphasis on the working qualities than on conformation, while the IRK's first objective was a uniform type and conformation. In contrast to the

Two highly important and very dominant early Rottweilers are Ralph v Neckar (left),

and Leo v. Cannstatt (right).

Jack v Schifferstadt, 8945, dog, born February 12, 1922. By Sieger Lord v.d. Teck, 413 ex Alma v Schifferstadt, 897. Breeder, Ignaz Bertram. Owner, P. Klee, Schifferstadt.

IRK dogs, the DRK dogs had predominantly Pointer-type heads.

When the ADRK was organized, its motto became "Rottweiler breeding is and shall remain working dog breeding"; i.e., breeders were supposed to concentrate on conformation and utility, this of course after elimination of the most glaring faults which were prevalent in the breed, such as over and under-shot bites, Pointer heads, steep hindquarters, etc. Only a few breeders stuck to their old ways, such as the kennels of Pfalzgau and Rennplatz. The former failed to eliminate the leggy Specimens that were also lacking in substance, and the latter produced most of the dogs that were weak in character.

In the IRK the breedings were primarily based on Leo von Cannstatt (29), see Chart 1, to which was added the Teck blood, mostly with Sieger Lord von der Teck (413).

It was he who was responsible for the speedy improvement of the breed, primarily by giving it powerful jaws and a broad upper head. Lord von der Teck was a son of Sieger Lord Remo von Schifferstadt (130), whose height, a bit over twenty-eight inches, was subject to much debate. He did gain recognition, however, which was not exactly to the detriment of the breed.

In the DRK Sieger Russ vom Bruckenbuckel had been used dozens of times and had sired several good Rottweilers. In addition to that there was Ralf vom Neckar (2), a sire also much in demand.

Later Max von der Strahlenburg was in the lead. Rhino von Kork (4013) SchH 3 (that was even known in the IRK as a good working dog) also contributed to the early breedings of the DRK. But the real top guns were in the IRK.

A few notes based on examination of the 1924 ADRK Zuchtbuch (Stud Book) are interesting. One notices that many things we take for granted today are not evident in the early book. For one thing, the breed was still actively being constructed. Officials were evaluating dogs about whom no breeding particulars were known. The Stud Book was still open. One assumes that if it looked like a Rottweiler, then the dog or bitch was admitted with birth date, father's and mother's identity all unknown. Dogs which had only one parent identified were also evident. Bitches were bred before the age of two years, and litters of ten or twelve were not uncommon, both items of restriction later on in the breed's history.

The most popular stud was Sieger Arco Torfwerk (955), with seventy-three litters in three years. His son, Bar v.d. Harden

Above: Xerxes vom Jakobsbrunnen, 24973. Breeder, E. Bolinger, Stuttgart. Below: Bussi v Fuchseck, 4025, bitch, born October 21, 1921. By Arco Torfwerk ex Minna Wild, 2168. Owned by A. Christiani, Hamburg.

Above: Sieger Arco Torfwerk, 955. **Below:** Aron v Zuffenhausen, 4135, born December 2, 1921. By Lord Binder v Weilim Dorf, 1328, ex Base v Rennplatz, 1542. Breeder, Fr. Schollkopk, Zuffenhausen.

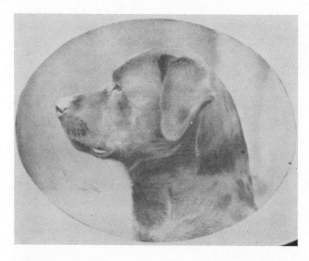

Sieger Arco Torfwerk, 955. Head study in profile.

(3557), at the tender age of three, had been used thirty-six times with result.

Lord von der Teck was used once more than his grandson, or 37 times. Lord Binder (1328) was used nineteen times. It is not uncommon today to see particular studs being widely used without great discrimination.

Great progenitors who leave their impression on whole generations of dogs, and may in some cases contribute to astonishing progress in breeding, are not just the results of the breeder's skill and industry, but are also to some extent gifts from heaven which are not bestowed upon a breed every day. In this period of prosperity, series of Rottweilers appeared who made an unforgettable name for themselves as progenitors and whose influence on the breed has continued to the present day. Pictures appearing early in the text were taken from the first (1924) ADRK (combined IRK/DRK) Stud Book. These are the dogs of note—the prolific producers from which our modern Rottweilers stem.

James and Norma Harwood have prepared for our readers the following three charts, which we are proud to present in the certainty that they will prove of interest and value to students of Rottweiler breeding and pedigrees. Following them at varying intervals throughout the text is a collection of pedigrees of many important Rottweiler sires and dams in the United States, traced back to their German heritage. This section is one of particular importance, and the dogs represented are in many cases pictured in the pages of this book.

Above: Sieglinde v.d. Steinlach, 4104. Bitch by Sieger Arco Torf-werk, 955 ex Affra v Sportplaz, 800. Owned by J. Kocher, Duss-lingen. **Below:** Sieger Arnim v Falkenstein, 2192.

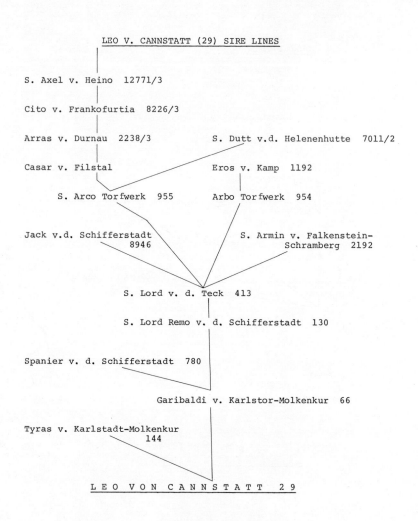

LEO V. CANNSTATT (29) SIRE LINES

S. Axel v. Heino 12771/3

Cito v. Frankofurtia 8226/3

Arras v. Durnau 2238/3   S. Dutt v.d. Helenenhutte 7011/2

Casar v. Filstal   Eros v. Kamp 1192

      S. Arco Torfwerk 955   Arbo Torfwerk 954

Jack v.d. Schifferstadt   S. Armin v. Falkenstein-
           8946   Schramberg 2192

          S. Lord v. d. Teck 413

          S. Lord Remo v. d. Schifferstadt 130

Spanier v. d. Schifferstadt 780

              Garibaldi v. Karlstor-Molkenkur 66

Tyras v. Karlstadt-Molkenkur
            144

      L E O   V O N   C A N N S T A T T   2 9

          C H A R T   1

Note: S. = Sieger
       Number after Registration number (such as /3) is Schutzhund
       degree which is shown in this form to save space. The same
       abbreviations are used on all charts.

LORD BINDER (1328) SIRE LINES

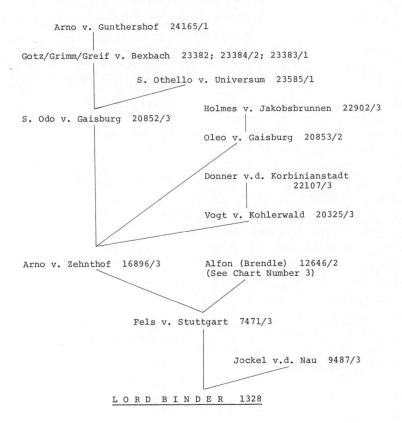

Arno v. Gunthershof   24165/1

Gotz/Grimm/Greif v. Bexbach   23382; 23384/2; 23383/1

S. Othello v. Universum   23585/1

S. Odo v. Gaisburg   20852/3

Holmes v. Jakobsbrunnen   22902/3

Oleo v. Gaisburg   20853/2

Donner v.d. Korbinianstadt
                  22107/3

Vogt v. Kohlerwald   20325/3

Arno v. Zehnthof   16896/3   Alfon (Brendle)   12646/2
                                (See Chart Number 3)

Fels v. Stuttgart   7471/3

Jockel v.d. Nau   9487/3

L O R D   B I N D E R   1328

C H A R T   2

Note: Lord's son Fels was linebred on Torfwerk and von der Teck
       stock, through the dam's side. See text for details. For
       details on Arbo Torfwerk 954, Eros v. Kamp 1192 and Lord
       v.d. Teck 413, see Chart 1.

ALFON (Brendle) 12646 SIRE LINES

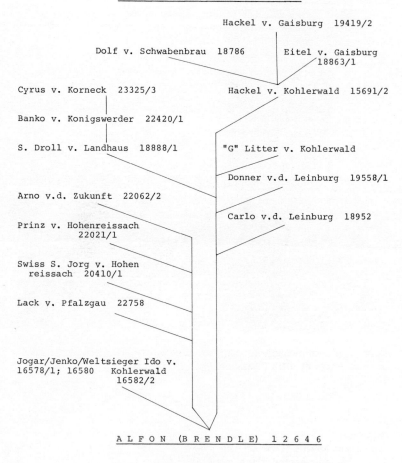

Hackel v. Gaisburg 19419/2

Dolf v. Schwabenbrau 18786

Eitel v. Gaisburg
18863/1

Cyrus v. Korneck 23325/3

Hackel v. Kohlerwald 15691/2

Banko v. Konigswerder 22420/1

S. Droll v. Landhaus 18888/1

"G" Litter v. Kohlerwald

Donner v.d. Leinburg 19558/1

Arno v.d. Zukunft 22062/2

Carlo v.d. Leinburg 18952

Prinz v. Hohenreissach
22021/1

Swiss S. Jorg v. Hohen
reissach 20410/1

Lack v. Pfalzgau 22758

Jogar/Jenko/Weltsieger Ido v.
16578/1; 16580   Kohlerwald
16582/2

A L F O N   (B R E N D L E)   1 2 6 4 6

C H A R T 3

Note: See Chart 2 for Alfon (Brendle) antecedents.

Dollo v Hartmannshofern, 16575, L.S. 1934. Owner, Alfred Richter, Munich. Photo by Willi Faussner, Munich.

Opposite:
James and Norma Harwood have prepared these three charts presented in the certainty that they will prove valuable to students of Rottweiler breeding and pedigrees. Another chapter of the book contains a collection of pedigrees of many important Rottweiler sires and dams in the United States, traced back to their German heritage.

CHAPTER 2

Breeding Rottweilers in Germany

$\mathbf{H}$ere in the United States the owner of a bitch decides to breed her, then sits down and makes a careful survey of the possible available studs. Pedigrees are considered as well as the conformation and show quality of the individual dogs, their temperament and character, soundness, and the success which they have been meeting as producers of quality stock. Usually one discusses all this and exchanges ideas with friends who are also breeders. When a decision has been reached, the owner of the selected stud is contacted, and with that person's additional approval, the alliance takes place. It is just that simple.

In Germany, however, things are quite different. A Rottweiler must go through specific tests and examinations to earn a degree of suitability for breeding if the litter is to be eligible for registration with the German Rottweiler Club (ADRK). Breeding activities come under the auspices of a Head Breed Warden and of regional Breeding Supervisors. It is their task to supervise all proposed breeding, breeding programs, keeping and rearing of dogs. Obviously, selection for these important posts carries a strong responsibility, plus a firm belief in the policies and aims of the ADRK. These people bring with them a solid background as breeders themselves, and years of experience during which they have gained the knowledge and expertise to equip them to assume this vast responsibility.

Head study of Ch. Liane vom Schloss Stauffenberg, a lovely bitch that did considerable winning in Germany, including the Open Class at the very large Bundessieger Show before coming to America following her purchase by Harry Z. Isaacs of Glyndon, MD.

Opposite:
Nelli vom Sillahop, photo taken by R.F. Klem in Stuttgart, Germany, 1965. Courtesy, Dorothea Gruenerwald.

Sieger Droll vom Landhaus, SchH I, number 18,888. D. Schweizer, Mohringen.

The Koerung (selection for breeding suitability) became effective in Germany in 1942, and in the Stud Book that year it was announced that, "Beginning in January 1944 only litters from dogs with Koerung or Zuchttauglichkeitspruefung can be registered." In order to attain Koerung, a dog must come before a judge who checks for appearance, condition, health, bearing, expression and conformation of the dog, the gait, and the temperament. Bloodlines are studied, and the suitability for breeding considered. When a dog has been approved for breeding at the Koerung, his vital statistics are then recorded and published in the Stud Book. Keeping a record permanently can be extremely useful to future breeders checking back on the credentials behind their dogs. It is interesting to learn that special comments and recommendations are made on these listings, such as a dog being "correct for breeding with a well boned bitch but not for a lightly boned one," or vice-versa, and other pertinent comments.

In order to become eligible for the Koerung, a dog must first have earned a training degree. He must be in good health, free of hereditary faults, of excellent character, and a talented working dog. Males younger than eighteen months and beyond eight years are ineligible for breeding, as are bitches less than eighteen months and beyond seven years.

Above: Lord Remo von Schifferstadt, 130. **Below:** Elko vom Kastanienbaum in Aachen, Germany, 1975. Courtesy, Dorothea Gruenerwald.

AHNENTAFEL

für den

Rottweiler

Der Hund darf erst zur Zucht verwen det werden, wenn er auf seine Zucht tauglichkeit geprüft ist und das Alte von 24 Monaten erreicht hat.

Name des Hundes: *CH* A x e l vom Schwanenschlag

Geschlecht: _____ Rüde

Farbe und Abzeichen: __schwarz mit braunen Abzeichen__

Wurftag: _____ 28. Juli 1969

Wurfjahr in Buchstaben: Neunzehnhundertneunundsechzig

Züchter) Name: _____ Frau Hildegard B r a n d t
des
Hundes) Wohnort: _____ 2841 W a g e n f e l d Bez. Bremen, Nr. 288

Eingetragen in das Zuchtbuch des ADRK

Band: **L III** _____ Nummer: __44778__

Die Ahnentafel hat nur Gültigkeit, wenn sie m beglaubigt und vom Züchter eigenhändig ur (Duplikat) bezeichnet ist. Sie gilt als Urkunde ändert oder mit ihnen Mißbrauch treibt, wird Ahnentafel an das Zuchtbuchamt zurückzugebe

Bei Verkauf des Hundes ist die Ahnentafel der wechsels auszuhändigen, beim Eingehen des zugeben.

I	Eltern	II	Großeltern	III	Ur-Großeltern	IV	Urur-Großeltern	
1 **Vater**		**3**		**7**	Kuno vom Weidbach 27 176 SchH 1	15	Bello von der Frühstückstube 34 960	3
	Fürst		Axel			16	Fee vom Weidbach 33 412 SchH 1	3
			vom Simonskaul					3
	von der		39 272 SchH 3	8	Alli vom Elmenau 37 583 SchH 1	17	Carlo von der Schildwach 32 910 SchH 3	3
						18	Edda vom Kanzachtal 36 337	3
	Villa Daheim	**4**		**9**	Internationaler Champion Lord vom Blankenhorn 35 785 SchH 2	19	Arno von der Wanne 32 041 SchH 2	3
	42 204 SchH 1		Blanka			20	Bertel von Nuifra 32 270 SchH 1	4
			vom Itzelbach					4
			39 080 SchH 1	**10**	Flori vom Kanzachtal 36 572	21	Castor vom Schussental 34 476 SchH 1	4
						22	Cita vom Kanzachtal 34 778	4
2 **Mutter**		**5**		**11**	Eddi von der Hobertsburg 36 930	23	Axel von der Kappenbergerheide 34 433 SchH 2	4
	Cora		Quinn			24	Andra von Bork 33 612 SchH 1	4
			von der Schwarzwiese					5
	vom		39 211 SchH 1	**12**	Olli von der Schwarzwiese 37 669	25	Lando von Jakobsbrunnen 35 699 SchH 3	5
						26	Affra vom Saalbau 35 048	5
	Grevingsberg	**6**		**13**	Quinto von der Solitude 38 609 SchH 1	27	Droll von der Brötzingergasse 36 212 SchH 2	5
	42 691		Britta			28	Fanny von der Solitude 35 565	5
			von der Zuflucht					5
			40 127	**14**	Dolly von der Hardt 36 313	29	Sg/WA 56 Hektor v. Burgtobel 32 969 SchH 1	5
						30	Anka von der Wanne 32 043	6

<table>
<thead>
<tr><th colspan="3">Erläuterungen über den Wurf,
zu dem dieser Hund gehört</th></tr>
<tr><th></th><th>Rüden</th><th>Hündinnen</th></tr>
</thead>
<tbody>
<tr><td>Wurfstärke b. d. Geburt .</td><td>5</td><td>5</td></tr>
<tr><td>Totgeboren . . . . . .</td><td>1</td><td>2</td></tr>
<tr><td>Getötet . . . .</td><td>1</td><td></td></tr>
<tr><td>Im Wurf belassen . . .</td><td>3</td><td>3</td></tr>
<tr><td>Verendet b. z. Eintragung .</td><td>1</td><td>0</td></tr>
<tr><td>Zum Zuchtbuch gemeldet .</td><td>2</td><td>3</td></tr>
<tr><td>Nicht nachgewiesen . . .</td><td></td><td></td></tr>
</tbody>
</table>

it dem Siegel des Klubs versehen, vom Zuchtbuchführer
iterschrieben oder vom Zuchtbuchführer als Abschrift
e im juristischen Sinne. Wer Ahnentafeln fälscht, ab-
strafrechtlich verfolgt. Beim Tode des Hundes ist die
en.

n neuen Eigentümer unter Eintragung des Eigentums-
Hundes ist sie an das Zuchtbuchamt des ADRK zurück-

	Ururur-Großeltern
1	Lump vom Oesterberg 32741
2	Karl Eulenspiegel 32814
3	Cuno vom Jakobsbrunnen 44630 SchH 1
4	Beni vom Weißbach 23625 SchH 1
5	Astor vom Weißhofertor 29938
6	Dori von der Nordstadt 29194
7	Sp/WA 1956 Hektor vom Burgtobel 32969 SchH 1
8	Cita vom Kanzachtal 34778
9	Genius von der Eichhalde 30487 SchH 1
0	Anny vom Salamander 28673 SchH 1
1	Lord vom Birkenbuck 27142 SchH 3
2	Edle vom Wallgraben 29585
3	Alex vom Köttgenweg 31407 SchH 2
4	Anni vom Forchenkopf 33158
5	Alex vom Goldboden 33538 SchH 2
6	Bella vom Klosterhof 28779
7	BS Igor vom Kohlwald 32149 SchH 1
8	Dolli von der Immenruh 32221
9	Alko von Wesel 31640 SchH 1
0	Cilli vom Birkenkopf 30146
1	Lux von Echterdingen 32668 S
2	Jette vom Jakobsbrunnen 34535
3	Sp/WA 1956 Hektor vom Burgtobel 32969 SchH 1
4	Cilla von der Schwarzwiese 32950
5	Alex vom Glastal 31011 SchH 1 CL
6	Asta von der Brötzingergasse 32457 SchH 1 CL
7	Bodo von der Laufenburg 33796 CL
8	Flora vom Silahopp 34127
9	Arras von der Schweizergrenze 29197 CL
0	Elli vom Burgtobel 28591
1	Genius von der Eichhalde 30487 SchH 1 CL
2	Anny vom Salamander 28673 SchH 1

Ergebnis der Zuchttauglichkeits-Prüfung

in .... am ....

Zuchttauglich – zur Zucht nicht geeignet

Körmeister oder Richter:

Bestätigung des Zuchtbuchamtes des ADRK

Stuttgart W, den ....

1. Körung in .... am ....

Für die Dauer von zwei Jahren angekört

(bis einschl. ....**)**

Körmeister:

Bestätigung des Zuchtbuchamtes des ADRK

Stuttgart W, den ....

2. Körung in .... am ....

Auf Lebenszeit angekört

Körmeister:

Bestätigung des Zuchtbuchamtes des ADRK

Stuttgart W, den ....,

Für die Richtigkeit der Angaben an das Zuchtbuchamt zur
Ausfertigung dieser Urkunde bürgt der Züchter durch Unterschrift

28. November 1969
Datum

Hildegard Brandt

Unterschrift des Züchters
(Ohne Unterschrift des Züchters nicht gültig)

Name: **Frau Hildegard B r a n d t**

Wohnort: 2841 Wagenfeld Bez. Bremen Straße: Nr. 288

Eintragungs- und Prüfungsbestätigung

Der oben bezeichnete **Rottweiler** ist am 26. November 1969 in das

Zuchtbuch des Allgemeinen Deutschen Rottweiler-Klub

unter Nr. 4 4 7 7 8 eingetragen worden. Die Abstammungs-

angaben sind nachgeprüft und ihre Richtigkeit wird hiermit

bestätigt

Das Zuchtbuchamt des ADRK

The Zuchttauglichkeitspruefung is another "means towards responsible breeding" in Germany. This is a stern character test to eliminate dogs of weak fighting instinct and shy character or nervousness. To pass this test the dogs must actually be sharp and display genuine fighting instinct; mere protectiveness is insufficient. Only dogs or bitches displaying no shyness or nervousness will pass this test, which calls for iron nerves and the true instinct of a fighter. Approval for the Zuchttauglichkeitspruefung is valid for three years, at the end of which time application must again be made. Approved dogs are to be mated only to others approved. And we understand that members not adhering to this rule will be dropped from the Club and their litter ineligible for registration. The pedigree form contains a note stating that dogs cannot be mated before they have been approved.

In further explanation, dogs that have passed the Zuchttauglichkeitspruefung are eligible to be bred, but a dog also must pass the Koerung to be especially recommended.

Accompanying this chapter is a "Koerschein fuer Rueden" which was issued on Fetz vom Oelberg and which gives his Koerung validation.

Also we bring you a sample of the Ahnentafel, which must accompany the dog when brought in for testing for the Koerung. This consists of the dog's pedigree and other vital information, and is issued by ADRK in somewhat the same manner as a registration certificate and certified pedigree would come from A.K.C., but with considerably more information on the background and heritage of the dog. The two pages (A and B) as printed are issued as one large sheet. Note on the right hand side the space to be filled in with the proper breeding approvals. "I Koerung" is temporary and must periodically be re-issued. "2 Koerung" is permanent for the duration of the dog's breeding age.

In order to breed Rottweilers in Germany, a person must have a registered kennel name. All breeders must be prepared to permit the Breed Warden or Breeding Supervisor upon request, to inspect premises where the dogs are kept. Should it be found that errors are occurring within a breeding program or in the housing of the dogs, a warning is issued stating the possible consequences should these unauthorized practices continue. If these errors remain uncorrected, it is then the duty of the Breeding Supervisor to report it to ADRK, by whom action may be taken.

Körschein für Rüden

als Bestätigung der vom Allgemeinen Deutschen Rottweiler-Klub (ADRK)
durchgeführten Körung für den Rottweiler

Körort: Utnd.-Bövin hausen
Körtag: 9. Juni 1963
Körmeister: Friedr, Berger

Gebrauchshundezucht / Körzucht / Leistungszucht   **Angekört** für   2 Jahre ab 14.7.63
bis einschl.13.7.65

(Name):   F e t z   vom Oelberg

Wurftag: 17. Oktober 1960 , ZB Nr.: 38 416   , Ausb.-Kennz.: Sch. 2

Vater: H e k t o r von der Solitude   36 481

[B o d o von der Laufenburg   33 796

F l o r a von Silahopp   34 127   ]

Mutter: D o r a von der Brötzingergasse   36 215

[A l e x von Glastal   31 011 Sch. 1

A s t a von der Brötzingergasse   32 457 Sch. 1   ]

Inzucht:

Züchter: Hermann K e i l i n g   Wohnort: Ersingen / Baden

Eigentümer: Robert   D r e b e n s t e   (Wohnort: Dortmund

Straße: Münsterstr. 16

(Bei Änderung des Eigentumsverhältnisses ist dem Zuchtbuchamt Stuttgart innerhalb längstens acht Tagen unter gleichzeitiger Einsendung dieses Körscheines Mitteilung zu machen.)

Nacheigentümer: (Zeitangabe) 9.4.64. Hch.Schimmel , Anschrift: Schwertkuhr
Hagerstr.... .. 22

Feststellungen bei der Körung:

I. 1. Gesamturteil über allgemeine Erscheinung und Verfassung, Gebäude und Gangvermögen, Gefügefestigkeit, Wesen und Kampftrieb:

mittelgroßer gut gebauter, gehaltvoller,trocken und fester Rüde mit
guten Kopf und dunklen Auge, gute Winkelungen mit ausgeprägter Muskulatur festen dicken und flüssigen Gängen, ausgeprägter Kampftrieb.

2. a) **Geschlechtsgepräge:** ausgeprägt, vorhanden.   b) **Konstitution:** kräftig, trocken, etwas derb, etwas fein.

3. **Wesen einschl. Nervenverfassung:** lebhaft, ruhig; aufmerksam; etwas zurückhaltend, gutartig; dreist, furchtlos, nervenfest und -frisch; leicht überreizt.

4. **Ausdruck:** rottweilermäßig, lebensvoll, geweckt, edel, etwas unfreundlich.

II. Gebäudebeurteilung im Stand:

1. **Gebäudeverhältnisse:** gestreckt, etwas lang, etwas kurz. Kräftig, reichlich schwer, schwer, mittelschwer, etwas leicht, gehaltvoll, ausreichend gehaltvoll, untersetzt (gedrungen), tief, etwas breit, etwas schmal, leicht flachrippig; guter Stand.

2. a) **Widerristhöhe:** 64 cm;   b) **Brusttiefe:** 31 cm;   c) **Brustumfang:** 91 cm;
d) **Körperlänge:** 73 cm.

3. a) **Knochen:** kräftig, mittelkräftig, etwas grob, etwas fein.

b) **Bemuskelung:** kräftig, genügend kräftig, trocken.

c) **Stand- und Bänderfestigkeit vorne:** sehr gut, gut, genügend.

d) **Stand- und Bänderfestigkeit hinten:** sehr gut, gut, genügend.

CHAPTER 3

Marianne Bruns: German Breeder, Fancier, Judge

Miss Marianne Bruns has, we are told, been dedicated to but one truly great love in her life—the Rottweiler. From the time that she was just a young girl in grammar school to the present she has remained one of the most dedicated Rottweiler fanciers to be found. To date she has bred forty-three registered litters, and her kennel name, "Eulenspiegel," is to be found in pedigrees of famous Rottweilers throughout the world wherever the breed is known.

Along with being a good breeder, Miss Bruns is a highly successful trainer of her dogs. Both beauty and working ability are required of Rottweilers in Germany in order that they may qualify to be used for breeding and their offspring registered.

Upon completion of her judging apprenticeship, Miss Bruns became a popular Rottweiler specialist judge, and she has officiated in that capacity frequently in Germany, Scandinavia and other European countries.

The esteem with which Miss Bruns is regarded by her fellow fanciers is proven beyond doubt by the fact that in the early nineteen-eighties, she became the first woman ever elected to become Chief Breed Warden and Chief Judge by the German Rottweiler Club (ADRK). A singular honor indeed!

Eulenspiegel Rottweilers are so named after the legendary Till Eulenspiegel, a jester and "teller of tall tales," who was buried in 1350 (and whose grave still can be visited) at the old city of Moelln

Who could overlook the intelligence of this gorgeous bitch? She is Gerte von Korneck SchH III, whelped in 1942, belonging to Marianne Bruns.

Opposite:
In the 1940s! Flori, Adda and Ena Eulenspiegel, all of whom figure prominently in the story of Marianne Bruns' famous Eulenspiegel Rottweilers.

Marianne Bruns very first Rottweiler in 1929! This is Tell, the
dog that led to half a century's
devotion to his breed.

in northern Germany where Miss Bruns makes her home. Surrounded by lakes and forests, graced by lovely churches and pic-
turesque towers, this is indeed a charming spot.

For Marianne Bruns it all started in 1929 when, with the pennies
she had earned by doing chores and had saved meticulously, she
decided to buy her father a Rottweiler puppy to replace their old
guardian and house dog. At seven weeks of age, "Tell" joined the
household; he became large, strong and impressive. When he was
a juvenile of one year, the Bruns sent him off to a trainer.
However, it was soon discovered that the dog did not respect this
trainer for long, as the trainer had made the mistake of punishing
the dog unjustifiably. But the dog had to be formally trained and
had to learn the requirements. The ten year old Marianne solved
the problem when she and Tell went to the local training class
together several times each month. In 1931 she took him to her
first exhibition, and they came home successful and happy.

In Tell's pedigree one found names like Sieger Arco von Torfwerk, a truly great transmitter of good quality; the brothers Lord
and Lenz, more formally Lord Remo von Schifferstadt and Lenz
von Schifferstadt, grandsons of the famous Leo von Cannstatt;
and dogs from the Felsenmeer kennel line. Miss Bruns fell head
over heels for the Rottweiler breed and for dog training
(Hundesport), but for quite a while nothing exciting or
remarkable happened. Occasionally a canine fancier friend

would bring a dog or puppy to Miss Bruns so that she would take care of it during their absence from home (boarding kennels did not exist during those days in Germany), and each time when the puppy or dog would leave her to go home, Miss Bruns would be heavy hearted and filled with sorrow. In 1941 the family had to part with Tell, and it was several months before a replacement came and it was quite a pitiful puppy which arrived—small, plagued by rickets, but with a great temperament. This was the period during World War II when there was just not enough food around to nourish a puppy properly, which undoubtedly caused the health defects. Just at that time Marianne Bruns came of age, and her first act, after having achieved majority, was to join the German Rottweiler Club (ADRK). Meanwhile the once pitiful puppy, called Hasso, had developed quite admirably, but in 1942 the German Army authorities came and took him away from his owners as they were in need of guard dogs.

So now the waiting game started all over again. Marianne Bruns finally got her first bitch, Gerte vom Korneck, from the first litter which was classified as Koerung and Leistungszucht, which signifies the highest degree of litter, as the Germans classify the litters depending on the titles and achievements earned by the dogs and their ancestors who breed the litter and whelp the litter. Gerte was rather small and soon after coming to the Bruns was afflicted with distemper which, fortunately, she survived. However, it left her with a certain weakness in her "backhand." This latter created a problem for her at the Schutzhund training and tests, especially when she had to scale the wall. Therefore it was necessary that she compensate for this by doing all other parts of the test so well that she could afford to lose some points during this particular exercise. Gerte is described by Miss Bruns as the most intelligent dog she has ever owned, and the two of them learned a lot from each other.

Also at this period Marianne Bruns learned a lot from the pioneers of the North German Rottweiler fanciers, taught her by such authorities as Hell, Cornehl, Passich, Mudra and Elbertrock. Gerte and Marianne succeeded in obtaining Schutzhund I, Schutzhund II and Schutzhund III titles, and they were at the top of the competition.

Adda Eulenspiegel next was added to the kennel, the only puppy from Marianne Bruns "A" litter. She is described as having been a "hardnosed and sharp bitch."

Above: Typical of the quality puppies born at Marianne Bruns' kennel in Germany is this one, Einzige Eulenspiegel, from Zierde Eulenspiegel. The pup is six weeks old in this picture. **Below:** Adda Eulenspiegel SchH II, from Marianne Bruns "A" litter.

Above: This beautiful bitch, Prima Eulenspiegel, was born in 1953 and is from Germany's famed Eulenspiegel Rottweilers belonging to Ms. Marianne Bruns. Below: A handsome side view of Marianne Bruns' Adda Eulenspiegel SchH II, whelped in 1944.

Flori Eulenspiegel SchH I, (standing), and Ena Eulenspiegel SchH I who entered prominently into the development of Marianne Bruns' kennel in Germany.

Exhibitions during these times were few and far between, but eventually Gerte became "angekoert" or "approved for breeding." But as so frequently happens with strong, robust bitches, in breeding there is not always a satisfactory result.

In the "B" litter came Barry, who had an extremely stable temperament and who accompanied a team of horses as a watchdog for several years and later, to the day of his death, was on duty with a security guard in a leather factory.

The "C" litter, out of Adda, turned into a real shocker, having several long-haired puppies in it. Adda had deliberately been bred to a half-brother as the Bruns wanted to ascertain whether or not their suspicion of longhairs in a certain line was justified, and indeed it turned out to be the case! Cilly from the "C" litter was a "blind-leader" dog for many years (comparable to our Seeing Eye Dogs in the United States).

The "D" litter, again from Adda, brought Miss Bruns only one bitch; all others were dogs. Unfortunately leptospirosis struck these puppies, and no medication whatsoever was available during these final war years and the period immediately following.

Especially was this true between 1946 and 1949, and it was heart-breaking to see the canine losses in Miss Bruns' section of Germany where every litter and many older dogs died of this terrible disease. Finally, in 1949, serum became available. Thus breeding began again at Eulenspiegel, and two litters were born, one from Gerte and one from Adda. The sire in both cases was the "Zonensieger" (a title given during those years after World War II as Germany was divided into four zones, English, French, American and Russian; in this case it denoted "Victor of the English Zone"), Faust von der Mark, SchH I. From each litter a bitch was kept, and it was through them that Miss Bruns achieved her initial breakthrough to success in the Rottweiler world!

These two bitches both gained their Schutzhund I titles at barely fourteen months of age. One of them, Ena, was named Best Juvenile and received the Hell Jubilee prize. Some years later, one of her grandchildren repeated that win. Ena's daughter, Sonne, was Number One at the World Victor Show in Dortmund in the young bitch class, and her other daughter, Prima was second

This is the great Bundessiegerin of 1954, Blanka vom Eppendorferbaum, SchH III. Owned by Marianne Bruns, Germany.

in the open class. Ena's dam was the beloved Gerte, who sad to report, died just a few days before Ena had completed her Schutzhund I title.

Ena Eulenspiegel is still to be found in pedigrees today via the kennel name "Fruehstueckstube" through such famous dogs as BS (Bundessieger—Victor of the Federal Republic of Germany) Igor von Hause Henseler and BS Emir von Freienhagen.

Two sons of Adda Eulenspiegel, Rex Eulenspiegel SchH III and Raudi Eulenspiegel SchH II, each received the predicate "very good."

In addition to Ena Eulenspiegel and Flori Eulenspiegel, Marianne Bruns also at this period owned another outstanding bitch, the Bundessiegerin 1954 (female Bundessieger) Blanka vom Eppenderferbaum SchH III, approved for breeding. From two of the bitches, one juvenile each was sent to England, Rudi Eulenspiegel and Quinta Eulenspiegel. Later, a Sonne Eulenspiegel daughter, Bim Eulenspiegel, also went to England. Sonne Eulenspiegel several times received the highest evaluation possible, V-I (excellent-I) and CACIB and a half-brother to Sonne became DDR Youthbest (German Democratic Republic Youthvictor). Cisco Eulenspiegel SchH III, a son of Sonne, became an International Champion.

Then there was a Flori Eulenspiegel daughter named Holle Eulenspiegel SchH I that also received V-I and CACIB.

Miss Bruns feels that she was less successful with her Blanka Eulenspiegel line. Nevertheless Blanka's son, Wuni Eulenspiegel, received a V rating and CACIB. He is said to be existing yet in a bloodline in Sweden.

During this period, within one year Miss Bruns lost three bitches "through illness and through deliberate poisoning"—the start of a very unlucky period for this talented fancier. Zierde Eulenspiegel, a daughter of Rex Eulenspiegel and Sonne Eulenspiegel, suffered a torn ligament in her knee and broke her hip. She had a Schutzhund III title and was approved for breeding. After she was cured she gave her owner one litter of two bitches, but only one of these could be saved. Bad luck continued; Miss Bruns had to change professions and move to a new residence, so her breeding program was interrupted, at least temporarily.

In 1959, Miss Bruns became a Rottweiler judge, at the same time as did two other very respected famous fanciers, Dr. Schmitz and Friedrich Berger. Shortly thereafter Miss Bruns was

Above: Cisco Eulenspiegel, an international champion, in the 1950s. Marianne Bruns, owner. **Below:** Flori Eulenspiegel SchH II, five years old here, was whelped in Germany in 1949. Sire, Zone Victor Faust von der Mark. Dam, Adda Eulenspiegel. Owner, Ms. Marianne Bruns.

Barbel von Grevingsberg, SchH I, approved for breeding. Photo courtesy, Marianne Bruns.

Representing Germany's fine Rottweilers in England! Quinta Eulenspiegel was imported by Joanne Chadwick from Marianne Bruns. **Below:** Zierde and Zenda Eulenspiegel, by Rex Eulenspiegel from Sonne Eulenspiegel. Owned by Marianne Bruns.

Halma Eulenspiegel, born in 1972, owned by Marianne Bruns. **Below:** Lunch time! Halma Eulenspiegel with her litter sired by Etzel von St. Andreasberg.

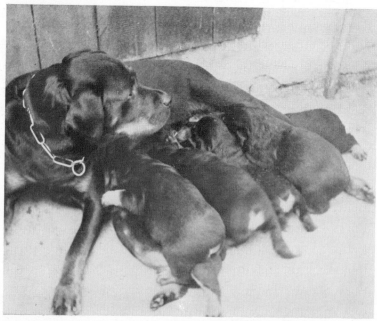

approved as a Koermeister, which is a Specialty judge who is qualified to officiate at special shows where dogs are measured and tested to decide if they are totally correct for breeding, in both physical conformation and in temperament.

From 1963 to 1965 the breeding program at Eulenspiegel was completely at a standstill. Then in 1968 a new start was made with a male. Unfortunately it became necessary for Miss Bruns to place the dog elsewhere as she had suffered an accident and was unable to control and train an animal of his strength. Even today, she says, "I am still carrying a torch for him, and will never forgive myself for not having placed him in a more suitable home, as I have heard via the grapevine that he suffered a stroke while working on the Schutzhund training grounds."

Next Baerbl v. Grevinsberg, SchH I, joined Miss Bruns, purchased as a proven matron that already had whelped three litters. She was the dam of Klubsiegerin and Bundessiegerin Dolly v.d. Meierei, SchH I, approved for breeding, whose brother Dack v.d. Meierei was also a V-rated dog with a Schutzhund III title. Dack was the sire of Anka and Asta vom Lohauserholz, both of which attained the titles of Klubsiegerin and Bundessiegerin and Schutzhund III. Unfortunately, and unknown to her, Baerbl already was ill when Miss Bruns acquired her. She produced one litter at "Eulenspiegel," two dogs and a bitch, of which only one survived, a male. This dog went to Finland and is being used in the Finnish breeding program.

Of this bitch, Miss Bruns writes "Baerbl was a most grateful dog, appreciated living in the home, and a short time after she joined us was able to obtain her 'approved for breeding' title. Oh, how much I could tell about both of them, Baerbl and Gerte, both of which I lost much too early."

Needing a new bitch, Miss Bruns next acquired Dina von Kaiserberg. She was three years old and was one of four sisters each with HD or HD + ratings, and all of them having achieved V ratings in the show ring. As a partner for Dina's first litter at "Eulenspiegel" Miss Bruns selected the Baerbl v. Grevinsberg son, Flash v.d. Meierei, SchH III, approved for breeding, sired by Brutus v. Georgshof, SchH III, approved for breeding. In this litter of six pups, Miss Bruns achieved a good mixture of desirable traits and elimination of faults. Hatto Eulenspiegel SchH I became a V-rated dog. Hoppla Eulenspiegel SchH I was also a V-rated dog and approved for breeding. Halma Eulenspiegel was

kept by Miss Bruns, and was rated high in the Youthclass. Halma has been an excellent producer; all the owners of Halma progeny praise the good temperament of these dogs. Halma is still in Miss Bruns kennel as this is written. She is now eight years old, "has been deliberately poisoned twice, and has had two caesarian births, once owing to a dead puppy a week overdue, once owing to a puppy which weighed eight hundred grams at birth and lived." Miss Bruns has not dared to breed her even once more and reproaches herself for not having kept a puppy out of her along the way, as she finds it impossible to buy back any of Halma's children, the present owners being so pleased with their great temperament.

Dina was bred again and produced this time, among others, Ilo Eulenspiegel and Ives Eulenspiegel. Both are HD + / – , both have achieved Schutzhund III, are approved for breeding, and have received V ratings. Ives is an International Champion. His son and daughter, Dingo vom Schweiger Wappen SchH III and the 1979 BS Dina vom Schweiger Wappen SchH III, are approved for breeding. Ives was sired by Astot vom Landgraben SchH III, who is a son of BS Dolly von der Meierei ex the Danish exhibition and working Champion Thor PH (Polizeihund—Danish title, Police Dog). Unfortunately Dina had to be put to sleep at ten years old; she was suffering from cancer. She certainly contributed well to her breed in the wonderful dogs and bitches she produced.

Miss Bruns now has two bitches in her kennels, Betta vom Schwarzwasser and Fledis vom Aalenersrion, both grand-daughters of Ives. Her future plans, so far as breeding goes, are uncertain due to illness. She can indeed rest on her laurels, if she so chooses, with the feeling of satisfaction that comes from truly worthwhile accomplishments. She has done inestimable good to the Rottweiler breed through her own dogs, her judging and her knowledge—a gentle, modest lady who truly exemplifies the highest type of dedicated fancier.

Opposite:
Above left: Joanne Chadwick, in England, owns this handsome German-bred Rottweiler, Rudi Eulenspiegel, imported from Marianne Bruns. **Above right:** Only three weeks old, these Rottweiler babies are from Halma Eulenspiegel, owned by Marianne Bruns. **Below:** Int. Ch. Ives Eulenspiegel, SchH III, approved for breeding to end of breeding age. Marianne Bruns, owner. A magnificent dog in type and quality.

CHAPTER 4

Working Dog Titles of German Rottweilers

Condensed, Translated and Explained by Dr. Evelyn Ellman—Rottweilers von Stolzenfels

You'll find them throughout the pedigrees of your Rottweilers, titles following the names of each dog's German ancestors. And you view them with pride, realizing that they indicate something special, something of importance. However, at times there is an unawareness, particularly among newer fanciers and those who do not understand the German language, of exactly what these titles indicate and how they have been achieved, the intelligence and effort involved on the part of the dogs, and the rules which govern them. We feel it essential that these titles be understood by everyone involved with this courageous and intelligent breed, and we are deeply appreciative of Dr. Ellman having prepared this digest and translation from the German Working Dog Rules for our readers. We hope that it will clarify for you all the noble character, stamina and intelligence indicated whenever you note the appearance of even the simplest of these titles!

—A.K.N.

The Governing Body for all Working Dog Degrees discussed in this chapter is the DVG, abbreviated from the Deutscher Verband der Gebrauchshundesportvereine fuer das Polizei and Schutzhundewesen. This might be translated "German Working Dog Association for Police and Schutzhund Clubs." The purpose of the

A gorgeous photo! Von Gailingen's Dark Delight, C.D. (left) and Ch. Von
Gailingen's Dassie Did It, litter sisters about 14 months old here. By Ch.
Srigo's Zarras v Kurtz ex Ch. Adka v Gailingen. Catherine H. Thompson,
owner, Freehold, NJ.

Opposite:
Bronze Plaque: the ADRK Award presented at the
Club Show in memory of Hans Korn, a founding father.

Willi Faussner, Sr., (left) and Hans Korn (back to camera) officiate at a 1954 Working Trial. Photo credit, Willi Faussner, Jr.

DVG is to encourage the training of working dogs and their handlers, as well as to be the service organization for the training of working dogs for the police departments and, at times, for the armed forces. The DVG is a member of the VDM, or German Kennel Club, which is the parent organization of all German dog clubs. The VDM, in turn, is a member of the FCI, or Federation Cynologique Internationale, which represents a number of countries, mostly European, which mutually agree on certain practices and breed identification.

The VDM unites the following Clubs:

The German Shepherd Dog Club (SV)
DVG (see above paragraph)
The German Doberman Pinscher Club (DV)
The Association of the German Working Dog (VLDG)
The German Rottweiler Club (ADRK)
The German Boxer Club (BK)

Approximately 20,000 members belong to the DVG. The Club is sub-divided into Landesgruppen (Regional Groups), which in turn are sub-divided into Bezirksgruppen (District Groups), which are further sub-divided into Zweiggruppen (Local Groups).

There are close to four hundred Local Groups which meet from twice weekly to twice monthly for training. The membership of the DVG is growing steadily. For participation it is not necessary that a dog be a purebred. Any dog that can do Schutzhund work is eligible for Schutzhund Trials. However, the dogs must have sufficient stamina to do the protection work and be capable of clearing a hurdle approximately thirty inches high, prerequisites which naturally prevent smaller dogs from participation.

The DVG offers the following degrees: Schutzhund A (SchH A), Schutzhund I (SchH I), Schutzhund II (SchH II), Schutzhund III (SchH III), the Faehrtenhund Degree (FH), which is an Advanced Tracking Degree, and two specialized Police Dog Degrees, the DPO I and the DPO II, similar to advanced SchH Degrees, as well as also three less frequently issued degrees and a certification, these latter as follows:

The Rettungshund Tauglichkeitspruefung, which certifies that the dog has been trained for Disaster Work. This degree covers endurance qualifications, obedience performed under severe distraction, running of an obstacle course and the location of hidden clothing or other articles.

The Verkehrssicherer Begleithund, which translates into "Degree for Traffic Sure Companion Dog," indicates that the dog has performed in obedience similar to that required for Schutzhund I except that jumping is not required. The dog works in both normal conditions and in heavy city traffic which causes severe distraction.

The Wachhund Title (WH) is issued to dogs which are tested in obedience routine and the guarding of areas and articles. It might be translated into Watch Dog Title.

The Ausdauerpruefung (AD) is an Endurance Test Degree, demanding that the dog will run beside a bike for fifteen kilometers at a speed of more than ten kilometers per hour. A ten minute rest period is permitted midway. Following completion of the trotting course, on cement, gravel and dirt roads, the dog must perform obedience and retrieve over a 1.00 meter high hurdle. The dog qualifies for this degree only if he displays no signs of exhaustion at the completion of all these exercises.

The Schutzhund degrees are the ones we find most frequently in our pedigrees in the United States as we trace back the ancestry of the dogs. Thus we shall describe their specifications in greater detail. They require that the dogs must perform in obedience,

Siegerin Dora von Burgtobel, 27644, SchH II. Breeder, Armbruster. **Below:** This magnificent dog is Sieger 1951, 1952 and 1953 Dieter von Kohlwald, 30650, SchH I.

Above: Vefa von Hohenreissach, 22,681. SchH I, Z.H.1. Breeder, Karl Osswald. **Below:** Siegerin Dolly vom Landhaus, SchH I, 18891.

tracking and protection. The dogs which most frequently earn these degrees are German Shepherds, Doberman Pinschers, Rottweilers, Boxers, Airedales, Hovawarte and Giant Schnauzers.

Schutzhund A: This degree is identical to Schutzhund I degree except that the requirements do not include tracking. Obedience and protection each are assigned a possible one hundred points, with a minimum of seventy points required for a passing score in obedience and eighty points in the protection trials.

Schutzhund I: There is an age requirement of fourteen months or older, and a temperament test to be administered to the participant. One hundred points are assigned as possible in each of these categories for tracking, obedience and protection and a minimum of seventy points must be achieved in tracking and obedience with eighty or better demanded in the protection trials.

For tracking, the dog, on a ten meter long tracking lead, must follow an unmarked track of no less than four hundred and no more than five hundred paces. This must be laid in place twenty minutes prior to the start of the exercise by the dog's own handler, who at the same time has dropped two articles which the dog must locate. This track includes two turns of ninety degrees.

In obedience, the dog is required to heel on and off lead at three different paces: slow, normal and fast. The dog also must walk calmly through a crowd. Gunshyness is tested with the dog off lead. If he shows fear when the gun is fired, he fails to pass. Another exercise demands that the dog sit down while heeling off lead, while the handler continues walking a distance of about thirty paces, and then returns to the still sitting dog. Again handler and dog will be walking. On the "down" command, the dog must drop to the "down" position while the handler continues for thirty paces, then faces and calls the dog to him. The dog is expected to come quickly and to sit facing his handler. Upon command, the dog must sit by his handler's heel. Now the handler throws an object belonging to him approximately eight paces ahead. Upon the command "bring," the dog retrieves and returns the article to the handler, in front of whom he sits. On command "out" the dog relinquishes the article to the handler. Next the dog must retrieve the article over a thirty inch jump that is one meter high and one and a half meters wide. He must also retrieve an article on the flat, in both cases relinquishing it at the "out" command. Next, upon command, the dog leaves his handler and proceeds at least

Ch. Koka's K's Degen v Burga, C.D., T.D., O.F.A. Photo courtesy, Felicia Luburich, East Brunswick, N.J.

twenty-five paces ahead; again he must "drop" upon command. Now the handler picks up the dog. This is followed by the "down-stay" with the handler approximately fifty paces away, his back turned to the dog. The dog must remain thus positioned while another dog goes through his paces.

During the protection exercises, the dog must locate an agitator who is hiding behind bushes or some other cover in the field. He announces his discovery by barking, but at this point is not supposed to bite. The agitator attacks the handler while the handler is heeling with the dog. Now the dog must attack the agitator, who then hits the dog with a switch. The dog must show no sign of fear and he also must stop immediately upon command of his handler. The agitator now starts to run, behaving in an aggressive manner. The handler sends the dog after the agitator to attack and to hold him.

Above: A Schutzhund area and dogs in Germany. The holding kennels are dark boxes. Photo, courtesy Barbara Dillon. Below: Panamint Ideal Impression at one year of age. Her titles include C.D. and T.D.X. Barbara Dillon, owner.

The Schutzhund II trials can be entered only following completion of the Schutzhund I training, and after the dog has gained that degree. These trials are a somewhat more advanced version of what has already taken place, with some additional more complicated exercises. The same number of points applies in each category as above.

This time, in tracking, the dog must locate two articles over an unfamiliar trail approximately six hundred paces but not more than seven hundred paces. The track must be at least thirty minutes old. Once more the dog is on a ten meter lead and he must manage two ninety degree angles, one going off to the left, the other to the right.

In addition to the test for gunshyness and the basic obedience exercises as in Schutzhund I, the dog must now perform three retrieving exercises using wooden dumb-bells of various weights. On flat ground one weighing one kilogram (2.2 pounds) must be retrieved. Next he must retrieve one weighing 650 grams (1 pound 7 ounces) in a free jump over a hurdle 1.60 meters high and 1.50 meters wide. Finally he must scale a wall 1.60 meters high (64 inches) and retrieve an object belonging to his handler. For Schutzhund II, the pacing and drop to a down command is extended from twenty-five to thirty paces.

In protection, again the dog must locate an agitator, at whom he barks but whom he does not bite. The handler commands the dog to guard the agitator while the handler checks out the hiding place. The agitator will attempt to escape, and the dog is expected to seize the agitator and prevent it. As soon as the agitator stops in his tracks, the dog, without being told, is expected to stop attacking. Now the agitator will attack the dog with a stick or a whip. The dog is to attack the agitator to prevent further aggression. During this exercise, the agitator hits the dog several times. Next the dog is expected to transport the agitator for approximately forty paces. The handler will command the agitator to walk ahead while he and the dog follow at a distance of five feet. The agitator now will attack the handler. The dog is taken off lead and is sent after the agitator. The dog must prevent the agitator from leaving by holding him until the handler calls off the dog.

Schutzhund III demands that the dog must have attained a Schutzhund II title. Here, too, there are the three categories with a possible score of one hundred points in each, and the same minimum requirements.

Could there possibly be a more lovable puppy than this one? Centa von Stolzenfels, Am., Can. T.D. snapped informally as a 9 week oldster, lives in Massachusetts and belongs to Walter Wernig.

In tracking, the dog now must locate three articles placed by a stranger on an unfamiliar track which extends between twelve hundred and fourteen hundred paces in length and has been laid at least fifty minutes before the start of the exercise.

There are two additional obedience exercises. The dog must come to a stand while being heeled at both a normal pace and a running pace. During the former, the dog will be picked up by his handler. During the latter, the handler will call the dog to him. The dog is then required to retrieve over flat ground a dumb-bell weighing two kilograms, and in a free jump over a hurdle that is 1.00 meter high and 1.50 meters wide to retrieve a dumb-bell weighing 650 grams. Over a scaling wall 1.80 meters high, he also must retrieve an article belonging to his handler. The "go away" exercise is extended to forty paces. Then there is a long "down" fifty paces away from the handler with the handler out of sight of the dog. Again the dog must remain in his "down" while another dog goes through his paces.

Protection scores in Schutzhund III include the judging of the overall combativeness of the dog during each of the exercises. First the agitator is once again located in his hiding place and barked at but not bitten by the dog. Next the dog is left to guard the agitator, who has emerged from his hiding place, while the

Ch. Dunja v d Flugschneise, C.D., Ro-1403T, rated "V" (Vorzuglich) excellent, in Germany before being imported by Rodsden. Joan R. Klem, owner, Wheaton, Illinois. Sired by 1978 Bundessieger Benno v Allgauer-Tor, SchH III, FH from Bonny v Haus Schottroy, SchH I. Dunja is handled here by Cindy Meyer under judge Langdon Skarda.

Champion Panamint Anytime Anywhere, C.D., T.D. Owned by Barbara Dillon, Baring, Washington.

handler searches the hiding place. The agitator will now attempt to flee, and the dog must prevent this flight. The agitator now threatens the dog with a stick or a whip. The dog must immediately react by attacking the agitator. Next the dog is to transport the agitator for fifty paces, dog and handler following at a distance of five paces. The agitator attempts to attack the handler. The dog prevents this by firmly grasping and holding the agitator. Handler and dog now escort the agitator to the trial judge where they leave him; then dog and handler start to leave the area. The agitator again attempts to flee, and the handler sends the dog after him. The dog must catch the agitator, using the shortest route. The agitator will try to intimidate the dog by threatening him. The dog must not stop his attack nor be influenced by that of the agitator. When the agitator stops his flight, then the dog ceases his attack. During this exercise, the handler is approximately forty paces away. The agitator will make one more final attempt to hit the dog, and the dog must again stop the agitator from succeeding. After that, the handler will call off the dog and leave the area with him, the dog still off the lead.

We hope that this explanation will provide all of you who cannot read the DVG rules in German a better insight into the true achievements these DVG titles represent.

Ch. Dieter vom Koningsberg, C.D. A German import by Dolf v Weiherbrunnele, SchH III, F.H. ex Jutta v Rodenstein. Dieter, the sire of 16 champions, was imported by Barbara Dillon for her Panamint Rottweilers.

CHAPTER 5

Rottweilers in the United States

Although it is generally accepted that Rottweilers were unknown in the United States prior to the mid-1930s, Jim Harwood has found a reference to one, complete with its photo, in the June 1929 issue of *Dogdom* magazine. Only a head-study of the dog appears, and it is unidentified beyond saying that it would be seen in the Borough of Queens, New York, at dog shows in the future!

On searching through my file of catalogues from the Westminster Kennel Club Dog Shows, I find that Rottweilers were represented there with two at the 1937 event: one in American-bred Dogs and Bitches and one in Open Dogs and Bitches (the sexes were not divided for the breed at this show at that period). The first one, a bitch, named Irma v Steinbach, had been whelped on September 4th, 1929 (thus was eight years old at the time). She had been bred by J. Kocher, sired by Franzl v d Kinzeg from Zilly v d Steinbach. The other, a dog whelped October 21st, 1932, sired by Jank v d Steinbach from Nora v d Landeck, was named simply Prince. Both were owned by Robert Sieber, and this gentleman was the breeder of Prince. The two were also entered in the Brace Class competition.

A great and famous Rottweiler, Ch. Don Juan, U.D., is owned by Mrs. Margaret McIntyre, Enumclaw, Washington. He is pictured here at ten months of age at a match show where he placed in the Group. The magnificent quality of this fabulous dog is clearly evident, even at the early age depicted here. He was, some years back, featured in a story in the *New York Times* written by Walter Fletcher.

Opposite:
Ch. Srigo's Garner v Zaghin, by Ch. Srigo's Bernard
v Derbis ex Heide v Zaghin.

There were no Rottweilers entered for Westminster in 1943, 1944 and 1947, which are the only three catalogues I still have from Westminsters of the 1940s.

There was one Open Bitch in 1954, Lisa Af Dannevang, born January 28th, 1952, by Timm ex Stella of Ally. Owner Geraldine Carter, breeder Peggy Inman.

Two years later, two Rotts. 1956. William C. Stahl had Rex von Stahl, bred by Hubert and Albert Riester, by Joseph v Hohenzollern of Giralda ex Asta of Roberts Park with (back again) Lisa Af Dannevang.

Mr. Stahl remained active in the breed over a number of years. The sire of the dog interests me, as he belonged to Mrs. M. Hartley Dodge, Jr., of Madison, New Jersey, the lady who gave the Dog Fancy the fabulous Morris and Essex Kennel Club Dog Show at her beautiful estate, Giralda Farms. Mrs. Dodge was the first of my own personal friends to own Rottweilers, and no breed ever could have had a more devoted fancier! How often I have sat with her as she lamented the lack of early interest in the breed and wished for it to have the wide recognition and big show entries she felt that it deserved. I wonder if she would really be that happy were she to know the fast and sudden upsurge being "enjoyed" today! Mrs. Dodge had at least several Rotts around Giralda Farms, where they were admired and appreciated.

In 1957, the Rott entry had grown to seven for Westminster. There was a class dog, Reidstadt's Rudiger, owned by Joanne Marsh, bred by John and Cecilia Reed, plus four class bitches: two in American-bred and two in Open. Two "specials" appeared this time, both belonging to Mr. Stahl, one co-owned with Mrs. Stahl. The latter was Champion Pomona, October 12th, 1955, breeders Mr. and Mrs. T.O. Wall, by Asso v Wittelsback ex Champion Valeria. The dog "special" was Champion Rex von Stahl, C.D., that had competed in the Open Dog Class in 1956.

In 1959 there appeared several names that have remained consistently active in the breed. Again seven entries, two of them Open Dogs, two Open Bitches and three "specials". The Open Dogs were Mrs. Bernard Freeman's Gerhardt von Stahl, bred by the Stahls, by Champion Rex von Stahl ex Champion Pomona, and Charles J. McKelvy's Jaro von Schleidenplatz, by Alf von der Burg Hohenstein ex Enka vom Schleidenplatz.

One Open Bitch was Srigo Kennels' Reidstadt's Helisand, John and Cecilia Reed, breeders, entered in an earlier Westminster by

The first known reference to the Rottweiler in America appeared in June, 1929, in the publication, *Dogdom,* a widely read all-breed dog magazine of that period. Only partial view of the dog is shown, and he is not further identified, beyond the information that he "will be seen in the Borough of Queens area, New York at shows in the future." The usual reference to Rottweilers in the United States begins in the early 1930s.

Photo, courtesy Jim and Norma Harwood.

Above: Four-month-old Rottweiler puppies from the mid 1950's owned by Mrs. Geraldine Rockefeller Dodge are (from l.): Arko, Argus, April and Autumn of Giralda. Sired by Ch. Krieger von Hohenreissach from Gretchen of Giralda, these puppies were from a litter of twelve, all living. Photo, courtesy Edwin A. Sayres, Jr., and Dr. Joseph Sayres. **Below:** Proudly we present this photo of Ch. Krieger von Hohenreissach taken in 1956 when he was three years old. This noted and magnificent dog belonged to Mrs. Geraldine Rockefeller Dodge, Giralda Farms, Madison, N.J. Photo, courtesy Edwin A. Sayres, Jr. and Dr. Joseph Sayres.

Joanne Marsh. It is hardly necessary to remark on the fame that has been earned by Srigo Rottweilers over the years, and that the kennel is still active after two decades of producing top flight Rotts. The other Open Bitch was Mrs. John K. Meiner's Dagmar von Schildgen. The "specials" were the same two as in 1957 from the Stahls, and Rudiger belonging to Joanne Marsh.

Meanwhile, in California, considerable important activity had been taking place. Noel Jones was a highly regarded American Kennel Club licensed handler, and he was the original individual, still alive, who began the breed on the Pacific Coast. The first two champions were of his breeding.

Mr. Jones has told us an amusing story (which I am certain was anything but amusing to the people involved) about the Rottweiler that was actually the first of the breed to fill the requirements for A.K.C. championship. This dog, Astra von Weinsberger-Tal, was purchased from Helen Heid for W.M. Bruenig. Mr. Jones won three five point majors in rapid succession with the dog, but then the wins were disallowed as the German papers were still in the process of registration, and permission had not been obtained to show the dog in the interim.

Thus Champion Zero became the first recognized American Kennel Club Champion in the Rottweiler breed.

The next, Mr. Jones tells us, was Cito v d Hohenzollern, which he recalls as having belonged to Mrs. Heid.

Mr. Jones goes on to speak of the dog, Champion Kurt, that he gave to Harry Kramer because he could not afford to show him for himself. This was the first Rottweiler to win a Working Group, which he did under Mrs. Dodge at the San Mateo Show. Mr. Jones tells us, "He was probably the best Rottweiler on the West Coast, and could win today in spite of our imports. He had 'ham' and live spirit. Too many are dull."

Noel Jones' first Rottweiler was Cuna v d Schwartzen Eiche, which came from Mr. Eichler in Wisconsin. Cuna was a daughter of Herlinde v d Schwartze Eiche, the first Rottweiler in the U.S.A. to gain a U.D.T. title. Cuna, says Mr. Jones "raised my first son, Ross," and "Delga raised my second son, Noel Jr." Ross, incidentally, still retains his love of the breed, and received one from Barbara Hoard Dillon. A gift to him for his 37th birthday, Delga also produced some excellent Rottweilers for Noel Jones, including his famous "Z" litter, which included Zero, Zepp, Zada, Zenda, etc.

Noel Jones handled or bred or did both with the following noted Rottweilers of early days. Champion Hannibal, described as "Dr. Durfee's dog," Champion Eric, Cliff Bunker's dog, called by Mr. Jones "a great one," and Champion El Pago Baca, owned by Erna Pinkerton. He comments, "Erna Pinkerton probably did more for Rottweilers than anyone during the 1950s."

Noel Jones was actually the founder of the club that had originally been destined to become the Parent Club for Rottweilers in the United States had it succeeded following its organization back in the 1940s. Known as the Rottweiler Club of America, it started off with an enthusiastic group and a busy program, holding frequent match shows in Mr. Jones' backyard. He, Barbara Hoard Dillon (who purchased her first Rottweiler from him), and Nancy and Andrew Cooper are the only ones of the original members still alive. Unfortunately, a political situation is said to have taken place, and the Club dissolved into various "cliques" en route to eventual extinction.

I believe that the Colonial Rottweiler Club, founded in 1956, is the oldest of the present Rottweiler Clubs, followed by Medallion in 1959.

Reaching the 1960s, we find Champion Jaro v Schleidenplatz going Best of Breed at Westminster that first year of the new decade. This was Charles McKelvey's well known dog, shown by Jack Houser of Moss Bow Foley Dog Shows now, who was then a highly successful professional handler. Liesel v Kuhlwald was entered there by John E. White, sired by Ali v Martinsburg ex Elfe v. Kuhlwald. Warner Gessner had Cora aus der Leubachstadt and Alf von der Kugellagerstadt in from Chicago.

Jaro was the only Rottweiler entered for "specials" at Westminster in 1961. Mrs. Bernard Freeman had Gerhardt von Stahl (Champion Rex von Stahl ex Champion Pomona) as an Open Dog. Srigo Kennels, always a big entry through the years at Westminster, had two bitches which were also shown as a brace. I feel quite certain, as I look at these catalogues, that Felicia Luburich must have bred, owned and/or handled more Rotts at these prestigious shows than the combined total of any other breeders! Those she showed in 1961 were Missy von Stahl (also from Pomona, obviously a successful producer) and Reidstadt's Helissend.

Seven Rotts made up the total 1962 Westminster entry. Jaro was again a "special," joined by Mrs. Freeman's Gerhardt von Stahl

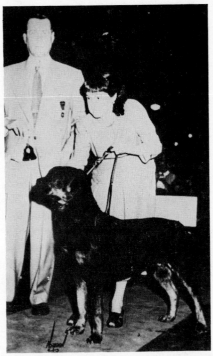

Ch. Zero, the first recorded Rottweiler Champion of Record in American Kennel Club records, completed his title in 1949. By Kris from Delga. The judge is James Walker Trullinger. **Below:** Mrs. Dorit S. Rogers contributed this picture of famous German import, Cuno v Kronchen, sire of Ch. Drossel, Ch. Danka v Molzberg and Am., Can. Ch. Drauf v Molzberg.

From the 1960's. Ch. Srigo's Creshenda v Misle, by Ch. Dervis v Wyershof x Ch. Missy v Stahl, the latter one of Srigo Kennels' earliest bitches and a dominant producer. Felicia Luburich, owner.

Opposite:
Above: In the tradition of his ancestors, Ch. Dolf Fuller von Stolzenfels is harnessed to a cart. Note the puppies in the young passenger's arms. Dolf belongs to Jack P. and Dr. Evelyn M. Ellman, Augusta, Michigan. **Below:** Head study of Ch. Lorelei, bred and owned by von Gruenerwald Kennels, photographed at ten years old.

Ch. Arras v Stadthaus, a
famous producer and show
dog of the early 1960s. By
Rex v Kohlwald, 33736, from
Olga v Bruckenwirt.

Ch. Dervis vom Weyerhof in
1961. By Carla v d Gathe
33898 ex Anka v Gansebruch
34326. Photo, courtesy James
and Norma Harwood.

Ch. Arno v Kafluzu at seven
years of age. See the quality
of this beautiful dog, and the
handsome picture he makes,
side view.

which now was a Champion, the same two Srigo bitches as the previous year and three Open Dogs: Rocky of King Merritt owned by Helen R. Charnas, Schon of Townview owned by Carole Jo Nichols and Caesar Leo owned by William S. Bartley.

Seven must have been the magic number for Rotts at Westminster of this period, as so often that was the number listed. In 1963 they consisted of an American-bred dog, Arkos of Camidon, by Champion Gerhardt v Stahl from Adella v Hohenreissach. Three bitches came from Srigo Kennels, they being Missy v Stahl with her two daughters, sired by Champion Dervis v Weyershof, and another from this litter belonging to Mrs. Helga Schroeder. Champion Gerhardt v Stahl was Best of Breed for Mrs. Freeman. This was apparently the first Westminster trip for Rodsden, as P.G. Rademacher and R.F. Klem had the other "special" in their Champion Quelle von der Solitude. Srigo Kennels again had an entry in the Brace Class.

In 1964 the Rottweiler entry advanced to ten, and this year there were several interesting advertisements in the catalogue from Rottweiler breeders, the first time this had happened. Rodsden, Srigo Kennels and Mrs. Freeman were those represented, with Srigo offering its new importation at stud, Champion Arno v Kafluzu.

There was also a long list of trophies for Rottweilers offered through the auspices of the Colonial Rottweiler Club. Donors were Mr. and Mrs. Sam Zinnanti (he was President that year), Srigo Kennels, Mrs. Helga Stoessler, Mr. and Mrs. J. Koeniger, Mr. and Mrs. Ernest Rau, Dr. and Mrs. Fred Knockem, Mr. and Mrs. Leo Gorney, Mr. and Mrs. Albert Gaiser, Karen Rau (Wunderkinder), Carolyn Allen, Mr. and Mrs. Paul Elkin, Mr. and Mrs. Richard M. Reinhardt, Debbie Mulvey (Grunberg), Mr. and Mrs. Thomas Arcidiancon, and Frank Hearn.

There were three Open Dog entries this time. Sam Zinnanti's Arkos v Camidon, Mr. and Mrs. Leo Gurney's Rigomar v Rau of Wunderkinder, and Alfred Gaiser, Senior and Junior, had their Srigo's Derekas v Arnos.

Three bitches were Lazelle S. Knocke's Srigo's Darla v Missle in American-bred, Srigo's Amai v Missle and Srigo's Diensta v Missle, both from Missy, sired by Aervis and Arno respectively.

The "specials" were Champion Schon of Townville, owned by Carole Jo Nichols, Champion Isolde v Rau of Wunderkinder owned by Karen Rau, Champion Missy von Stahl owned by Srigo

Ch. Zola is the second recorded A.K.C. champion Rottweiler in the United States, and the first of her sex. Like Zero, the first recorded A.K.C. champion of the breed, she was sired by Kris from Delga.

Above: Excellent Rottweiler action is being illustrated here by Am., Can. Ch. Bingo vom Hohenreissach, owned by Darlene Adam of Winston-Salem, North Carolina and handled here by Judith Ann Coen. It is easy to see how this dog finished his title at 13 months of age with 5 majors, and has two Working Group firsts among his credits! **Below:** Five-month-old Southwood's Faline of Tobant learning about "show posse." Owner, Sherri Page.

Am., Can. Ch. Negus vom Hohenreissach II, C.D., C.D.X., the first Rottweiler owned and trained by Judith Ann Coen, Baltimore, MD, was the High Scoring Rottweiler, Shuman System, for Obedience in 1970 and 1971 in the United States and Canada. It is believed that he was the second Rottie to earn an All-Breed Highest in Trial, which he did at Barrie 1971.

Kennel and Champion Srigo's Crescendo v Missle owned by Mrs. Stoessler.

The Rodsden advertisement in the 1964 Westminster catalogue expressed regret for the fact that their International Champion and Bundessieger for 1960, 1961 and 1962 that had arrived from Europe several months previously had been too late to have the opportunity for qualifying in time to be entered at this show.

The Westminster entry rose to thirteen for 1965. Two dogs, one in American-bred, Srigo's Erna v Lorac owned by Dr. John Ippolito, one in Open, Srigo's Bernard v Dervis owned by Richard Bernhardt, three in American-bred, all of which were either owned or bred by Srigo (what a truly GREAT producing kennel!) and one in Open, Fabiana v Rau of WunderKinden.

Srigo had four representatives in "specials". Their own Champion Srigo's Diensta v Missle and Champion Srigo's Amai v Missle, Mrs. Lazelle E. Knocke's Champion Srigo's Darla v Missle. And Helga Stoessler's Champion Srigo's Crescendo v Missle. Edward H. Beretta of Pawtucket, Rhode Island had a dog that was to become well known to visitors at this show, Champion Ferdinand v Dachsweil, a son of Jaro ex Follow Me's Michele, bred by Betty Reinhardt. Carole Nichols had Champion Schon. Mr. and Mrs. Leo Gorney had Champion Bigomar v Rau of Wunderkinder.

In 1966 there was a page from Srigo in Westminster's catalogue, with a report of numerous exciting wins through the year. Half a page appeared from Rodsden's and a quarter page from Mrs. Freeman. Champion Ferdinand v Dachsweil was Best of Breed in an entry of thirteen, which included, from the "specials" class, Champion Rodsden's Felicia, owned by Mary Jayne and Meyer Sachs, that had been the 1965 Colonial Specialty Winner at Trenton. This was a daughter of Champion Baron of Rodsden, C.D. from Champion Quelle von der Solitude, plus Champion Srigo's Econnie v. Lorac owned by Lucille and Donald Kurtz, Winners Bitch at the Colonial Specialty and second in the Working Group at Penn Ridge from the classes; also the Bernhardts' Champion Srigo's Bernard v Dervis, Lazelle, S. Knocke's Champion Srigo's Darla v Missle and Champion Srigo's Amai v Missle owned by Srigo Kennels—some very challenging competition.

There were three in Open Dogs. Kimba v Kaltental owned by Ida Marcus, Zito v Kursaal, Bart Chamberlain and Condor v d Lowenau, Stanley Paul Jones. In American-bred there was one bitch, Srigo's Faxonia owned by Srigo Kennels. Three were in Open, Mrs. Alice Jernigan's Srigo's Eloric Missle Again, Mrs. J.B. Syne's Rodsden's Jafra (by Harras) and Lulu M. Stettes' Townview's Hide A Way Mecca.

The Gruenerwalds came to Westminster in 1967, bringing with them Cache v Gruenerwald in American-bred Dogs and Champion Lorelei as a "Special." It was not too usual in those days for fanciers to come so far, even for Westminster, and I am certain that the Easterners enjoyed meeting these Colorado breeders who have been so highly successful over the years and seeing their Rotts.

Mrs. Bernard Freeman had her Champion Gerhardt von Stahl's son, D'Artagnon of Camidon, entered in Open, a young dog that went on to an excellent career. Kenneth Laub had Srigo's Garner

Srigo's Heart of Gold, third in the 1979 Sweepstakes. Felicia Luburich handling. **Below:** Ch. Srigo's Spruce v Kurtz, by Ch. Srigo's Garner v Zaghin ex Ch. Econnie v Lorac. Bred, owned and handled by Felicia Luburich.

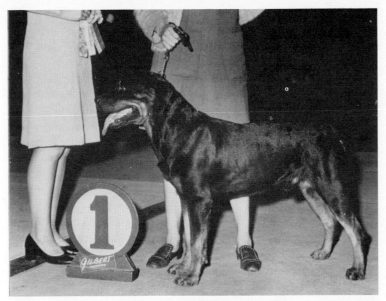

Above: Felicia Luburich owns Ch. Srigo's Kerno v Kurtz, by Bundessieger Ch. Erno v Wellesweiler from Ch. Srigo's Econnie, C.D. **Below:** Ch. Cache von Gruenerwald pictured winning Best of Breed at Ventura Kennel Club, July 27, 1968. Owner Dorothea Gruenerwald, Colorado Springs, CO.

115

v Zaghin. Srigo had its import, Casper v d Lowenau, by the noted German sire Harras v Sofienbusch and Barbara Wood, and Debbie Mulvey had Grunberg Anker v d Adel.

Mrs. Freeman also had an Open Bitch, Priska von Kyrsaal. Mrs. Alice Jernigan had Srigo's Eldorac Missle Again and Mrs. Patricia Lecuyer had Northwind's Tina in this class.

The seven "special" were the aforementioned Champion Lorelei, Edith Drewer's Champion Srigo's Eshenda v Lorac, James E. Ryder's Champion Srigo's Garrett v Zaghin, Donald and Lucille Kurtz's Champion Srigo's Econnie v Lorac, Debbie Mulvey's Champion Grunberg Andra von der Adel and Lulu M. Stettes' Champion Townview's Hide A Way Mecca. You will note that some of these had appeared previously at Westminster in the class competition and were going on from there to be "specialed."

Opening the catalogue for Westminster 1968, we note an advertisement from Mrs. Bernard Freeman announcing the arrival of International Champion, Bundessieger and World Sieger Erno von Wellesweiler, Schutzhund III, to join the Rottweilers already in her kennel—an extremely important addition to the breed in the United States. Erno was entered as an Open Dog at this event, and we regret that our catalogue does not have the awards marked. There was an Open Bitch entry from Mrs. Freeman, too, Belinda of Canidom, a daughter of Gerhardt. Also Mr. Roger Pile had Srigo's Amabel v Missle and Rebecca Threapleton had Townview's Melissa.

Champion Ferdinand v Dachsweil was back as a "special." We have noted that this dog, which was handled by Tom Glassford, during 1966 had sixty-two Bests of Breed including Westminster, Chicago International, Trenton (Colonial Rottweiler Club Specialty), Westchester, Philadelphia, Baltimore, etc, plus three Working Group placements.

Also at Westminster in the 1968 "specials" list, one finds Champion Srigo's Elorac Missle Again, Champion Srigo's Eshenda v Lorac, Champion Srigo's Econnie v Lorac, Champion Srigo's Garner v Zaghin and Champion D'Artagnon of Canidom.

The decade of the 1960s finished up with only seven "specials" entered for the 1969 Westminster. Mrs. Freeman had three of them: Champion Erno v Wellesweiler, Champion D'Artagnon (with Stuart Sliney, now of Moss Bow Dog Shows, listed as handler) and Champion Priska, which also listed Tom Glassford

A bitch that really made her presence felt in the Rottweiler ring during the 1960s. Ch. Srigo's Econnie v Lorac, C.D., bred by Felicia Luburich, shown here. Owned by Lucille and Donald Kurtz.

Ch. Arno v Kafluzu, Best of Breed from the Open Class over "specials" at the 1962 Colonial Rottweiler Club Specialty, his very first point show. His daughter was Winners Bitch and Best of Opposite Sex. Felicia Luburich, handler and co-owner.

A very handsome head study of a Group Winning Rottweiler, Ch. Wind-makers Arlo der Gremlin owned by Jim and Wanda White.

Opposite:
Above left: Debbie Mulvey of Grunberg Rottweilers is credited with having introduced the breed in Vermont when she moved there from Connecticut. This was her foundation bitch, Valeska v Rau of Wunderkinder. Val produced Ch. Grunberg Andra v.d. Adel, breeder-owned and Ch. Grunberg Anker v.d. Adel, C.D., owned and handled by Ruth and Arthur Twiss. Ch. Andra produced the first Rottweiler "super tracker," Grunberg Brummel v.d. Adel, Am., Can. T.D., owned and handled by Ruth and Arthur Twiss. **Above right:** Ch. Srigo's Eshenda v Lorac, Best of Opposite Sex at Westminster over "specials" from the American-bred Class in the 1960's, and Reserve Winners Bitch at the Colonial Rottweiler Club Specialty. By Ch. Arno v Kafluzu ex Srigo's Constance v Misle. **Below:** Ch. Rodsden's Kluge v d Harque, CD, Ro 50, owned by Rodsden. Sire: Int. Ch. 3-yr. Bsgr. Ch. Harras v Sofienbush SchH I. Dam: Ch. Quelle vd Solitude, CD.. Kluge became the 1960's Top Producing Stud dog.

119

to handle, as did Champion Olli v Silahopp belonging to E. Miller and James Rosenbaum, Champion Rodsden's Echo Abby and Champion Srigo's Garrett v Zaghin.

1970 had little in the way of new Westminster developments beyond the fact that the "specials" competition was truly spectacular. Dick Cooper was listed as handler on Dr. and Mrs. Olson's Champion Rodsden's Duke Du Trier. The Gruenerwalds had Champion Cache con Gruenerwald entered as did Mrs. Freeman Champion D'Artagnon, Champion Erno and Champion Priska. Champion Srigo's Garret v Zaghin represented Srigo Kennels. Champion Rodsden's Acho Abby was in for Abigail Blackwell. In class competition, Karen Rau had two entries. The Kurtzes had one, and Mrs. Freeman had one in co-ownership with Mrs. Geoffrey Nightingdale.

Mrs. Freeman judged the breed at Westminster in 1971 and certainly had some beautiful quality from which to make her selections. Duke Du Trier, back again. Champion Srigo's Madchen v Kurtz and Champion Srigo's Merno v Kurtz and the appearance of what was to become America's first Best in Show Rottweiler, Champion Rodsden's Kato v Donnaj, C.D., owned by Jan Marshall. Four dogs and two bitches made up the remainder of the entry. Two of the dogs were owned or handled by Felicia Luburich. Samson von Rodsden was handled by Alan Levine for Fred Barandes. And Evonne Chashoudian had Duarte von Altmeister on from California for Annie Dees Anderson. The bitches were Srigo's Quindle v Kurtz and Srigo's Paint Your Wagon.

Duke Du Trier, handled by Richard Orseno, was Best of Breed, as he had been the previous year handled by Dick Cooper.

New names that are by now familiar to our present day fanciers began appearing in the Westminster entry lists by 1972. Harry Isaacs with his importation, Liane vom Schloss Stauffenberg (Bulli vom Hungerbuhl—Asta vom Schloss Werenwag) followed this one the next year with Caro vom Zimmerplatz and by 1974 was showing both of these as "specials" with Erno vom Ingenhof (Dux v Stuffelkope—Dedda vom Kursaal) in the dog classes. Mr. Isaacs is a loyal Rottweiler enthusiast with a keen, active interest in the breed. His frequent trips to Europe give him a good opportunity to evaluate what is taking place in Rottweiler circles there, and it is always worthwhile discussing Rotts with this gentleman.

James and Norma Harwood were showing in the early 1970s, too! Axel von Gailingen, bred by Cathy Thompson, by Champion

Left: Lori and son, the latter at 9½ months old, photographed July 1, 1966. Dorothea Gruenerwald, owner. **Right:** Ch. Olga von Gruenerwald finished her championship with a 4 point major and Best of Breed from Judge Robert Wills at Oakland County Kennel Club, January 21, 1978. Alan and Karen Kruse owners.

Dux von Hungerbuhl ex Champion Natasha vom Hohenreissach. Jim Harwood is a former President of the American Rottweiler Club and, as already noted, has contributed to this book with photos and historical facts.

Breeders who had considerable impact on the future of Rottweilers in the United States, and who were active during the 1960s and 1970s were Paul and Norma Harris of the Kuhlwald Kennels. This couple started out breeding Greyhounds for the Florida racetracks; then they also started breeding Rottweilers, importing a number of very good German dogs and bitches. Among them were Fetz vom Oelberg, SchH II, a dog with the Lebenszeit Angekort (Lifetime Breeding Approval) from ADRK before coming to America. Also the German "V" dog ("Excellent") Bodo vom Stuffelkopf. Others included Jetta vom Oelberg, Bill von der Grurmannsgeide, Assi vom Dahl, Kathi von der Hobertsburg, Jarro von der Hobertsburg, and Axel vom Schwanenschlag. These dogs were instrumental in establishing the Kuhlwald line, which is to be found among some excellent present day Rottweilers. As mentioned in her kennel story, Dorit Rogers, of the Bergluft Rottweilers, founded her kennel on Kuhlwald lines. It is Mrs. Rogers who handraised the last litter, their "T" litter, for the Harrises. They never saw these puppies. Unfortunately there was a divorce in the family, which evidently ended interest in the dogs.

CHAPTER 6

Top Ten Rottweilers:

1973 through 1979

W e are deeply indebted to the American Rottweiler Club Top Ten Committee, to its Chairman, Kathy Evans, and to Cathy Thompson who was responsible for getting to us the following tabulations covering the above stated years. We can think of no better way to put our finger on the pulse of what Rottweilers and which bloodlines have been winning during the decade of the 1970s—valuable information to breeders, exhibitors, and those who just enjoy following developments within the breed.

BEST OF BREED. Number of Rottweilers in competition, minus one.

BEST OF OPPOSITE SEX. Number of Rottweilers in competition of that same sex, minus one.

IF BEST OF OPPOSITE SEX WAS A CLASS ANIMAL. The number of animals of that sex, plus the number of specials of the same sex, minus one.

IF BEST OF OPPOSITE SEX DEFEATED BEST OF WINNERS. Then both sexes of class animals, plus specials of the same sex, minus one.

IF BEST OF OPPOSITE SEX WAS A CLASS ANIMAL THAT WAS ALSO BEST OF WINNERS. Then both sexes of class animals, plus specials of the same sex, minus one.

BEST OF
BREED

GILBERT PHOTO

Ch. Bergluft's Cliff, despite limited showing, was among the Top Ten Rottweilers in 1975. Jack Patterson handling for owner Mrs. Dorit S. Rogers.

Opposite:
Another of Jan Marshall's famous Best in Show winning Rottweilers, Am., Can. Ch. Donnaj Vt. Yankee of Paulus, C.D.X. Yank is a grandson of the first Best in Show Rottweiler, Ch. Rodsden's Kato v Donnaj, CDX, TD., also owned by Mrs. Marshall. Yank's first Best in Show was won at the Ladies Dog Club June 2, 1979, the largest show ever to have been won by a Rottweiler at this writing.

Basically this comes out to be one point for each Rottweiler defeated.

The numerals following each dog's name indicate these facts. Column one: number of dogs defeated. Column two: number of wins. Column three: number of times Best of Breed. Column four: number of times Best Of Opposite Sex.

TOP TEN DOGS FOR 1979

	Dogs Defeated	No. Wins	BOB	BOS
1. Ch. Oscar v h Brabantpark C. Hurley and M.S. Grossman.	974	55	55	—
2. Ch. Rodsden's Ansel v Brabant.H.E. and R.A. O'Brien.	869	54	53	1
3. Ch. Rodsden's Bruin v Hungerbuhl, CD.J. and G. Kittner.	774	68	68	—
4. Ch. Donnaj Vt. Yankee of Paulus, CDX.J.M. Marshall.	583	27	26	1
5. Ch. Erno v d Gaarn.A.M. Earp.	361	12	11	1
6. Ch. Mannsunn's Annotation P.G. Oesterman, Sr.	276	33	33	—
7. Ch. Srigo's Flight of the Eagle, CD.A.L. Rikel.	267	24	22	2
8. Ch. Bethel Farms Apollo R.D. Bolden and P. Weller.	193	15	15	—
9. Ch. Haserway's Polo Bear C T. and S. Stephenson.	178	13	13	—
10. Ch. Wotan v Kastanienbaum.H. and F. Mikoleit.	176	9	9	—

TOP TEN BITCHES FOR 1979

	Dogs Defeated	No. Wins	BOB	BOS
1. Ch. Andan Indy Pendence v Paulus.Mrs. B.C. Tilghman	406	33	16	17

2. Ch. Radio Ranch's
Christmas Spirit.T. Sallen
and B. Jones 261 23 3 20

3. Ch. De Riemer's Sjefke,
CD.R.M. Anderson and T.
Wade. 223 24 4 20

4. Ch. Weissenburg's Blau
Max.P. and D. Diamond. 182 13 8 5

5. Ch. Marja Elka v Heidel.J.
Puglise. 160 23 9 14

6. Ch. Czarina v Stolzenfels,
CD.J.P. and Dr. E.M.
Ellman. 156 8 2 6

7. Ch. Ebonstern Kzabear
V.D. Liege, C. Wheeler,
and B. and B. and S.
Spooner. 149 20 9 11

8. Ch. Annika v Schmetterling
Mrs. A. Kahler. 148 15 3 12

9. Ch. Dacca M von Golden
West, CD.M. and E. Good-
farb. 143 15 2 13

10. Ch. Bella von Meadow.V.K.
Hutto. 139 10 3 7

TOP TEN DOGS FOR 1978

1. Ch. Phaedra's Amax of
Sunnyside.Mrs. B.M.
Tucker. 512 36 32 4

2. Ch. Gatstuberget's Eskil
Jarl, C.D. M.S. Grossman. 430 37 33 4

3. Ch. Panamint Otso v
Kraewel, UD.H.A. and B.J.
Hendler. 353 14 12 2

4. Ch. Burley v Morgan
Carroll, C.D.B. and B.
Carroll 350 19 18 1

5. Ch. Rodsden's Ansel v
Brabant H.E. and R.A.
O'Brien. 299 27 27 —

125

Ch. Rodsden's Bruin v Hungerbuhl, CD. Ro-1189. An outstanding American-bred, Bruin goes back thru a fine working dog heritage to Harras on his dam's (Ch. Rodsden's Frolich Burga, CD, TD Ro-649) side and is a son of Dux. Bruin is the Top winning Rottweiler in the US, 1979-'80 and has placed Best In Show 25 times so far. Owned and bred by the Kittners.

Opposite:
Above: A superb homebred bitch, bred and owned by Jack P. and Dr. Evelyn Ellman, Ch. Czarina von Stolzenfels takes Best of Opposite Sex at the Medallion Rottweiler Club's Specialty, June 10, 1978, at Wheaton, IL, in an entry of 106 including 39 for "specials" competition. **Below:** A memorable moment in Rottweiler history: Judge Ed Dixon presents the Best in Show award to Am., Can. Ch. Srigo's Flight of the Eagle, Am., Can. CD, a dual champion owned by Mr. and Mrs. Arthur L. Rikel, Butler, PA. Bred by Felicia Luburich.

Ch. Centurian's Che Von Der Barr, Ro-757, winning the Working Group at Skokie Valley. Che, a dominant producer and highly successful show dog, belongs to Josej and Donna Hedl, Chicago, IL.

TOP TEN DOGS FOR 1978 (cont.)

6. Ch. Centurian's Che Von Der Barr. J. and D. Hedl	297	36	32	4
7. Ch. Rodsden's Bruin v Hungerbuhl, C.D., J.M. and G.M. Kittner	253	29	29	—
8. Ch. Blitz von Gailingen.Dr. D. Hodinar and L. Lieberman.	245	19	18	1
9. Ch. Bingo von Hohenreissach.D.F. Adam.	239	13	13	—
10. Ch. Donnaj Vt. Yankee of Paulus, CDX.J.M Marshall.	229	22	21	—

(All of these dogs had at least one Group placement)

TOP TEN BITCHES FOR 1978

1. Ch. Haserway's Razzle
   Dazzle.P.G. Sr. and C.M.
   Oesterman.   278   29   15   14

2. Ch. Chelsea De Michaela
   W.C. and I.G. Rhodes.   259   15   4   11

3. Ch. V Gailingen's
   Welkerhaus Cia.Mrs. R.
   Welker.   249   24   2   22

4. Ch. Radio Ranch's Kari On
   T.L. Sallen.   221   27   1   26

5. Ch. Bella von Meadow.V.K.
   Hutto.   169   17   2   15

6. Ch. Hella v Marchenwald
   M. Marcus.   137   3   1   2

7. Ch. Czarina v Stolzenfels,
   C.D. J.P. and Dr. E.M.
   Ellman and D. Boik.   132   10   6   4

8. Ch. Ebonstern Itzabear v d
   Liebe.C. Wheeler and B.
   and S. Spooner.   131   12   5   7

9. Ch. Centurian's Cassandra
   R. Noll and P. Weller.   121   17   2   15

10. Ch. Taba v d Keizerslanden
    C. Hurley and M. Grossman.   112   15   4   11

TOP TEN DOGS FOR 1977

1. Ch. Centurian's Che V.D.
   Barr. J. and D. Hedl.   549   55   53   2

2. Ch. Burley v Morgan
   Carroll, CD.B. and B.
   Carroll and C. Lindsey.   455   25   24   1

3. Ch. Phaedra's Amax of
   Sunnyside.Mrs. B.M. Tucker.   442   44   43   1

4. Ch. Gatstuberget's Eskil
   Jarl, CD.M.S. Grossman.   397   32   23   4

5. Ch. Panamint Nobel v
   Falkenberg, CD.S.L. and C.
   Johnson.   211   20   20   —

129

The handsome head study shown here is of Ch. Radio Ranch's Axel v Notara owned by Pamela Crump Weller, Radio Ranch.

6. Ch. Donnaj Vt. Yankee of Paulus, CD.J.M. Marshall.	193	16	16	—
7. Ch. Brattana's Gus De Michaela.J.C. and A.C. Bratt.	154	8	8	—
8. Ch. Panamint Otso v Kraewell, CDX,H.A. and B.J. Hendler.	139	6	6	—
9. Ch. Radio Ranch's Axel v Notara.G. Crump and P. Weller.	138	17	15	2
10. Ch. Rommel v Reno.J.E. and J.H. Zimmer.	136	11	10	1

TOP TEN BITCHES FOR 1977

1. Ch. Andan Indy Pendence v Paulus.A.D. Tilghman.	374	33	18	15
2. Ch. Panamint Pakt v Rheintal.P. Taylor.	265	35	5	30
3. Ch. Vala v Kursaal.F. and H. Mikoleit and M. Schmidt.	140	12	—	12
4. Ch. Ebonstern Halalujah V D Liebe.C.E. Wheeler.	135	16	1	15
5. Ch. Merrymoore's Charisma.M. Douglas and C. Mann.	108	15	5	10
6. Ch. Northwind's Just Blew In.J. Nichols.	97	7	2	5
7. Ch. Panamint Saphir v Rheintal, CD.L.E. Ang.	86	3	1	2
8. Ch. Gatstuberget Asa v Kleinholz.M. McIntyre.	82	5	4	1
9. Ch. Barenhof Amby v d Arrow Ranch.Mr. and Mrs. F.L. Crawford.	78	12	2	10
10. Ch. Radio Ranch's Kari On T.L. Sallen and P. Weller.	59	9	—	9

TOP TEN DOGS FOR 1976

1. Ch. Burley v Morgen
   Carroll, CD.B. and W.
   Carroll and C. Lindsey.   583   56   54   2

2. Ch. Radio Ranch's Axel v
   Notara.G. Crump and P.
   Weller.   338   39   38   1

3. Ch. Centurian's Che. V.D.
   Barr.J. and D. Hedl.   229   35   33   2

4. Ch. Panamint Orso v
   Kraewel, CDX,H.A. and
   B.J. Hendler.   208   12   12   —

5. Ch. Bingo von
   Hohenreissach,D.F. Adam.   191   26   24   2

6. Ch. Gastuberget's Eskil
   Jarl, CD.M. Grossman.   141   15   11   4

7. Ch. Titan Sujon.J.
   Mammano   117   6   6   —

8. Ch. Eigenschaft's Chase
   J.M. Depew.   114   13   11   2

9. Ch. Panamint Nobel v
   Falkenberg.S.L. and C.
   Johnson.   112   12   12   —

10. Ch. Adler v Andan, CD
    A.D. Tilghman.   89   12   12   —

TOP TEN BITCHES FOR 1976

1. Ch. Panamint Pakt v
   Rheintal.P. Taylor.   124   23   8   15

2. Ch. Christa v Odenwald.A.
   Bassett and M. Schmidt.   87   10   —   10

3. Ch. Riegele's Agreta Maid
   R. Timmerman.   73   9   1   8

4. Ch. Bea Mathilda v Haus
   Kalbas H. Stark and S.
   Rinkin.   63   14   4   10

5. Ch. Andan Indy Pendence
   v Paulus.Mrs. A.D.
   Tilghman.   61   12   4   8

132

Fred Habit

Sire and dam of Ch. Radio Ranch's Axel v Notara are Ch. Nomad v d Harque and Ch. Kuhlwald's Tara of Ronlyn, the latter a Top Producer.

6. Ch. Rodsden's Beorn, CD.I. Goodrich.	56	7	4	3
7. Ch. Trollegen's Aparri, CD Mrs. C. Hurley.	48	7	—	7
8. Ch. Ebonstern Crote v Klahnerhof.R. Rawson and C. Wheeler. *	47	7	—	7
8. Ch. Hella v Marchenwald M. Marcus. *	47	9	5	4
9. Ch. Cilkka v Kursal.M. Schmidt. *	46	4	—	4
9. Ch. Georgian Court Bliss v Altar.E. Alplin. *	46	10	4	6
10. Ch. Brady Haserway v Haus Kalgas.Mrs. J. Griffin, Jr.	42	6	3	3

*Note that there are ties for the 8th and 9th placements.

Am., Can. Ch. Bingo vom Hohenreissach, Working Group winner, and winner of three Colonial Rottweiler Club area-supported shows. He completed his championship at 13 months of age. Owned by Darlene Adam, Winston-Salem, N.C., handled by Judy Coen to a BOB under Judge Roy Ayers.

TOP TEN DOGS FOR 1975

1. Ch. Burley v Morgen Carroll, CD. B.J. and W. Carroll.	421	40	40	—
2. Ch. Duke's Derek v Altmeister. I. Ruder.	288	46	45	1
3. Ch. Erno v Ingenhof C. Hill.	170	25	25	—
4. Ch. Srigo's Viking Spirit J.V. Reid.	156	24	24	—
5. Ch. Uwe v Kursaal, SchH I M. Schmidt.	125	6	5	1
6. Ch. Adler v Andan. Mrs. A.D. Tilghman.	105	19	19	—
7. Ch. Panamint Banner v Hohenwald. J.H. and E.H. Woodward.	104	7	7	—
8. Ch. Bingo v Hohenreissach D.F. Adam.	97	11	10	1
9. Ch. Rodsden's Rough Diamond. C. Bailey and S. Rivkin.	94	20	19	1
10. Ch. De Riemer's Driekus B.C. and S. Horn.	91	4	4	—

Ch. Gastuberget's Asa v. Kleinholz, C.D., taking Best of Breed at the Del Monte Kennel Club show, May 1977. Asa is one of the many outstanding Rottweilers owned by Mrs. Margareta McIntyre.

TOP TEN BITCHES FOR 1975

1. Ch. Riegele's Agreta Maid
   R.C. Timmerman.   127   20   6   14

2. Ch. Brady Haserway v
   Haus Kalbas.Mrs. J.T.
   Griffen, Jr.   106   17   6   11

3. Ch. Bea Mathilda v Haus
   Kalbas.H. Stark and S.
   Rivkin. *   90   11   3   8

3. Ch. Kitty v Kursaal.M.
   Schmidt.   90   8   4   4

4. Ch. Panamint Linde v
   Rheintal, CD. B. Hoard and
   R.E. Thatcher.   85   15   4   11

5. Panamint Pari v Rheintal
   P.C. Burns.   75   2   1   1

6. Ch. Rodsden's Beorn, CD
   J. Goodrich.   71   15   8   7

7. Ch. Panamint Jolle v d
   Eichen, CD. A. Varana.   69   13   8   5

8. Ch. Rodsden's Tally v
   Hungerbuhl, CD. R. and S.
   Taylor.   65   11   8   3

9. Ch. Panamint Pakt v
   Rheintal.P. Taylor.   63   13   3   10

10. Ch. Asta v Forstwald, CD
    J. Klem and S.
    Rademacher.   42   3   —   3

*Note tie for #3.

CHAPTER 7

Tribute to Best In Show Dogs

As this book is being written, there have been eight different Rottweilers which have won Best in Show honors at all-breed events in the United States. The author feels a special tribute is due these dogs for their quality and for their accomplishments. We list them here in the order of their earliest Best in Show wins.

On May 29th 1971 came the breakthrough when Jan Marshall owner-handled her American and Canadian Champion Rodsden's Kato v Donnaj, C.D.X., T.D., to the first Best in Show won in this country by a member of the breed.

Strangely enough, on the very same weekend but one day later another Rottweiler gained the Best in Show award in all-breed competition. This time it was Champion Rodsden's Duke Du Trier, an older full brother to Kato, Olson owned, Orsino handled. This dog subsequently gained two additional Bests in Show, bringing his total to three. These dogs were bred by Laura Coonley of Wheaton, Illinois, sired by Champion Rodsden's Kluge von der Harque, C.D. from Champion Franzi vom Kursaal.

Then came the Duke's son, Champion Duke's Derek v Altmeister, also handled by Richard Orsino.

Fourth in line was Champion Shearwater's Cochise, owned by Shearwater Kennels and handled by Alan Levine.

The fifth, in 1975, was a German import, Champion Arno v Ingenhoe. Owner, Hill. Handler, Kim Knoblock.

The first brace of Rottweilers to win Best Brace in Show, at Oakland Kennel Club in 1964. Ch. Panamint Ragnarok (left) and Panamint Christal owned by Panamint Kennels, Barbara Hoard Dillon.

Opposite:
Am., Can. Ch. Rodsden's Duke du Trier, Ro-107, taking Best of Breed at the Golden State Rottweiler Club Specialty, July 30, 1970, in conjunction with Santa Barbara. Four-time Best in Show winner and second Rottweiler ever to gain an all-breed Best in Show award in the U.S.A., he is owned by Dr. and Mrs. Nelse O. Olson, Bremerton, WA, handled by Richard Orseno.

Am., Can. Ch. Rodsden's Kato v Donnaj, CDX, TD is America's first Best in Show winning Rottweiler, and the only Rottweiler of eight that have won this title to have achieved it owner-handled. Kato, a truly great example of the breed, belongs to Mrs. Donald S. Marshall, Woodstock, VT. Twenty-five Working Group placements won by this dog include five Group firsts. He has also accumulated 80 Best of Breed wins.

Am., Bda. Ch. Adler von Andan, CD, bred and owned by Mrs. Benjamin C. Tilghman, Centreville, MD, claims a Bermuda Best in Show win and ranked in the American Rottweiler Club's Top Ten Dogs for 1975 and 1976. Sired by Am., Can. Ch. Rodsden's Kato v Donnaj, CDX, from Ehrenwache's Andernach.

The sixth Rottweiler Best in Show winner was Champion Donnaj Vt. Yankee of Paulus, C.D.X., in June 1979. Owned by Jan Marshall, bred by Pauline Rakowski, handled by Mel Goldman. A grandson of Kato, the first Best in Show Rottweiler in the United States.

In July 1979 came the seventh Rottweiler to go Best in Show, Champion Rodsden's Bruin v Hungerbuhl C.D., bred and owned by Jeffrey and Geraldine Kittner and handled by Brian Meyer. Bruin went on to gain a total of five times Best in Show.

Eighth in line was the Dutch import Champion Oscar v.h. Brabantpark belonging to Clara Hurley and Michael Grossman, handled by Corky Vroom.

It is interesting to note that only Jan Marshall's Kato won his Best in Show owner-handled, and that only Kato and his grandson, Yank, both belonging to Mrs. Marshall, have, as well, advanced obedience degrees and that the Kittners' Bruin has a companion dog degree.

CHAPTER 8

Rottweiler Specialty Clubs in The United States

Following is a list of Specialty Clubs devoted to Rottweilers and located in various sections of the country. If you need help with a problem, want to find out where puppies are available, or any other information pertaining to the breed, contact the person listed for one of these clubs and I am certain that assistance will promptly be forthcoming. If you are a new Rottweiler owner, or about to become one, you will find that membership in a Specialty Club can be both beneficial and rewarding. Most of these clubs provide training classes, educational programs and worthwhile breed newsletters or other publications.

AMERICAN ROTTWEILER CLUB.
Mrs. Jane Pampalone,
631 West 11th Street, New York, N.Y. 10009.

COLONIAL ROTTWEILER CLUB.
Mrs. John H. Wehrle,
5 Monnett Street, Little Ferry, N.J. 07643.

DOGWOOD ROTTWEILER CLUB.
Mrs. S. Roehr,
112 Springview Drive, Gainesville,
Georgia 30501.

The spectacularly beautiful bitch Ch. Srigo's Madchen v Kurtz, handled by Felicia Luburich, East Brunswick, NJ at the Colonial Rottweiler Specialty Show judged by Earle Adair. Madchen has just been selected for Best of Opposite Sex. Owned by Lucille and Donald Kurtz.

Opposite:
Felicia Luburich with one of the handsome young homebreds from her kennel. Srigo's Where Eagles Dare goes Reserve Winners Dog at the Colonial Rottweiler Club Specialty Show.

Konder von Stolzenfels wins first in the 6-9 month Puppy Class at the Medallion Rottweiler Club Jubilee Specialty Show 1979. Owned by Terry and Betty O'Brien. Judging is Heinz Eberz, Germany.

Opposite:
Above left: Ch. Arno v Kafluzu, German import, goes Best of Breed over "specials" from the Open Class at the 1962 Colonial Rottweiler Club Specialty. At six years, 11 days of age, his first point show was a success! Felicia Luburich, handler. **Above right:** Ch. Radio Ranch's Zephyr, with co-owner handler Bob Noll, wins the puppy class at the Colonial Rottweiler Club Specialty. Owned by Mr. Noll and Pamela Weller. **Below:** At the first Rottweiler Futurity held in the United States, Aug. 3, 1979, this photo (by Zak) shows the Medallion Rottweiler Club's Grand Prize Futurity Winner, Ch. Erdelied Astraea, CD. Owner-handled by Ms. C.L. Rawlings, bred by Joanna M. Sawyer. The judge is noted Rottweiler breeder Mrs. Margareta McIntyre. "Star" completed her championship at 15 months old with four majors out of seven shows.

Another smashing puppy from Srigo Kennels. This one is Srigo's Joy To The World, making a superb picture of excellence at the Trenton Kennel Club Colonial Rottweiler Specialty Sweepstakes, May 1979. Felicia Luburich, owner-handler.

GOLDEN STATE ROTTWEILER CLUB
Mrs. Marina Weeks,
3230 West 134th Place, Hawthorne, California 90250.

HOUSTON BAY AREA ROTTWEILER CLUB.
Barbara Albert,
18923 Mirror Lake, Spring, Texas 77373.

MEDALLION ROTTWEILER CLUB.
Carol Krickeberg,
Rte. 1, Box 25, Pluno, Illinois 60545.

ORANGE COAST ROTTWEILER CLUB.
Roxane Peterson,
6850 Cameo, Alta Loma, California 91701.

ROTTWEILER CLUB OF GREATER DETROIT.
Barbara Hooper,
11869 Flanders, Detroit, Michigan 48205.

TEXAS ROTTWEILER CLUB.
Ms. Debbie Gallegos,
928 Eventide, San Antonio, Texas 78209.

TIDEWATER ROTTWEILER CLUB.
Mrs. Leslie Fulcher,
1133 Homestead Drive, Virginia Beach, Virginia 23462.

WESTERN ROTTWEILER OWNERS.
Lucy Ang,
P.O. Box 2945, Sacramento, California 95814.

CHAPTER 9

American Rottweiler Club

In the summer of 1971, delegates from the various local Rottweiler Clubs previously established on the East and West Coasts and in the Mid-West met to informally discuss the formation of a National or Parent Club for the breed. This was the beginning of the American Rottweiler Club, or A.R.C. as it is known.

Actually, the Rottweiler Club of America, sanctioned by the American Kennel Club in 1947-48, was chartered to serve as the Parent Club but had ceased to exist through lack of activity. Therefore, A.K.C. suggested that a new Parent Club be formed. Such an undertaking, quite naturally, progressed slowly and methodically.

After the delegates had approved the A.K.C. recommended Constitution and By-Laws for the Club, charter memberships were opened to individuals throughout the United States. William Stahl, one of the delegates and founder of the Colonial Rottweiler Club, was elected first President of the American Rottweiler Club in 1974. At that time, charter membership totaled 359.

After the Club began functioning, one of the first projects was a revision of the Breed Standard. When the Rottweiler qualified for breed conformation competition in 1935, A.K.C. partially adopted the then current German Standard as the American Standard. Subsequently, although revisions of the German Standard were made over the years, none were made in the United States. The

Srigo's Joy To The World taking first in Bred-by-Exhibitor at the American Rottweiler Club Specialty Match, 1980. Felicia Luburich, breeder-owner-handler.

Opposite:
Two super puppies relaxing at home. Srigo's I Am Invincible, Best in Sweepstakes winner at the Colonial Rottweiler Club 1979 show with his litter sister, Srigo Imitation of Life, Best in Match winner at the American Rottweiler Club National Specialty Match, 1978.

American (A.K.C.) Standard for the breed needed to be specific regarding size, correct gait, temperament, and, most important, disqualifying faults in order to assist judges and breeders in assessing the ideal Rottweiler. The task was arduous and lengthy. But five years and four revisions later, a new Standard of the Breed was approved by the membership of the American Rottweiler Club and by the American Kennel Club in 1979. With the increasing popularity of the breed, the timing was appropriate.

The American Rottweiler Club has now held the required series of Match Shows to qualify itself to hold Specialty Shows. These Match Shows have taken place in various sections of the United States, affording the members opportunities of meeting one another and participating in Club activities. In 1981 it will hold its first Independent Specialty in the Boston, Massachusetts, area. The current membership (Summer 1980) stands at 750 and includes Rottweiler fanciers from all of the United States, Canada, Australia, Germany, France, Puerto Rico, Jamaica and El Salvador.

As part of the educational program, the American Rottweiler Club published ROTTWEILER PICTORIALS #1 and #2. While President of the Club (1975-1977) Mrs. Dorothea Gruenerwald conceived the ROTTWEILER PICTORIAL project for the Club. ROTTWEILER PICTORIAL #1 (1975-76) contained 325 pictures and three generation pedigrees of champion and obedience titleholders. It is no longer in print. ROTTWEILER PICTORIAL #2 (1978) was an expansion, with over 400 pictures and pedigrees, plus a section devoted to Producers of Merit and deceased Rottweilers that had contributed materially to succeeding generations of winners. Both PICTORIALS have been extremely well received. They have provided the newcomer to the breed with valuable insight into the past and present breedings, and the inquiring public an opportunity to assess various bloodlines throughout the United States and abroad. The Club is indebted to Miss Ann Maurer, Editor of both PICTORIALS.

The bi-monthly Newsletter, ARK, has grown from a six page edition to a sixty page volume of reference. It has won two awards from the Dog Writers Association of America for excellence in the category of National Club Newsletter, Printed.

Future projects of the American Rottweiler Club include the publication of an Illustrated Standard, Breeder's Directory, Breeder Guidelines and ROTTWEILER PICTORIAL #3.

150

Ch. Colonel Crunch belongs to Tobar Rottweilers, owned by Barbara Baris and Thomas J. Condon at Oxford, CT. Handled by Marty Silver.

COLONIAL ROTTWEILER CLUB

On May 4th 1980, the Colonial Rottweiler Club held its twenty-first Specialty Show, in conjunction with the Trenton Kennel Club All-Breed event at West Windsor Township, New Jersey.

Founded in 1956, Colonial's first Specialty took place three years later. We follow with a list of the Rottweilers which have won this prestigious event.

1959. Champion Reidstandt's Rudiger.
1961. Champion Jaro vom Schleinenplatz.
1962. Arno vom Kafluzu.
1963. Dervis vom Weyershof.
1964. Champion Schon of Townview.
1965. Champion Rodsden's Felicia.
1966. Champion Ferdinand von Dachweil.
1967. Champion Ferdinand von Dachweil.
1968. Champion Ferdinand von Dachweil.
1969. Rodsden's Panzer von der Harf.
1970. Dago von der Ammerquelle.
1971. Champion Rodsden's Duke du Trier.
1972. Champion Srigo's Garret v Zaghin.
1973. Champion Srigo's Madchen v Kurtz.
1974. Champion Titan Sujon.
1975. Champion Srigo's Viking Spirit.
1976. Champion Titan Sujon.
1977. Champion Donnaj Vt. Yankee of Paulus.
1978. Champion Hella vom Marchenwald.
1979. Champion Donnaj Vt. Yankee of Paulus, C.D.X.
1980. Champion Donnaj Vt. Yankee of Paulus, C.D.X.

Officers of the Colonial Rottweiler Club as of May, 1980 are as follows: President, Mrs. Henry R. Walls, Jr.; Vice-President, Mrs. Benjamin Tilghman; Treasurer, Mrs. Ainsley Sawyer; Secretary, Mrs. John M. Wehrie.

The Colonial sponsors a highly successful Specialty Show and Sweepstakes. This year's event drew eighty-six for the Sweepstakes, with one hundred and ninety-nine in the Regular Classes in May, 1980.

DOGWOOD ROTTWEILER CLUB

What an energetic group of fanciers makes up this Club! During January 1977, a dedicated number of Rottweiler enthusiasts established it as an organization for the purpose of advancing the interest of its breed through worthwhile educational meetings and specific activities.

Meetings take place monthly, with programs and special events scheduled throughout the year. The Dogwood Rottweiler Club offers voting memberships open to everyone 18 years of age or older. Non-voting memberships are open to interested parties of all ages. Since the bulk of the membership resides in the Atlanta area, most Club activities are centered there; however, members are listed from other sections of the country, too.

Events sponsored by the Dogwood Rottweiler Club include Working Group matches, all-breed matches, show training classes and all-breed obedience classes. This Club believes that wherever possible their activities should be open to every breed, owing to the demand for high quality dog related programs in Atlanta. The Club's public Obedience Classes were the first hosted by a Rottweiler Club and were capably taught by a nationally famous trainer.

Members and friends of DRC recently were invited to attend a Schutzhund lecture and demonstration put on by the Greater Atlanta Schutzhund Association. The response is reported as having been tremendous, with much insight gained into this unique and important sport. As a direct result of so enthusiastic a turnout, the Dogwood Rottweiler Club has planned a Fall Tracking Seminar/Clinic featuring several instructed training sessions, the last of which is to be a Tracking Match, certifying dogs for an American Kennel Club Trial. Interest in this has been expressed by owners of several other breeds, so the decision has been to go "all-breed" with this seminar, too.

Participation by the Specialty Club took place in the Atlanta Kennel Club's big 100th show in December 1980. More than 20 trophies were offered in competition for the Rottweilers. Welcome packages were provided for exhibitors, literature was circulated among the spectators, and Rottweiler benches attractively decorated.

Appreciation is expressed to Dogwood members in the form of plates crested with the Club logo for any American Kennel Club title won and for certain SchH titles earned by their dogs during the year. These plates also can be won at certain selected shows. They are sandcast of an alloy of ten different metals, and no two of them are exactly alike.

A Newsletter is published monthly, featuring articles of general interest along with up-to-date show reports, stud book listings, OFA Certifications and coming events.

The Club's DOG WORLD advertisement, first published in January 1980 in an effort to provide information and assistance, has proven highly successful. It now runs continuously, bringing good response and new friends.

Secretary of the Dogwood Rottweiler Club is Ms. Alison Lowe, 640 South Indian Creek Drive, Stone Mountain, Georgia 30038.

GOLDEN STATE ROTTWEILER CLUB

In June of 1962 the Golden State Rottweiler Club was founded, and by the end of that year the name had been officially adopted, representing a total membership of sixteen.

At this time only very few Rottweilers were to be found in Southern California. Thus the goal of Golden State's "founding fathers" was to provide an atmosphere of camaraderie and friendliness towards all Rottweiler owners, while at the same time working for the promotion of wider public recognition of the breed. The early members also were aware of the necessity of improving the available breeding stock and providing a source of mutual advice, support and education to its own members and the general public. With this thought in mind the monthly publication "Golden State Rottweiler Newsletter" began, since renamed to its present title, "The Guardian Newsletter of the Golden State Rottweiler Club." This publication is now sent to nearly four hundred members and subscribers around the world.

By 1966 the club membership had grown to eighty people and had expanded well beyond its original territory of Southern California. As interest in the breed and the number of club members increased, American Kennel Club recognition became the Club's goal, which was fulfilled in 1969 when Golden State's first Annual Specialty Show received approval. To date, ten Specialties have followed for this energetic club made memorable by steadily increasing entries plus outstanding and famous judges.

As the Club matured and its membership increased it was realized that if the excellent qualities of mental and physical soundness which had come as a legacy from the German breeders were not to be lost, it would be necessary to adopt safeguards to assure sound breeding practices. Thus, in 1968, a

Club Policy was adopted with respect to hip dysplasia, and in April 1969 a Code of Ethics was adopted regarding the breeding of Rottweilers. The aim of both steps was to improve the physical soundness of the breed.

Awareness has also existed of the necessity for preserving mental soundness as well, Members have been encouraged to obedience train their Rottweilers and are proud to say that many of their dogs have achieved high honors in Obedience work, some going on to Schutzhund and Tracking. Golden State believes that "Rottweiler breeding is working-dog breeding" and that sound temperament is as important as beauty.

Along with growth of the Club from a local Southern California group to one with National and even International membership, there has been accompanying recognition of the fact that to maintain and improve the quality of Rottweilers, fanciers must educate themselves in the areas of genetics, animal behavior and animal nutrition. Accordingly a number of seminars have taken place, with wide membership attendance and with outstanding speakers, authorities on the breed both from here and abroad.

Golden State pays tribute to some of their especially energetic and enthusiastic members. One of them, Margareta McIntyre, has become a highly respected and knowledgeable judge. Another, Clara Hurley, has developed a most useful genetic tool known as the "Biodex," from which every potential Rottweiler breeder can benefit by information on the hip dysplasia background of prospective breeding partners.

This "Biodex" we understand is the solitary source for information as complete as it is regarding the Rottweiler O.F.A. status in the United States. It is thus of inestimable value to breeders to whom the matter of hip dysplasia is given the deep concern this serious problem merits. The "Biodex" is an easily understood code which permits a breeder to ascertain at a glance what the hip x-rays reveal as reported by the O.F.A. regarding individual animals, ancestors and littermates. These O.F.A. findings have been public knowledge since January 1974. Earlier information is available only if released by the owner.

Golden Gate has been fortunate in obtaining numerous judges from the breed's homeland, as well as other noted foreign and domestic judges, too, making a well rounded balance of qualified people whose critiques and opinions can benefit the breeding programs of the membership.

Shown at the American Rottweiler Club National Specialty Match Show, Atlanta, GA are (from l.): Felicia Luburich, breeder-owner-handler; Ch. Srigo's Zoom v Kurtz, Highest Score in Obedience; Srigo's Imitation of Life, Best in Match at 4½ months over adults with an entry of more than 50; Cathy Thompson, friend and helper.

MEDALLION ROTTWEILER CLUB

It was on July 11th of 1959 that a meeting was held, in the Chicago area, for the purpose of organizing what has become the Medallion Rottweiler Club. Charter Members were Dr. and Mrs. James Alexander, Mr. and Mrs. P. Fitterer, Mr. and Mrs. Ludwig Gessner, Mr. Werner Gessner, Mr. and Mrs. Richard Klem, Mr. and Mrs. Franz Liebfried, Mr. and Mrs. Seymour Levine, Col. and Mrs. Leon Mandel, Mr. and Mrs. Perrin Rademacher, Mr. and Mrs. John Refieuna, Mr. and Mrs. Eugene Schoelkopf, and Mr. and Mrs. William Stark.

Medallion is one of the three Rottweiler Clubs currently holding Specialty Shows in the United States, the others being the Colonial Rottweiler Club and Golden State Rottweiler Club. These three groups have worked together in many ways, including bringing noted European authorities here to officiate as judges at Specialty Shows and Match Shows. Additionally all three have adopted Codes of Ethics with which their members have agreed to comply. Their singleness of purpose for the good of the breed is further illustrated by the fact that these three Clubs share a monthly advertisement in DOG WORLD magazine offering authoritative information about the breed.

In 1969 the Medallion Rottweiler Club held its first Specialty Show. In 1979, the eleventh Annual Specialty Show was presented, the third to have been held as an Independent Specialty Show rather than in conjunction with an all-breed event. To summarize a bit on these eleven Specialties is interesting.

The first was held on July 6th 1969, in conjunction with the Wheaton Kennel Club Dog Show, Wheaton, Illinois, as were the three immediately following. Then in 1973 an exciting milestone was reached: Medallion's first Independent Specialty. This took place as part of a gala Rottweiler weekend, quite appropriately, since it was the occasion of the very first such event held solely by the Specialty Club. A Show Committee of Medallion members assumed complete responsibility for selection of a site, judge, stewards, ribbons, trophies, catalogue advertising, equipment, publicity and hospitality. No small task, particularly when being assumed for the first time! Adding to the appeal of the weekend were a Friday evening pre-show dinner, with an interesting program, and an after-dinner get together. The Specialty was on Saturday, at the DuPage County Fairgrounds, Wheaton, Illinois, with judging by a famed German authority, and on Sunday a Breed Survey and Temperament Test such as are done in Germany, including examination of each Rottweiler's calmness, previous training, protective instinct and aggressiveness, were held. Understandably the two-day event drew exhibitors and spectators from all parts of the United States!

In 1974 the Sixth Annual Specialty took place in conjunction with the Stone City Kennel Club All Breed Show. The Seventh, in 1975, returned to the Wheaton Kennel Club, but with some exciting innovations. A two day group of events once more were planned: Saturday the Specialty, Annual Meeting and a dinner and on Sunday Medallion's first Rottweiler Rodeo, a fun-filled day with dog/owner races and games held at Featherhead, Wheaton, Illinois.

It was again in conjunction with Wheaton Kennel Club for the Eighth Annual Specialty in 1976, with a judge from Sweden officiating in the classes. The innovation for this occasion was the addition of a Puppy Sweepstakes which was extremely well received. And, as the previous year, the second day of the weekend saw a Rottweiler Rodeo and other "fun and games."

Medallion Rottweiler Club's Ninth Annual Specialty, in 1977, was also its second Independent Specialty, and was held outdoors at the Holiday Inn, Itasca, Illinois, with separate judges for dogs, bitches and Puppy Sweepstakes. Exhibitors and spectators, it is said, will remember the rain as it has so rarely occurred at events held by this Club. The Annual Meeting and dinner again followed in the evening. The second day of the Second Independent Specialty weekend took place at Featherfield, with an American Kennel Club Sanctioned Obedience "A" Match in the morning, followed by a mini-rodeo in the afternoon.

The Tenth Annual Specialty in 1978 was again in conjunction with Wheaton Kennel Club. The three-day weekend consisted of a Judging Seminar on Friday, the Specialty with Annual Meeting and dinner the second day. This featured the initial presentation of awards to those Rottweilers elected to the Hall of Fame and Honor Roll, a much prized honor! And on Sunday at Featherfield, an Obedience demonstration.

In 1979, the Club's Eleventh Annual Specialty and third Independent Specialty celebrated the Club's Twentieth Anniversary. Events covered a three-day period, with still another "first" for Rottweilers in the United States: the Futurity Stakes on Friday, and, for the first time at an Independent Specialty for Rottweilers, an Obedience Trial—both of these at DuPage County Fairgrounds—Saturday the Specialty, with separate German judges for the Dog Classes and the Bitch Classes with the Annual Meeting and dinner immediately following the judging and on Sunday, Rottweiler character testing as done in Germany and Holland.

In addition to its Specialty Shows, Medallion makes it a practice to support with trophies and entries various all-breed events in the Mid-West.

Medallion has published a Tenth Anniversary Book (1959-1969) and a Twentieth Anniversary Book (1969-1979), both of which are extremely interesting and informative. They also issue a bi-monthly newsletter and provide a "New Member Information Kit" which is sent to all new members and which includes a membership card, membership list, Rottweiler Standard chart, A.K.C. Standard, ADRK Standard and breeding rules, Medallion Rottweiler Club's Constitution and By-laws, Dictionary of Dog Terms and Code of Ethics.

WESTERN ROTTWEILER OWNERS

This active and progressive group was founded in October 1962, with an initial membership of 17 persons. Now, in 1980, the membership census stands at 351.

In 1962 the officers were: President, Erna Pinkerton; Corresponding Secretary, Dorothy Cholet; Recording Secretary, Margaret Perry; Treasurer, Robert Cholet; News Editor, Ken Hoard; Assistant Editor, Wright Huntly; Membership Chairman, Jack Dumas.

The 1980-81 officers of the Western Rottweiler Owners follows: President, Margaret Teague; Vice-President, Dick Bjornestad; Recording Secretary, Lucy Ang; Corresponding Secretary, Colleen Wetmore; Treasurer, Peggy Bird; Directors: Doris Baldwin, Beverly Hendler, Hildegard Mikoleit, and Thelma Wade; Membership Chairman, Charlotte Twineham; Hospitality Chairman, Danielle Green; Benching Chairman, Marlene Lore; Trophy Chairman, Steve Whitney; Homefinding Chairman, Judy Bjornestad; Librarian, Keith Twineham; News Editor, Jean Forster; Assistant News Editor, Mid Rothrock.

The goal of Western Rottweiler Owners is to promote the enjoyment, improvement and preservation of the Rottweiler. WRO has implemented this goal by directing its efforts towards the education of prospective Rottweiler owners. An excellent booklet prepared by them and published in January 1979 has been a tacit realization of their education goal. "On Owning a Rottweiler" was compiled by Margaret Teague, Lucy Ang and Susan DeHaan, with contributions by Barbara Hoard Dillon and Thelma Wade.

Approximately fifteen hundred copies of this booklet already have been sold.

Western Rottweiler Owners support the breed entry at the Annual Golden Gate Kennel Club benched show in February; this entry has reached the one hundred mark in the last few years.

CHAPTER 10

Rottweilers in Canada

On our frequent judging trips to Canada, we note good quality and keen competition in the Rottweiler rings. There are numerous dogs from the United States shown there in competition with those that are Canadian-owned, and interest in the breed would seem reasonably high both for conformation and obedience.

There is a Rottweiler Club of Canada, the Secretary of which is listed as Brian J. Smith, Box 447, Dundale, Ontario LOG IKO.

Canadian Champion Rintelna the Dragoon had done a sizable amount of winning for owners Pat Johnson and Jim Schwartz, whose kennels are in Winnipeg. Dragoon holds the distinction of being the first Canadian-bred Rottweiler to have won an All Breed Best in Show in Canada, an achievement in which his owners take pride. This fine Rott also has won the Rottweiler Club of Canada Specialty when it was judged by Mrs. Bernard Freeman.

Kyladie Kennels are breeding Rottweilers in Alberta and have been doing so since 1977. Aime and Adele Brosseau had started out with English Cockers and were into showing them. They decided to try their luck with the first of their Rottweilers, although he had been originally purchased primarily as a pet and companion. Soon this dog became Champion Hallenhof's Gentleman Bayre, C.D., doing extremely well and finishing second top Rottweiler in the breed for 1978. Bayre is Canadian-bred,

A substantial, well-balanced and handsome dog is Am., Can. Ch. Srigo's Flight of the Eagle, Am., Can. CD as well as Canadian Best in Show winner. Owned by Mr. and Mrs. Arthur L. Rikel and bred by Felicia Luburich. He is pictured winning Best of Breed, Sept., 1979, Butler County Kennel Club from Judge Bob Moore.

Opposite:
A beautiful headstudy of the handsome Canadian Ch.
Hallenhof's Gentleman Bayre, CD, Canada's Number
Two Rottweiler for 1978. Owned by Mr. Aime and
Mrs. Adele Brosseau, Devon, Alberta, Canada.

161

Ero v d Mauth in Germany prior to shipping out to Canada. **Below:** An unposed snapshot of the Rikels' Am., Can. Ch. Srigo's Flight of the Eagle, Am., Can. CD.

Above: Winning Best Brace of Rottweilers are Kyladie's Mister Arcturus CD (left) and Can. Ch. Kyladie's Arabesque owned by Aime and Adele Brosseau, Alberta, Canada. **Below:** Winning Best Puppy in Group is Can. Ch. Kyladie's Anette's Baybe, at ten months. Mr. Aime and Mrs. Adele Bosseau, owners.

Above: This handsome group of Rottweilers was featured on a Christmas card sent to their friends from Jessnic Kennels, owned by Jessica Nichols, Burnsville, NC. **Below:** Can. Ch. Hallenhof's Braye, pictured at 10 months, one of the splendid breeding bitches at Kyladie Kennels owned by the Brosseaus at Devon, Alberta.

but his pedigree consists mainly of American dogs, including Rodsden's Kluge v d Harque, Harras von Sofienbusch and Rodsden's Goro v Sofienbusch.

The Brosseaus next purchased a bitch from the Cantass Kennels in Ontario which they bred to Bayre. This produced a litter that now consists of four Bench Champions and four Obedience Champions.

At their first National Specialty Show, the Brosseaus entered four six-month-old puppies and won every class in which they were entered. Additionally they came away with Winners Bitch, Reserve Winners Bitch and Best Puppy. They also took Best Brace and the Sire and Get Classes, which truly is not bad going at all.

The puppies from this litter have grown up to become Champion Kyladie's Arabasque, that finished at nine months, Champion Kyladie's Avitar the Wiz, C.D., finished at thirteen months, Champion Kyladie's Starmaster Antares, Champion Kyladie's Baybe, that took Best Puppy in Group at Saskatoon, Kyladie's sister Arcturus, C.D. and Kyladie's Beowulf the Brave, C.D.·

The Brosseaus are extremely conscientious breeders whose kennel policy is that all puppies sold, even their best, go to homes where they are considered pets. They hope in the years to come to do right by these beautiful dogs which they so greatly enjoy. They are working towards improving the temperament and size of their line as they feel that this is the area in which most modern Rotts fall short. They also try to educate the judges regarding what is considered correct type in the ring, and that should be ROTTWEILERS, not heavy Dobes or light Mastiffs.

We certainly feel that breeders of such determination and true love for their dogs are an asset, and we look to many future generations of Kyladie Rottweilers in the winners circle.

Other Canadian Rottweiler breeders include LaVerne and Helen MacPherson and their Heamac Kennels in Ontario, Carol Kravets at Windsor, Ontario and more in all the various Canadian Provinces.

CHAPTER 11

American Rottweiler Kennels Past and Present

There is no better way to describe the progress of a breed than by telling you of the individual breeders and kennels that have contributed along the way. On the following pages we are proud to present resumes of many important Rottweilers and of the background which contributed to their success. All are not still active, but each has contributed to the well-being and development of these splendid dogs, and many continue to do so. Study these pages well and you will come away with an increased knowledge of where the best Rottweilers have been bred, the forethought and study expended towards progress, and the exciting results in the form of the generations produced.

We tell you of the long time breeders, but we pay tribute to the comparative newcomers, too. On their shoulders rests the task of carrying on and preserving what has already been accomplished and the responsibility for the future well-being of the breed.

ANDAN

Mrs. Benjamin C. Tilghman is owner of the von Andan Rottweilers which make their home at Centreville, Maryland. Six champions to date have been raised at this fine kennel, while two others from the von Andan line have been shown to their championship and are owned there, and there are some fine young dogs looking ahead to the future.

Two foundation bitches at Bergluft Rottweilers are litter sisters, Ch. Drossel vom Molzberg and Ch. Danka vom Molzberg at four years of age, photographed about 1971. Mrs. Dorit S. Rogers, owner, Sewickley, Pennsylvania.

Opposite:
Ch. McCoy Von Meadow, WD 527172, RO 1145, finished his championship with all majors. Producer of championship OFA offspring. This beautiful headstudy of a handsome dog belongs to Donna and Bob Wormser.

Pauline Rakowski, Middletown, NJ owns these handsome Rottweiler babies. Photographed at six weeks old, they are a litter by Ch. Rodsden's Ikon v d Marque C.D. from Ch. Amsel Von Andan, C.D.
Opposite:
Mrs. Benjamin Tilghman with her Ch. Andan Vesta von Paulus, RO 1297, by Ch. Rodsden's Ikon v d Harque, C.D., RO 355 ex Ch. Amsel von Andan, C.D., RO 300. Vesta is pictured winning Best of Breed at the Mason and Dixon Kennel Club, 1980.

Pride of place among Mrs. Tilghman's Rottweilers goes, of course, to the justly famous American and Bermudian Champion Adler von Andan, C.D. This magnificent son of American and Canadian Champion Rodsden's Kato von Donnaj, C.D.X., T.D. from Ehrenwache's Andernach has distinguished himself with the following accomplishments. Adler ranked in the Top Ten Dogs by the American Rottweiler Club in 1975 and 1976. He was the first and still remains the only Rottweiler to have won an All-Breed Best in Show at the prestigious Bermuda Kennel Club events, which he did in November 1975. He is a member of the Medallion Rottweiler Club's Hall of Fame Honor Roll. He won Best Stud Dog and Best Veteran Dog at the Colonial Rottweiler Club Specialty in 1977. This is a record in which any breeder can take well merited pride.

The other homebreds belonging to Mrs. Tilghman that have distinguished themselves in the show ring are Champion Amsel

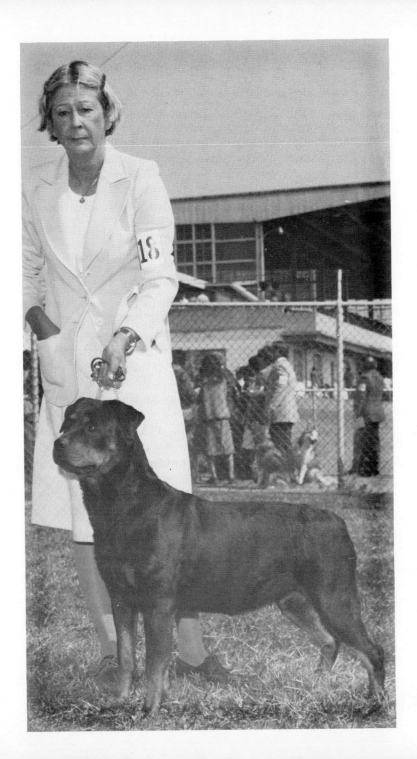

von Andan, C.D., Champion Abenteur von Andan, Champion Baron Kato von Andan, Champion Brav von Andan and Champion Britz von Andan.

The highly successful bitch American and Bermudian Champion Andan Indy Pendence v Paulus is a daughter of Champion Amsel von Andan, C.D., as is Champion Andan Vesta von Paulus. Indy completed her title in September 1976 at fourteen months of age. In 1977, with eighteen Best of Breed awards and fifteen times Best of Opposite Sex, she won the American Rottweiler Club Award as Number One Rottweiler Bitch in the Country. In addition she was Number Five Rottweiler and the only bitch on the list of the WORKING DOG MAGAZINE system.

During 1978, Indy was Best of Breed nine times, Best of Opposite Sex eight times (including Westminster), took a Group 3, spared time out for motherhood, but still wound up the Number Ten Rottweiler in the Country, KENNEL REVIEW System. In 1979 she was fifteen times Best of Opposite Sex (again including Westminster and the Colonial Rottweiler Club Specialty which this time had one hundred and fifty entries), plus seventeen times Best of Breed. She was the Number One Rottweiler Bitch again that year, too, and became a member of the Medallion Rottweiler Club Hall of Fame Honor Roll.

Indy's overall record includes a total of forty-four times Best of Breed, thirty-eight times Best of Opposite Sex.

Champion Andan Vesta v Paulus became a champion undefeated from the Open Class at seventeen months, was Best in Sweepstakes at the Medallion Rottweiler Club Specialty in 1977 and Best of Opposite Sex at the Colonial Rottweiler Club's Match Show in March 1977.

By the time you read this book, a young dog and bitch from this kennel should be really making their presence felt in the show ring. They are both sired by Adler. Altair von Andan, the dog, won first in his Puppy Class of fifteen at the Colonial Specialty, Trenton, in 1979, and is now, at time of writing, waiting to grow up. The bitch, Daba von Andan, is a daughter of Vesta. She took first in her Puppy Class also at Trenton's Colonial Specialty, 1979 with an entry of fifteen and took a five point major at Maryland Kennel Club in November 1979 in an entry of forty-five, where she climaxed the day by going on to Best of Breed over a specials entry of 12. An English judge, Mary McPhail, officiated at this one.

All set to go sledding! Bergluft's "F" litter at seven weeks old, born Dec. 2, 1976, by Ch. Radio Ranch's Axel v Notara from Ch. Bergluft's Carla. Dorit S. Rogers, owner.

BERGLUFT

Bergluft Kennels, Registered, was established by Mrs. Dorit S. Rogers in 1962, breeding and training German Shepherd Dogs for conformation and obedience.

In 1965 the first Rottweiler, Champion Kuhlwald's Little Iodine, C.D., was acquired at the age of ten weeks from Kuhlwald Kennels of Florida. She was one of the three foundations bitches of the "Bergluft" line. Little Iodine was raised, trained and shown by Mrs. Rogers to her titles. She was bred only once, to Champion Axel vom Schwanenschlag, and produced the Kuhlwald "T" litter. These puppies were hand raised by Mrs. Rogers. Four champions came from this mating: Champion Kuhlwald's Troll, Champion Kuhlwald's Tara, Champion Kuhlwald's Tobrina and Champion Kuhlwald's Trakehner, the latter becoming foundation stud dog at "Bergluft".

The second foundation bitch, Champion Drossel vom Molzberg, was purchased in 1968 at the age of six months from Molzberg Rottweilers of Tumwater, Washington. "Big Donka" was also owner-handled to her title. She was bred to Champion Axel vom

Am. Can. Ch. Drauf vom Molzberg, 26½ inches tall, weighing 120 pounds, Drauf is a litter brother to Ch. Drossel and Ch. Danka v Molzberg. Drauf belongs to the McCormicks, Vancouver, B.C. Photo, courtesy Mrs. Dorit S. Rogers.

Opposite:
Mrs. Dorit S. Rogers owner-handling Ch. Danka vom Molzberg to Best of Breed at Licking River Kennel Club, April 13, 1974.

Dojean's Adventorous Miss going Best of Breed for a three point "major" at Tacoma, WA, June, 1967. The dam of Ch. Drossel and Ch. Danka vom Molzberg and Am., Can. Ch. Drauf v Molzberg, she had eleven points when she died in a fatal accident at five years of age. Photo, courtesy Mrs. Dorit S. Rogers, Bergluft Rottweilers, Sewickley, PA.

Schwanenschlag and produced a litter of four champions. There were Champion Bergluft's Cliff, Champion Bergluft's Cai, Champion Bergluft's Centa, and Champion Bergluft's Carla who is owned by Mrs. Rogers.

Champion Drossel's second breeding was to Champion Kuhlwald's Trakehner, and the resulting litter was small. One bitch from it was sent to South America and was bred to produce one of the first litters of Rottweilers in Brazil.

In August of 1968, Mrs. Rogers purchased her third bitch, Champion Danka vom Molzberg, a litter sister to Champion Drossel, at the age of nine months. Champion Danka also was owner-handled to her championship. She was bred only once, to Champion Kuhlwald's Trakehner, and that breeding produced Champion Bergluft's Fee, Champion Bergluft's Fara, and Champion Bergluft's Gunda.

There are three other youngsters, from Carla's "G" litter, that have championship points, and one has her Companion Dog degree.

Mrs. Rogers takes pride in the fact that "Bergluft" still is consistently producing the large, heavily boned Rottweilers of years ago. Her dogs are not offered at public stud, and her dedication to the Rottweiler means very selective breeding only when placement in quality homes is assured.

Ch. Drossel vom Molzberg finishing her title under Maxwell Riddle at twenty months old. Mrs. Dorit S. Rogers, owner-handler.

BETHEL FARM

Bethel Farm Rottweilers are owned by Robert and Lavinia Bolden of Tabb, Virginia, a small but highly successful kennel which breeds only one or two litters each year.

Foundation bitch at Bethel Farm is Champion Graudstark's Irma La Deuce, C.D., Ro 752, a 1978 Kennel Review Awards System Top Producer. In her first litter, known as the "A" litter, sired by the late Rottweiler George Anderson, Ro 760, Irma produced six champions; these included the famous Champion Bethel Farms Apollo which is co-owned by Bethel Farm and Radio Ranch Rottweilers (the latter belongs to Pamela Weller.) In the past year as this is written, Apollo has won seventeen Working Group placements and has been 48 times Best of Breed.

This "A" litter did not stop with Apollo. The champions from it have reached a total of six. They include, firstly, Bethel Farms Adra that has multiple Best of Breed wins and was Best of Opposite Sex at Westchester 1979. Secondly, Bethel Farms Angela, that gained her title in six shows within 15 days. Bethel Farms Axan is number three in this group and was Best of Opposite Sex at Channel Cities and Santa Barbara in 1979. Bethel Farms Ali has multiple Best of Breeds and a Group Fourth, and lastly Bethel Farms Annon has multiple Best of Breed credits, too. Small wonder that this litter has been referred to as one of the most outstanding in Rottweiler history.

Irma now has a total of seven finished champions to her credit, along with four others that have major points. With a third litter maturing nicely, she will certainly gain a position high on the list of outstanding all-time Rottweiler producing bitches, a goal towards which Bob and Lavinia Bolden are striving.

The Boldens have been active in Rottweilers since about 1973. Bob is past-present of the Merrimac Dog Training Club and its Obedience Trial Chairman this year.

Currently Bethel Farms Angela's first litter is being watched carefully as the puppies develop. Hopes are especially high for one of these puppies, Bethel Farms Estelle, that at ten months old looks very promising.

Opposite:
Ch. Bethel Farms Angela, by the late George Anderson from Ch. Graudstark's Irma La Deuce, C.D., is owned by Bob and Lavinia Bolden and handled by Bert Halsey. Angie gained her championship in 6 shows in 15 days, her wins including four "majors."

Donna and Bob Wormser are the breeders of these adorable 8-week old Rottweiler puppies. Their sire is Ch. McCoy von Meadow; their dam, Ch. Orlando von Ocala.

BLUE MEADOW FARMS

Donna and Bob Wormser have owned Rottweilers for about 10 years at their beautiful Blue Meadow Farms in Ocala, Florida, and have been Rottweiler breeders now for about six years. Owing to the problem of hip dysplasia within the breed, they use only O.F.A. rated dogs and bitches in their kennel activities.

The Wormsers show consistently in Florida, Georgia, Alabama and upon occasion in the Carolinas. Wendy Wolforthe handles the dogs in the ring, and through her 20 years' experience as a Rhodesian Ridgeback breeder and as a leading Professional Handler, has been a good friend and valued advisor to the Wormsers in planning their breeding programs and guidance with puppies.

Several noted champions have been bred by Mr and Mrs. Wormser, 96% Certified Rottweilers, including three "excellent" ratings. Donna Wormser is proud to say, after raising and buying many Rottweilers, that she and her husband now have firmly established their basic kennel with only extremely sound dogs. All of the Rottweilers at Blue Meadow Farms are champions, and it is Mrs. Wormser's belief that only champions should be bred to champions, the policy followed at her kennel.

Champion McCoy Von Meadow is an outstanding example of the Rottweilers being raised at Blue Meadow. Truly a handsome dog with an exciting show record, he is siring Rottweilers of correct type and high quality.

178

Another excellent example of the Rottweilers at Blue Meadow Kennels is Ch. Margarita v Meadow, by Ch. McCoy v Meadow ex Ch. Gisela v Anderson, going Best of Breed at 13½ months. Handled by Wendy Wolforthe for owner Donna M. Wormser.

Ch. Merrymore's Ultimatum finishing her championship at the Macon Kennel Club under judge Roy Ayres. "Ultie" was Best of Opposite Sex for a 4-point major defeating 13 bitches. Susan C. Catlin, owner, Kennesaw, GA.

DER CATLIN

Mrs. Susan C. Catlin of Kennesaw, Georgia, acquired her first Rottweiler, an eight weeks old puppy, in 1973. This was destined to become Champion DC's Rostock of Queensburg, and she was a daughter of Champion Merrymoore's Invincible ex Merrymoore's Glad About Gal.

The first litter to be whelped at Der Catlin Kennels, or DC as Mrs. Catlin abbreviates it in naming her dogs, arrived in 1976 from the foundation bitch she had purchased, as a two year old, from the famous Merrymoore Kennels. Champion Merrymoore's Ultimatum completed her title in 1977. From breeding both of these bitches, "Rosh" and "Ultie," Mrs. Catlin has produced three lovely champion bitches. Ultimatum now has a total of four champions to her credit and a C.D.X. holder (from a breeding previous to Mrs. Catlin's purchase of her), and grandchildren taking points and Reserve Winners from the Puppy Classes.

Sadly, Champion Ultimatum died of cancer in January 1980. She left behind her a legacy of outstanding progeny and descendants. She herself had been highly successful in the show ring, gaining her championship quickly in stiff competition.

Champion Der Catlin's Cologne v.d. Oder completed her championship with all majors owner-breeder handled at seventeen months. She is co-owned by Mrs. Catlin with Keith and Pat Marston, and good things are expected of her as a producer. She gained her championship under noted judges in keenest competition.

As this is written hopes are high for the young Trollknoll's vd Domino and for several others from this same litter.

Although relatively young in her breeding program, Mrs. Catlin is deeply dedicated to her wonderful breed. She has exhibited in more than two hundred shows and is being extremely selective in her breeding program, having so far produced but four litters. She looks forward to many more years of exhibiting and breeding excellent Rottweilers and continuing to enjoy their camaraderie, love and sense of humor.

A member of the American Rottweiler Club for the past seven years, Mrs. Catlin was a founding member of the Dogwood Rottweiler Club and is its Corresponding Secretary.

Susan C. Catlin with her arms full of baby Rottweilers, these two being 5 month bitches by Ch. Southwood's 'H.H. Blue, C.D. from Ch. DC's Antje vom Rostock.

Am., Can. Ch. Northwind's Helga, an outstanding bitch and a splendid producer. Helga is a daughter of Best in Show winner Am., Can. Ch. Rodsden's Kato v Donnaj, C.D.X., T.D., and is co-owned by R. Powell Monegue and Jan Marshall. Helga already has three champion offspring plus some half dozen others with points to their credit.

DONNAJ

After ten years of breeding, training and showing German Shepherd Dogs, Mrs. Donald S. Marshall, owner of Donnaj Kennels, at Woodstock, Vermont, acquired her first Rottweiler. This dog eventually became American and Canadian Champion Rodsden's Kato v Donnaj, C.D.X., T.D. He was bred by Laura Cooney of Wheaton, Illinois, sired by Champion Rodsden's Kluge v.d. Harque, C.D. ex Champion Franzi vom Kursaal, and came from a litter of five champions. Kato became the first Rottweiler ever to win a Best in Show in the United States, and the only one of eight Rottweilers that have gained the top award to have done so owner-handled. Shown over a five year period, only eighteen to twenty shows a year, and always handled by his owner, Kato piled up the impressive record of eighty times Best of Breed, 29 Working Group placements including first on five occasions, plus the aforementioned Best in Show—a remarkable and excellent dog.

Sadly Kato was stricken with rheumatoid arthritis at six years of age, and the cortisone treatments caused him to become

Above: America's first Best in Show winning Rottweiler illustrates his versatility by returning to one of the jobs for which his ancestors were noted. Ch. Rodsden's Kato v Donnaj, C.D.X., T.D. pulling the milk cart. Kato was one of a litter of five champions bred by Laura Cooney. Mrs. Donald S. Marshall, owner, Woodstock, Vermont. **Below:** Winning the Working Group at the prestigious Bucks County Kennel Club Dog Show, May 1980, is Am., Can. Ch. Donnaj Vt. Yankee of Paulus, CDX, handled by his owner, Mrs. Jan Marshall of Woodstock, VT.

sterile, just at the time when his worth as a sire was being recognized. He sired ten litters prior to this time, mostly sold as pets as no kennel had used him at stud, but seven of his champion offspring, four of them bitches, founded five highly successful kennels. These are von Paulus, Mondberg House, Arrow Ranch, Donnaj and Powsell.

Mrs. Marshall's second Rottweiler, bred by Pauline Rakowski, is a son of Champion Axel v Schwanenschlag from Champion Amsel Von Andan, C.D. The latter bitch is a Kato daughter, thus Mrs. Marshall's current Best in Show winner is a grandson of the original one and is certainly carrying on the family tradition! This is Champion Donnaj Vt. Yankee of Paulus, C.D.X. Born on the Fourth of July in 1975, Yank, as he is called, made his show debut at the Colonial Rottweiler Club 1976 Specialty by winning Best in the Sweepstakes. At the 1977 Colonial Rottweiler Club Specialty, Yank returned to go Best of Breed, Highest Scoring Rottweiler in the Obedience Trial, and first in the Working Group, all owner handled. In 1978 he was Best of Opposite Sex at this Specialty, then returned in 1979 and 1980 to go Best of Breed there on both occasions.

Yankee has been rated Number Three Rottweiler in the United States for the past three years for Group wins as of September 1980. He was also in the American Rottweiler Club Top Ten for Best of Breed wins in 1977, '78, '79 and '80.

Like Kato, his grandsire, Yank is a Best in Show dog. When he took this top award at the Ladies Dog Club in June 1979, it was the largest dog show in the United States ever to have been won by a Rottweiler.

As could be expected, Yank is proving himself to be a sire of tremendous quality. His twelve champions that have finished so far include two that have placed in Working Groups. With one of these sons, Champion Donnaj Crusader, Yankee became part of the third Rottweiler Brace, and the first, other than on the West Coast, to win Best Brace in Show, which took place at the prestigious Eastern Dog Club event on December 15th 1979.

Shortly after her acquisition of the then seven weeks old Yankee, Mrs. Marshall was able to buy, and then to co-own, a beautiful Kato daughter: American and Canadian Champion Northwinds Helga. This handsome bitch has proved to be a good investment, being the dam of three champions now with numerous others pointed. Her young son, American and Cana-

184

A magnificent Rottweiler depicting well what is considered correct in the breed. Ch. Axel vom Schwanenschlag, imported from Germany by Paul and Norma Harris, is pictured here with Norma Harris at the Maryland Kennel Club Dog Show, Nov. 28, 1971. Photo, courtesy Mrs. Dorit S. Rogers.

dian Champion Donnaj Green Mtn. Boy, already is making his presence felt with Working Group placements and seems to be off to a splendid start of an exciting career.

The breeding program at Donnaj is limited to one litter each year. Unfortunately Helga has lost two litters to viruses but another is on the way now; this is eagerly anticipated as it is the last time it is planned to breed her. We hope that all goes well!

Jan Marshall says, "I have been fortunate to have owned (been owned by) two great Rottweilers. I hope one day to be the breeder-owner of a truly memorable Rottweiler!" We wish it for her, too.

A magnificent headstudy by famed photographer Joan Ludwig of the noted Rottweiler, Ch. Gatstuberget's Esbjorn Jarl, C.D.X., owned by Mrs. Margareta McIntyre.

GATSTUBERGET'S ROTTWEILERS

Mrs. Margareta McIntyre comes from a family who owned its first Rottweiler in Sweden back in 1935. Since then she has almost steadily had at least one Rottweiler, with the exception of only occasional very short periods of time.

The first member of the breed she purchased in America was a bitch and was never shown, which Mrs. McIntyre acquired in 1950. The imported dog Aviemore's Don Juan came to her from Sweden in August of 1961. Don Juan was the first Rottweiler to earn the titles Champion and Utility Dog in the United States, and he further distinguished himself as the sire of six champions.

Mrs. McIntyre's first homebred litter was born in 1966, of which Don Juan was the sire. In November of 1969 she purchased Freeger's Ingela from Mrs. Bernard Freeman. She considers Ingela to be her foundation bitch, and it is on her bloodlines that she will continue to build in the future. Unfortunately Ingela only produced twelve live puppies. However, seven of them became champions and obedience title-holders as follows:

American and Canadian Champion Freeger's Leif Gatstuberget, C.D.X.

Champion Freeger's Lisa Gatstuberget.

Freeger's Lotta Gatstuberget, C.D.X., winner of the Will Judy Award.

Champion Gatstuberget's Eskil Jarl, C.D., Number Two Rottweiler, All Systems, in 1977.

Champion Gatstuberget's Esbjorn Jarl, C.D.X.

Champion Gatstuberget's Elegant Essi, U.D.T.

Champion Gatstuberget's Erike, C.D.

Ingela was the Top Producing Rottweiler Dam, *Kennel Review,* 1975 and 1976. And she has the distinction of being a member of the Medallion Rottweiler Club's Hall of Fame. This lovely bitch died on August 18th 1980 at nearly eleven years of age.

Mrs. McIntyre owns a daughter of Ingela, Gatstuberget's Giselle Gamine, that, due to a leg injury at an early age, cannot be shown. She is, however, the dam of two litters, the puppies from which are still too young to have made names for themselves.

Another of Mrs. McIntyre's Rottweilers is Champion Gatstuberget's Asa v. Kleinholz, Number Seven Rottweiler Bitch in the Nation for 1977, the dam of one litter to date. Of this litter one bitch has finished, two other bitches have their majors and two dogs are close to becoming champions. Four of these have obedience degrees. Three are working in Open and one still is in Novice. Since only six live puppies were born in this litter, these records are especially outstanding.

Champion Gatstuberget's Esborn Jarl, C.D.X., is also owned by Mrs. McIntyre, who owner-handled him to his titles. Others with which she has done likewise include Champion Don Juan, U.D.; Champion Birgitta of Gertase, C.D.; Champion Freeger's Ingela, C.D.X.; and Champion Gatstuberget's Asa v Kleinholz, C.D.

Mrs. McIntyre holds membership in the three Rottweiler Clubs that have adopted strict Codes of Ethics, these placing specific restrictions on a breeding program. For example, members of these clubs cannot use a dog for breeding, nor a bitch, until he or she has reached the age of two years and has been certified by the O.F.A. Additionally Mrs. McIntyre guarantees in writing all of her puppies to be free of hip dysplasia and all disqualifying faults. As she says, not exactly a money making enterprise!

In addition to Rottweilers, Mrs. McIntyre has owned and shown Miniature Dachshunds. She began exhibiting in 1961. She was a co-founder of the Golden State Rottweiler Club in 1962 and has served this organization as President, Secretary, Treasurer, Membership Chairman and Show Chairman over the years. Also she was co-founder in 1972 and first Secretary of the American Rottweiler Club, as well as first Chairman of its Standard Revision Committee.

Mrs. McIntyre was approved in 1975 by the American Kennel Club to judge Rottweilers. During the same year she was approved as well by the German Rottweiler Club (ADRK) to judge the breed at all F.C.I. affiliated countries. She is also on the Board of the American Dog Owners Association as of 1980.

For many years Mrs. McIntyre lived in Southern California. Now she and her husband have moved to the beautiful state of Washington, where they presently are building a new home and where the Gatstuberget's Rottweilers will be located in the future.

GERMELSHAUSEN

Although she acquired her first Rottweiler in 1975, Mrs. Betty Bilsky, Germelshausen Rottweilers, located at Longmeadow, Massachusetts, did not breed her first litter until the Spring of 1980. Her kennel is a small one, presently consisting of two noted champions and a most promising puppy.

Top dog at Mrs. Bilsky's is the excellent Champion Dedan der Denker von Paulus, a son of Champion Rodsden's Axel V H Brabant from Champion Liberty Bell von Paulus. He completed his championship in 1979 when only 15 months of age. Since then he has been successfully shown as a "special."

Then there is the lovely bitch, Champion Shana Tova von Paulus, C.D., a litter sister to the Best in Show winning Champion Donnaj Vt. Yankee of Paulus, Champion Indy Pendence von Paulus and Champion Liberty Bell von Paulus.

At the time of writing this, Mrs. Bilsky is watching with keen excitment and anticipation the development of a puppy, from Shana Tova sired by Champion Ero von der Mauth, for which she has high hopes. This is Thor von Germelshausen.

Ch. Dedan Der Denker von Paulus finishing his title at 15 months handled by Mel Goldman for owner, Mrs. Betty Bilsky.

Ch. Shana Tova von Paulus, C.D., litter mate to Ch. Donnaj Vt. Yankee of Paulus, Ch. Indy Pendence von Paulus, and Ch. Liberty Bell von Paulus. Shana is handled by Mel Goldman for owner, Mrs. Betty Bilsky.

Opposite:
This is the handsome Ch. Dedan Der Denker von Paulus (Ch. Rodsden's Axel V H Brabant ex Ch. Liberty Bell von Paulus) belonging to Mrs. Betty Bilsky, Longmeadow, MA. Pictured winning Best of Breed at Elm City Kennel Club, July 1980, he is handled by Mel Goldman.

191

Grunberg Brummel v.d Adel, Am. Can. T.D. with his sister Ebby, the little bitch referred to in the Tracking chapter. Owned, trained and handled by Ruth and Arthur Twiss.

Ch. Grunberg Andra v.d. Adel, owned by Debbie Mulvey, is the dam of the first Rottweiler "super tracker", Grunberg Brummel v.d. Adel, Am. Can. T.D., owned, trained and handled by Ruth and Arthur Twiss, Reading, MA.

GRUNBERG ROTTWEILERS

The Grunberg Kennels, owned by Debbie Mulvey and located at Waterbury Center, Vermont, played their part in establishing some fine Rottweilers in the New England area although they are no longer actively breeding.

The foundation bitch was Valeska v Rau of Wunderkinder, from the historic litter of 1962, bred by Karen Rau of the Wunderkinder Kennels in Connecticut. The sire was Champion Dervis v Weyerhof, Top Rottweiler for 1962. Dam was Champion Romona's Heidi of Townview, which produced four champions in her only litter. This "wonder litter," from which Val came, included the four champions three of which were Specialty winners; a fifth retired one point short of the title and a sixth with "major" points.

At the age of two years, Val was bred to Wilhelm of Townview, that was Best in Match at the 1964 Colonial Rottweiler Club Match Show judged by Gerd Hyden of Sweden. He was rated "excellent" by this well-known authority. Wilhelm was the son of Group winning Champion Jaro v Schleidenplatz, Top Rottweiler for 1958, 1959 and 1961. From this litter of six came the first two Grunberg Home-Bred champions: a bitch, Champion Grunberg Andra v.d. Adel, retained by her breeder and finished with four "majors" in just six shows at the age of 19 months, and a male, Champion Grunberg Anker v.d. Adel, C.D. An adult when he was acquired by his owners, Art and Ruth Twiss, Anker was finished in very limited showing with four "majors" (owner handled from the American-Bred Class) and a total of eight Bests of Breed.

In 1964 the "B" litter at Grunberg was produced out of Champion Andra by German import Bodo v Stuffelkopf, that was rated "V" (excellent) each time shown in Germany. From this litter of six came Grunberg Brummel, American and Canadian Tracking Dog. Brummel was the fourth Rottweiler to earn an American Kennel Club Tracking Dog Title and the first Rottweiler to earn his Canadian Tracking Dog Title, which he did at the Montreal Tracking Tests. Brummel's record of 13 A.K.C. Tracking Tests passed with never a failure stands unbroken in his breed to this day. In 1971 he passed more Tracking Tests than any other dog of any breed.

Several later dogs and bitches from the "C" and "D" litters were shown and pointed, but the above are the "standouts" for which this kennel is noted.

Am. Can. Ch. Northwinds Danka, Am., Can. C.D., owned by Jessnic Kennels. Whelped July 12, 1970 by P. Hickman, Danka completed her Canadian championship undefeated in the classes. She is also a multiple Best of Breed winner in Canada. In four litters totaling 29 puppies, Danka has produced 19 champions (of which three hold the title in both the United States and Canada) and two Schutzhund bitches.

JESSNIC

Jessnic Rottweilers, established around the 1975-1976 period, are owned by Jessica Nichols at Burnsville, North Carolina.

Ms. Nichols' breeding program started with the purchase of a lovely Canadian-bred bitch, Northwind's Just Blew In. Owner-handled, "Just" completed her championship at fifteen months old by winning four majors; she became the Nation's Number Six Rottweiler bitch in the United States in seven shows when she gained multiple Best of Breed wins.

The great producing bitch, American and Canadian Champion Northwind's Danka, American and Canadian Companion Dog, was a gift to Ms. Nichols in 1976 when Danka's former owner, Mrs. P. Hickman, moved to make her home in Europe. Danka was bred four times. The first litter, by the Best in Show winning Champion Rodsden's Kato of Donnaj, produced American and Canadian Champion Northwind's Helga, C.D.; Canadian Champion Northwind's Heiko; and Northwind's Hasso, Canadian C.D. Her second litter was by Champion Igor von Schauer, from which came American and Canadian Champion Northwind's Ilsa; American Champion Northwind's Ideal; American Champion Northwind's Indigo, Schutzhund I, Tracking Dog; Canadian Champion Northwind's Icon; Canadian Champion Northwind's Inca; and Canadian Champion Northwind's Ingo.

Danka next was bred to American and Canadian Champion Ero v d Mauth. This produced American Champion Northwind's Just Blew In, C.D.; American Champion Northwind's Jasmine; Canadian Champion Northwind's Jaro; Canadian Champion Northwind's Jank; Canadian Champion Northwind's Jewel; Canadian Champion Northwind's Joker; and Canadian Champion Northwind's Juno, Schutzhund I.

For the last litter, Danka returned for the second time to Champion Igor v Schauer. Mrs. Hickman had wanted her bred this way again, and Ms. Nichols, who had just acquired Danka at the time, took care of the breeding, whelping and selling of the pups for Danka's former owner. This litter was headed by American and Canadian Champion Northwind's Kaiser of Mallam, C.D.; American Champion Northwind's Kaleb of Topside; American Champion Northwind's Kara; and American Champion Northwind's Kriemhild, C.D.

Thus Danka's total get, from 29 live puppies, bred four times, has added up to ten American Champions to date, eleven Canadian Champions, three American and Canadian Champions, two Schutzhund I title holders; two American Companion Dog title holders; and two Canadian Companion Dog title holders—a bitch that has, indeed, contributed well to her breed!

Top dog at Jessnic is American and Canadian Champion Northwind's Kaiser of Mallam, Danka's son by Igor, co-owned by Ms. Nichols and Joyce de Vries. Awarded the Number One Rottweiler in Canada for 1978 by the Canadian Kennel Club, Kai also has done himself proud here in the States where, owner handled, he

Am., Can. Ch. Northwinds Kaiser of Mallam in full extension, showing the good action that has won him acclaim from numerous judges. Jessica Nichols and Joyce de Vries, owners.

gained championship in ten shows, all major wins. Starting out as a "special" in mid-March of 1980, by September 1980 he was the #5 Rottweiler in the United States in the Canine Chronicle listings.

Ms. Nichols takes pride and pleasure in showing and finishing the championships on her own dogs. We have already mentioned that she did so with "Just" and "Kai." Added to that, she piloted Champion Northwind's Kaleb of Topside to the title in twelve shows. And Jessnic's Alouette, as we write this, has just one point to go at seventeen months.

The goal at Jessnic is not to see how many champions can be finished from each litter regardless of quality, but rather to improve and maintain and adhere to the true, correct Rottweiler Standard—because their owner is a dedicated lady who really cares about this unique and magnificent breed.

LYN-MAR ACRES

The Rottweilers at Lyn-Mar Acres Kennels, owned by Mrs. Margaret S. Walton at Mt. Holly, New Jersey, came about following the loss of the Walton's beloved Doberman Pinscher, Salty, during the 1950s. Salty had been a show dog, guard, friend and companion. The Waltons searched widely for a suitable "second Salty," but to no avail. While attempting to locate one, however, a call came from a friend who had just lost an old German imported Boxer bitch, which they also were looking to replace. This friend had already compiled a list of breeds the family did *not* wish to own for various reasons. But the Waltons and friend had a good idea! Since the friend's husband was a pilot with an oil company, and put down at Amsterdam on his return from the fields, Peg Walton suggested that he visit the Dutch Kennel Club, inquire about Rottweilers and get a list of breeders in that country.

The rest is history! He brought back a dog with which everyone concerned promptly fell in love, and subsequently, in 1958, he brought back to the Waltons a bitch puppy registered by her breeder only as Britta. She was sired by a grandson of Landes and Landesleistungssg Blitz v.d. Wesermarsch and out of Jutta v.d. Brantsberg, a granddaughter of Kamp Arno v Glastal. Although the Waltons never bred Britta, she really sold them on her breed and its quality and intelligence to the extent that Lyn-Mar Acres has never been without one since. In fact usually there have been more than one to be found at the Walton's home.

The second bitch that came to Lyn-Mar Acres was also of German breeding, and when bred to Champion Ferdinand v Dachsweil produced a litter of seven. Three of the four dogs gained their championships, and the three bitches each had a major or better but, for various reasons, never were finished.

Champion Lyn-Mar Acres Arras v Kinta certainly made his mark on the breed! Although he sired only thirteen litters, in them he produced twenty champions. Among them were two Working Group winners, including one that went on to Best in Show.

The Rottweilers presently in residence as house dogs at Mrs. Walton's are: Champion Lyn-Mar Acres Chesarras v Amri, and Champion Lyn-Mar Acres Ruffian v Amri, both sired by Arras; Lyn-Mar Acres Britta v Caslexa, by Champion Axel v Schwanenschlag (Germany) ex Champion Lyn-Mar Acres Cassie v Amri; Lyn-Mar Acres Cardo v Bridar and Lyn-Mar Acres Cosi v

Ch. Lyn-Mar Acres Arras v Kinta by Ch. Ferdinand v Dachsweil ex Rodsden's Grosskind v Harras, owned by Miss Joni L. Walton taking Best of Breed over specials, at his first show, Westchester 1969. Handled by Mrs. Margaret Walton.

Bridar, sired by Champion Lyndhausen Free Spirit (an Arras grandson) ex Lyn-Mar Acres Britta v Caslexa (an Arras granddaughter) and Lyn-Mar Acres Phaedra v Stolzenfels, sired by Champion Imor von Stolzenfels ex Champion Holly von der Grunen Grenze (Germany).

PANAMINT

Barbara Hoard Dillon began her justly famous Panamint Rottweilers back in 1948 when she acquired her foundation bitch. The kennel name was registered with the American Kennel Club in 1953.

Zada's Zenda was the foundation bitch, and she was whelped in July 1948. Her owner, Barbara, handled her personally through to her Championship and Companion Dog titles. She was the first C.D. titled Rottweiler and the sixth to gain a Championship in the United States.

Zenda was bred by Nancy and Andrew Cooper, who lately acquired a puppy from Barbara after many years without a member of the breed. She made her first appearances in match shows sponsored by the fledgling Rottweiler Club of America, which was founded by Noel Jones, and in whose Burlingame, California, back yard the early matches took place. Barbara became one of the charter members of this Club. Of those originally involved with it, only Barbara Dillon, Nancy and Andrew Cooper, and Noel Jones are still alive, and of them, Barbara is the only one who has been consistently active with Rottweiler exhibiting, training, breeding, etc, since 1948. Unfortunately the Rottweiler Club of America "died" in about 1956 due, Barbara tells us, to a clique which eliminated many of the original members to a point where "the membership seemed to be numbered only from four to six, who then rotated the offices and would accept no applications to revive the Club."

Barbara acquired the Rottweiler dog, Zuke, that was from the first litter bred by Noel Jones in 1947. Zuke acquired a few points under her handling, but since Barbara was still a teenager living at home at the time and Zuke did not get along well with her mother, they found him another home where he would be the only dog. His sire was Kris and the dam Delga. The first Panamint litter was whelped in March of 1952, from the original bitch, Zenda, sired by Champion Hannibal. One bitch was kept from that breeding, Kezia v Heidenmauer. She had gained part of her necessary points towards championship when she developed a fatty tumor on her hind foot. It proved impossible to be removed completely. Its constant re-growth caused her no real trouble, but it was disfiguring and thus ended her show career.

Claus v Schildgen was acquired from W.F. and Mary Ann De Vore in 1952 and handled by Barbara to his championship. Unfor-

Ch. Panamint Christal, owned by Barbara Dillon, was sired by Emir v Kohlenhof ex Am., Can. Ch. Panamint Ragnarok.

Opposite:
Above: Nine-week-old puppies are pictured here courtesy of Barbara Dillon. **Below:** Am. Can. Ch. Panamint Antje produced eight champions for Barbara Dillon. Antje was sired by the German import, Ch. Emir v Kohlenhof, SchH I ex Ch. Panamint Ragnarok, dam of eight champions. Owned by Barbara Dillon, Panamint Kennels.

Panamint Rottweiler puppies by Black v Golderbach, Barbara Hoard Dillon, owner.

tunately, he died in 1961 after having been boarded for a few weeks. At the time the fatal illness was diagnosed as distemper. Kezia bred to Claus in 1958 produced Panamint Ragnarok, which became an American and Canadian Champion.

It was about 1958 that the German male Emir v Kohlenhof, SchH I, came to stay at Panamint off and on over a period of several years, during which time his owner continued an army career. Emir became a Champion and the sire of a number of litters. Later he was purchased by the handler, Fay Owyoung. Barbara's Panamint Ragnarok was bred to him in 1960, producing a litter from which two bitches were kept, Champion Panamint Antje and Champion Panamint Christal. Antje added on the title Canadian Champion, as her mother had done, too.

In 1962 Panamint acquired two importations, both males, from Holland, the first Rottweilers to be imported here from that country. One was Fernando v d Sheriff, sired by Champion Balder v Habenichts out of Bauxite v d Woelwijk, and thus a direct descendent of the "hero" of the book by Jan Rheenan about his Rottweiler Rik, entitled *My Friend Rik*. Ferdy later was placed with the Schafroth family. Barbara says "he was not of show or breeding quality for us, he was over 30″ tall and over 175 pounds weight. In build he resembled more the Giant Mastiffs rather

202

Lap dogs can be Rottweilers, too. Barbara Dillon owns this handsome one at Baring, WA. **Below:** Rottweilers *do* mix well with other breeds if brought up to do so. The friend in this case is a Bedlington Terrier. Photo, courtesy of Barbara Dillon, Panamint Rottweilers, Baring, WA.

than a Rottweiler." He was further described as being of super temperament and most impressive to all novices.

The second male was Bullino v d Neckarstroom. He was exhibited to his Canadian and American Championships. "A most impressive, blocky male bred by C.A. Laamers. Bullino lived to be thirteen years old and had to be put to sleep to end further suffering and a loss of his special dignity." Bullino was bred with Ragnarok in 1964, and Barbara kept the bitch, Panamint Cheyenne Autumn, another one to gain championship honors.

In 1964 the co-owned bitch Canadian Champion Panamint Sunday Special, C.D., gained her title to become the first Rottweiler in Canada to earn a Companion Dog degree. She also was Top Rottweiler in Canada for two years and was the first Rottweiler to place in the Working Group. She was whelped in 1962 from Champion Ragnarok and Champion El Fago Baca.

In 1965 Panamint again imported several Rottweilers from Germany. These included Dingo v Kupferdach and his sister, Datmar. Both dogs gained American Championships. Dingo died from a possible heart attack before he was three years old. Datmar was at Panamint until her last days, or about ten years of age.

In co-ownership, about 1967, Panamint imported the male Lenlee Cheron from England. He was given to his co-owner, and Barbara never used him at stud in her own kennel.

In 1967, in lieu of a stud fee for Bullino, a bitch puppy was kept from the English bitch Asta of Aarons. This was Russell's Herzchen, that became the first Rottweiler in the United States to win a Tracking Dog title.

The German bitch Datmar was bred in 1968 to Bullino, and the linebred Panamint Torkeln v d Eichen was kept. She gained her championship and lived to a fine old age, having died at the age of eleven just prior to the Dillon's move to Washington.

Cheyenne Autumn was bred with the German import Champion Falk v Kursaal, SchH I, owned by Dorothy Stream in 1969, and Champion Panamint Shasta Sage was a result. She was eight years old when she died of kidney failure. At the request of friends who wanted them for guard dogs and protectors, Barbara imported two males from Germany for this purpose. Bodo v Uhlbachtal became the protector that his owners here needed to foil several holdups at their restaurant. In fact, he has been singlehandedly credited with preventing the possible killing

A handsome dog with a multitude of titles! Int. CACIB, Am., Can., Mex. and Bda. Ch. Jack v Emstal, Am., Can. CD, Mex. PC. He belongs to Barbara Dillon, Panamint Kennels, Baring, WA. **Below:** A scene at a Finnish dog show, courtesy of Barbara Dillon.

Above: At the playground is pictured Panamint Pfalz v Rheintal. Photo, courtesy of Barbara Dillon. **Below:** Panamint Wanda v Watzenhof at 27 months. Photo, courtesy of Barbara Dillon, Baring, WA.

of his mistress one night. Black v Golderbach, the other dog, became the guardian of some seven acres of his owner, the President of National Semi-Conductor. He was used at stud a number of times on Panamint bitches and some others, producing some good offspring.

In 1969 Panamint imported and co-owned the German bitch Bella von Steinach. She gained championship with ease but was never bred because of a physical obstruction. At the same time, Panamint imported and kept Cilly v Uhlbachtal that became another owner-handled champion. Cilly died in 1979.

Dieter v Konigsberg was imported from Germany in 1970. This dog had considerable impact on the breed, siring sixteen champions. He gained Championship and C.D. honors here and died in 1979.

Again at the request of friends, Panamint imported Bar v Emscherwald and his litter sister, Britta v Emscherwald. Bar was injured at his owner's home and never shown. Britta became an estate guard and personal companion.

Littermates again came from Germany in 1971. The dog, Bandit v Salamandertal, owned by a very fine family, was of unstable temperament and was never allowed to be bred. The litter sister, Bambi, gained her championship here.

In about 1970, the German male Troll v Hook became available from his owners in Michigan. Mrs. Dorothea Gruenerwald and Barbara Dillon decided to purchase him for the value of his bloodlines. He had never been trained for showing, and his new owners found it a bit difficult to do so when he had reached six to seven years of age, so he gained only a few points here.

Champion Panamint Shasta Sage, producer of seven champions, was bred to Champion Dieter vom Konigsberg in 1973. Both Panamint Legend and Linde v Rheintal, that went on to gain championships, were kept from this litter.

Linde was later placed, under co-ownership, with a family in Oregon.

In 1973, Panamint imported from Holland again; Barbara had been there earlier on a visit. This import was a male and he became Champion Donar v d Neckarstroom, a closely bred male on some excellent bloodlines and individuals. He easily gained his title, and stud use was permitted on a limited basis. He sired eight champions here. Donar now is retired and living with the Dillons on the farm in Baring, Washington.

Panamint Happy Talk watching out the window. Barbara Hoard Dillon, owner.

In 1975, Champion Cilly von Uhlbachtal was bred to Black v Golderbach; Panamint kept a bitch, Orenda v Kraewel. Barbara says "the 'von Kraewel' was a family name in Germany, and I'm not too sure how the relatives took the thought of naming the dogs that way. However, while Orenda was not a smash in the show ring, and she was not bred, her little brother, Otso, was quickly the one that made the family proud! He was owner handled to many a Best of Breed and Group placement, and to at least one Group First. Orenda, meanwhile, was a success in her own way as a companion to her owners until she died in 1980."

While in Germany on a trip, Barbara was introduced to one Gina v Ingenhof and had her sent on to Matt Parr of Cabo san Lucas. Later Gina changed homes, much to Barbara's regret. Through Barbara's good offices, Jackel v Ingenhof was also sent by his breeder to Matt Parr, and he was the guard for this gentleman's complex holdings in Cabo San Lucas.

Again visiting Germany in 1975, Barbara was offered the dog Jack v Emstal, SchH I. She had no place for another male at the time but she was quick to find a friend who would give the dog what he deserved. Jack lost no time in completing his American Championship, his Canadian, Mexican and Bermudian titles, and with his already gained three CACIB cards to his credit when he

Above: Rottweilers are helpful on the golf course, too. This one is pulling the golf cart. Photo, courtesy Barbara Dillon. **Below:** This is a longhaired Rottweiler of beautiful conformation. Unfortunately, this type of coat is a disqualification, and the dog may not be shown. Photo taken in 1971, courtesy, Barbara Dillon.

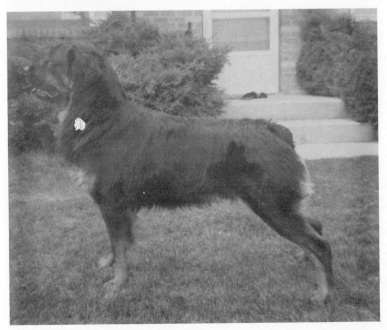

From television's popular series, "The Flying Nun," two of the stars, Sally Field and Ch. Panamint Apache Dancer.

left Germany, he earned the fourth for the International Championship. He is owned by Steve and Charlotte Johnson and Linda Schuman. Barbara comments "Jack has proven to be popular as a stud and as a household companion. I doubt if the Germans would look upon him now with favor as he has learned some tricks and gets along with all manners of animals at home" adding "but he is still a guard." On this same trip it had been hoped for a bitch for breeding from the Kastanianenbaum Kennels. Unfortunately, the bitch developed hip dysplasia after importation.

Later in 1975 Barbara made a return visit to Germany, where

she was apprenticing for a German Rottweiler Club (ADRK) judging license. At this time she acquired the puppy bitch Ella v Weilheimer Stuckl. The puppy was only seven weeks old when she left Germany with her new owners in the cabin of the Lufthansa flight. "She was quickly the darling of the crew, and actually while she was highly spirited, she was quick to catch on to why we rushed her off to the bathroom facilities every so often on the long flight home!"

In 1976, Jack v Emstal was bred to Champion Panamint Legend, and the Dillons have kept Panamint Forever Mine. She has acquired more than the necessary major points, but since their move the Dillons have not yet had the opportunity to get her back into the ring to finish.

Panamint Flint v Eichen and Panamint Apache Dancer were acquired by Ralph McCutcheon, the owner and trainer of the famous horse Fury and a number of other horse "stars." The last movie that Apache Dancer, or "Rote" as he was called, made was *Mustang Country* with Joel McCrea. While both dogs actually appeared in this film, it was Rote who was used for the majority of the close-ups. We understand that Ralph McCutcheon died prior to the making of this movie, and the beautiful and popular "Rote" did likewise shortly following its completion. "Rote" was well known for his television appearances, too, and will be remembered by the "dog aware" public as having been in the *Flying Nun* series with Sally Field and a number of episodes of *Bewitched* with Elizabeth Montgomery.

In 1978, Champion Panamint Legend and Champion Panamint Junker (Troll v Hook—Datmar v Kupferdach) were bred. The resulting litter was small in numbers but produced Panamint Ideal Impression that had gained her Tracking Dog title in just one trial by the time she was seven months old! She was the first Tracking Dog titled Rottweiler on the West Coast. The first in the country had been in the East also of Barbara's breeding: Champion Dieter v Konigsberg, C.D., out of Champion Panamint Icko v Hohenwald, C.D. Ideal Impression as we write this has also gained her Companion Dog title and is working on Companion Dog Excellent as well as her conformation title.

Over the twenty-eight years of Rottweiler breeding at Panamint, since the first litter in 1952, the policy has been to breed for the owners' pleasure and enjoyment, not for the public. None of the bitches have been permitted more than several litters in their lifetime. The dogs have been sparingly used at stud for only short periods of time. Mrs. Dillon's goal has been the personal satisfaction of proving her breeding theories and her faith in the quality of the Panamint dogs, which she has succeeded admirably in so doing as one can see by looking at the record!

From their own breedings at the kennel, Panamint has produced 43 American Kennel Club champions. "More than any other Rott breeder in the United States," to quote Barbara. Additionally they have bred or shown more than six Rottweilers to Canadian championships. Co-breeding with others has added about five additional titled dogs. Barbara has "lost track of" all the Obedience titles won through the years. There have been a number of Group winning and/or placing Rottweilers, too. The Panamint homebreds have been almost entirely owner-handled to their various titles and show ring successes!

As a judge, Mrs. Dillon points to her spectacular record as a breeder preceding the start of this interest. Hers is the longest consecutive record of exhibiting Rottweilers in the United States, as she has appeared in the show ring with Rotts of her own since 1948. Also she was a pioneer in the custom of X-raying for hip dysplasia, claiming to have done so well before any of the other U.S.A. breeders considered it necessary.

Mrs. Dillon holds the longest consecutive membership of any American in the German Rottweiler Club (ADRK) and possibly the longest of any member outside of Germany. Only she and Mr. Pasanen of Finland have received gold medals for this.

In addition to being approved to judge Rottweilers in the United States, Mrs. Dillon has her judging license to judge the breed in Germany or in any other country in the world where the rules of the Federation Cynologique Internationale are effective. She holds the longest membership of any American in the Dutch Rottweiler Club, as well as having been a member of the English Rottweiler Club since that organization's beginning. She had the honor of judging one of their Specialty Shows where she was greeted by two hundred entries.

Barbara Dillon is of German-American descent. Her paternal grandparents were German-born while her Mother's side of the family can be traced back to before the American Revolution. Thus she feels she has roots in both places!

At the Dillon's, there are never more than ten Rottweilers kept at one time; many of them are the older stock retired after their show careers.

Radio Ranch's Sam Huff at six weeks of age. Pamela Weller, owner, Radio Ranch Rottweilers.

RADIO RANCH

Pamela Weller of Chesapeake, Virginia, owns the Radio Ranch Rottweilers, so named due to her affiliation with WCMS Radio and *Metro Magazine* of Norfolk, Virginia.

Time, quality rather than quantity, and integrity to the breed is the basic philosophy at Radio Ranch in the raising of Rottweilers. From the beginning, with the purchase of Champion Zander of Rafter in 1969, to the present when Champion Radio Ranch's Axel V. Notara continues the tradition by continually siring championship quality puppies as well as good companions, those goals are being fulfilled.

The foundation bitch for Radio Ranch was Champion Kuhlwalds Tara of Ronlyn. She became an undefeated champion, completing her title in two weeks, leaving seven-week-old puppies at home. In her lifetime she produced only twelve live pups, of which six became champions, three of them Top Ten. The most famous of these is Champion Radio Ranch's Axel V. Notara. Axel's sire was Champion Rodsden's Nomad V D Harque, that won both "majors" from the Puppy Class, but unfortunately was used only four times at stud.

Radio Ranch's George Anderson, owned by Radio Ranch Rottweilers, Pamela C. Weller, Chesapeake, VA. George Anderson sired nine champions in only two litters. Two of these were in the Top Ten, one of them being Ch. Bethel Farms Apollo, handled to some exciting wins by Bert Halsey.

Ch. Kuhlwald's Tobrina, by Ch. Axel vom Schwanenschlag from Ch. Kuhlwald's Little Iodine, C.D., taking Best of Breed at the Berrien Springs Kennel Club Dog Show June 23, 1974. Hand raised by Mrs. Dorit Rogers.

Axel was *Kennel Review's* No. 1 Top Producer for the breed in 1979 and has been on the Top Producers list for three years. He was also No. 3 Working breed sire for 1979. As of this writing, Axel is the sire of 28 champions, which is even more exceptional since in keeping with the basic philosophy of quality not quantity, Axel is used at stud no more than an average of four times a year.

Among the champion offspring sired by Axel are three Specialty winners, an International Mexican and American Champion daughter, several Top Ten dogs and multi-Group placing Rottweilers. Champion Radio Ranch's Christmas Spirit, owned and handled by Tom and Marion Sallen of Tarpon Springs, Florida, just set a new record for the breed when she was named first in the Working Group handled by her owner. This made her the first owner-handled Rottweiler bitch to win a Working Group in the United States. It also gave her the distinction of being only the second Rott bitch in the history of the breed to have taken a Group First—truly an exciting honor. Spirit's other wins include Group 2 and Group 3 placements as well as Winners Bitch and Best of Winners at the Colonial Rottweiler Club Specialty. She was the No. 1 owner-handled Rottweiler bitch in 1979 and the No. 2 overall in only six months out as a "special".

Christmas Spirit is from a litter of six champions, including Champion Radio Ranch's Merry V Notara, Winners Bitch and Best of Winners at the Medallion Rottweiler Club Specialty in 1978.

Another daughter from this litter, Champion Radio Ranch's Gypsy V. Notara, was Best in Sweepstakes at the Colonial Rottweiler Club Specialty in 1977. Some notable sons are Champion Graudstark's Lugar and Radio Ranch's Weekend Warrior, Group placers. Champion Rocky V. Anderson and Champion Radio Ranch's Extra Special are others to watch for in the ring.

A very special dog that presented a tragic figure to Radio Ranch was George Anderson. He was purchased as a mature dog and sired only two litters but had accumulated 11 points towards championship before his untimely death. From the two litters there have been a total of nine champions. George was *Kennel Review's* 1978 Top Producer for the breed two years after his death. One of his more famous sons, which it is hoped will fill the gap left by the loss of his sire, is Champion Bethel Farms Apollo, a multi-Best of Breed winner and Group placer. He is co-owned by Radio Ranch and Bethel Farms of Newport News, Virginia.

RAVENWOOD

Len and Linda Griswold raise several breeds at their Raven-wood Kennels in Michigan City, Indiana: Alaskan Malamutes, Pembroke Welsh Corgis and Rottweilers. Their kennel slogan is "Special Dogs for Special People," and they truly live up to this in every way.

Ravenwood Rottweilers began in 1974 with the Griswolds' foundation bitch, Dagna Von Arktos, C.D. Dagna proved to be a very eager obedience student and zipped through to her C.D. title in three shows, going Highest Scoring Rottweiler at Hoosier Kennel Club Dog Show, Indianapolis, Indiana, when she was a mere thirteen months old. During this time she was also being shown in conformation. A sad and untimely tangle with a car resulted in a broken right rear leg for Dagna at fourteen months, which ended her conformation career and further obedience training.

Dagna did prove to be a superb producer of bone, substance and temperament in her puppies. From some of her first came Champion Ravenwood Black Gold, C.D., Champion Ravenwood Time Traveler, C.D. and Ravenwood Stardust, C.D. These were sired by Champion Pondutt Von Schweitzer, C.D. Although used as a stud by the Griswolds, Pondutt did not come to Ravenwood until he was six years old. He too was an extremely eager obedience dog, and earned his C.D. title, then went through to take the complete police training prior to reaching the age of eight years. Rott-weilers *never* are too old to learn!

Ravenwood has imported Rottweilers from England with which to complement its own domestic bloodlines. All imported Rott-weilers purchased by the Griswolds come from the Thewina Rott-weilers belonging to Ann Payne, who is a highly regarded and respected breeder in Great Britain. Champion Thewina Sundevil, C.D. finished at thirteen months and went on to complete his C.D., going Highest Scoring Rottweiler at the Glenbard All Obedience Trial in 1979. Another importation was Thewina Thundahawk that had the makings of a great show career, but, sad to say, she contracted the dreaded parvo virus and died.

Opposite: Ravenwood Kennels Obedience Drill Team: (l. to r.) Ch. Ravenwood Black Gold, C.D., Luna von Stolzenfels, C.D., Ch. Ravenwood Nightmare, C.D., and Ch. Pondutt Von Schweitzer, C.D. Owners, Len and Linda Griswold Michigan City, IN.

Above: Ch. Ravenwood Black Gold, C.D., practicing his weight pulling. "Luggie" will be competing in individual weight pulls shortly. Linda and Len Griswold, owners.

217

Ch. Thewina Sundevil, C.D., an English import pictured at 13 months, at which age this handsome Rottweiler became a champion. Thewina had gained both majors before reaching a year old, and was the Highest Scoring Rottweiler at the Glenbard Obedience Trial in Illinois in 1979. Owner, Linda Griswold.

Opposite:
Above left: Linda Griswold's Ch. Pondutt Von Schweitzer C.D. **Above right:** Ravenwood Night-Time Express at 20 months. Owned by the Griswolds, Ravenwood Kennels. **Below:** Ravenwood Nightmare, C.D., pictured at six months of age. This was the Highest Scoring Dog at the 1980 4-H Fair. Proud owner is Linda Griswold, Ravenwood Kennels.

Ch. Dux v Hungerbuhl, SchH I, RO 234, shown going Working Group II at age four after a very successful show career in Germany.

RODSDEN

The kennel prefix "Rodsden" was registered originally to the ownership of R.D. Rademacher and R.F. Klem. Following Richard Klem's death in 1978, ownership was transferred to P.G. Rademacher and Joan R. (Rademacher) Klem. Rodsden grew out of the Rademacher/Klem family's sharing of each other's interests. At various times these have included horses, waterfowl, dogs, fish and assorted types of wild animals—even including a wolf—all those creatures to which people with a special love of animals are usually attracted. In 1945 the family acquired its first Rottweiler thus began a love affair with the breed which has grown and endured until this very day.

In the early days American-bred Rottweilwers were very close-ly bred owing to the lack of breeding material available. There was an obvious need for new bloodlines. The first of many lucky breaks for Rodsden occurred in 1961 when an aunt of Richard Klem made a trip to Europe and was asked to "bring back a Rott-weiler puppy." It was not luck, however, but discrimination that led her to purchase this puppy from Jakob Kopf, the President of the ADRK. The four-month-old puppy which Aunt Charlotte brought back grew up to become famous as Champion Quelle v d Solitude, C.D., Best of Opposite Sex at the Colonial Rottweiler Club Specialty in 1963 and mother of the very first bitch ever to take Best of Breed at a Rottweiler Specialty (Colonial Rottweiler Club in 1965). This Best of Breed bitch, Champion Rodsden's Felicia, was sired by the first home bred Rodsden champion, Baron of Rodsden, C.D.

The second import acquired by Rodsden was Champion Bengo v Westfalenpark, C.D., brought over as a young adult.

The appearance and character of Quelle and Bengo convinced the Rademacher/Klem family that the American Rottweiler needed help from the breed's country of origin. So, on a trip to Germany in 1963, Joan Klem and Pat Rademacher were for-tunate enough to purchase Bengo's sire, the 1960-'61-'62 Bundessieger, Harras vom Sofienbusch, SchH I, and bring him to this country. Harras was used sparingly here but produced twelve American-bred champion offspring and, when bred to Quelle, produced in one litter: a Group placing dog in Hawaii, Rodsden's Kaiser v d Harque; the first Rottweiler to place consistently in Working Groups on the Pacific Coast, Champion Rodsden's Kurt v d Harque, Ro. 4; and Champion Rodsden's Kluge v d Harque, C.D., Ro-50, the Top Producing stud dog in U.S. Rottweiler history until 1980 when he was surpassed by a later Rodsden import, Champion Dux vom Hungerbuhl, SchH I, Ro. 234.

At the same time Harras was imported, Rodsden also brought over Champion Afra vom Hasenacker, SchH I, C.D., that had been the Young Siegerin in Germany the previous year. Afra bred to a later import, Champion Falk vom Kursaal, SchH I, produced Champion Rodsden's Lady Luck C.D., Ro-60, dam of twelve O.F.A. certified champion offspring.

Kluge, when bred to another Rodsden import, Champion Franzl vom Kursaal (littermate to Falk and to the 1966 Bundesseigerin, Flora vom Kursaal) produced the first two Best in Show Rott-

A beautiful winter scene of Ch. Falco von het Brabantpark, RO 286, pulling a young charge in a sleigh.

Opposite:
Above: Ch. Rodsden's Axel v h Brabant, RO 582, sired by Ch. Falco v h Brabantpark, RO 286, out of Ch. Rodsden's Lady Luck, CD, RO 60. **Below:** Ch. Rodsden's Kane v Forstwald, CD, RO 1574, goes back on his sire's side to Kluge and Harras, his dam being German import, CACIB V and Am. Ch. Asta v Forstwald, CD, RO 519. Kane won the 1979 MRC Specialty. Owned by Thompson and Klem, Rodsden's Rottweilers Reg.

223

weilers in the United States: Champion Rodsden's Kato v Donnaj, C.D.X., T.D., Ro-37, the first to win Best in Show, and Champion Rodsden's Duke du Trier, Ro-37, the first to win multiple Bests in Show. The litter also included the second Rottweiler bitch to take Best of Breed at a Specialty, Champion Rodsden's Kirsten du Trier, C.D.

Another tremendously influential Rodsden import came from the Netherlands, Champion Falco v h Brabantpark, Ro-286, sire of more than 28 champions to date.

Judicious use of their imports in combination with their American-bred stock resulted in approximately 35 winners in Best of Breed, Best of Opposite Sex, Winners Dog or Winners Bitch competitions at Specialties held by the Medallion Rottweiler Club, Colonial Rottweiler Club and Golden State Rottweiler Club. The first Rottweiler to win as many as five Bests in Show in this country was Champion Rodsden's Bruin v Hungerbuhl, C.D., Ro-1189. Certainly an impressive record, but this by no means is all!

The Rodsdens are equally proud of Rottweilers that have made special names for themselves in Obedience Competition. Champion Dirndl of Rodsden, C.D.X., T.D., is the first Rottweiler bitch to gain the Champion and C.D.X. titles. Their import Champion Axel v d Taverne, U.D.T., is the first male to earn Champion and U.D.T. titles. Champion Rodsden's Goro v Sofienbusch, U.D.T.X.,

Am., Can. Ch. Rodsden's Elko Kastanienbaum, CDX, TD, Can. CD, RO 1448. Elko is a wonderful family dog as well as an outstanding working and conformation dog and is at home with the Klem family.

This beautiful show female, Ch. Rodsden's Alexa v Brabant, CD, RO 574 is the loving companion and protector of owner, Laura Coonley.

SchH I, is the only Rottweiler to date to earn *all* the conformation *and* training titles possible in Canada, United States and Mexico, plus an International Championship. Champion Rodsden's Quelle v d Harque, U.D., SchH II, is the first American-bred Rottweiler to be awarded a SchH II title. Champion Rodsden's Willa v d Harque, U.D.T., is the first Champion—U.D.T. Rottweiler bitch.

Mrs. Klem comments, "None of these achievements would have been possible, of course, without the tremendous co-operation, loyalty and dedication of our many friends in the breed, both at home and abroad. We are very grateful for having learned so early that the Rottweiler is a truly superior breed, and for the continued support of the members of the Rademacher/Klem families and our friends who have made it possible for us to maintain an ongoing breeding program without having to resort to keeping our Rottweilers in kennels.

"And since the Rottweiler was designed to be primarily a companion/working dog, we are also very proud of the great pet/companion dogs we have produced. We judge our success in this area by the fact that a large percentage of our currently produced puppies go to owners who are living with and loving their second, and in many cases third, Rottweiler from Rodsden. These dogs are the backbone of the breed and a measure of success to which we are most devoted."

Ch. Dina v Schloss Rietheim, CD, by Bulli v Hungerbuhl, SchH II, ex Asta v d Albsicht goes Best of Opposite Sex under Judge Hyden at the Medallion Rottweiler Club Specialty, 1975. Ron and Sandy Taylor, owners; Ron Taylor handling.

SANRON

Sanron Rottweilers belong to Ron and Sandy Taylor and are located in Cynthiana, Kentucky.

The Taylors' First Rottweiler, purchased in 1972, was Champion Rodsden's Tally v Hungerbuhl, C.D., by Champion Dux v Hungerbuhl ex Champion Cora v Zimmerplatz. Tally was Winners Bitch and Best of Opposite Sex at the 1974 Medallion Rottweiler Club Specialty. She was one of the top Best of Opposite Sex bitches in 1975 and was retired in 1976.

During 1976 the Taylors bought Champion Dina v Schloss Rietheim from Joan Klem and Jane Wiedel. Champion Dina had

Sandy Taylor handles Ch. Sanron Juggernaut v d Harque to Best of Winners for four points at the Cincinnati Kennel Club Show, May 1980. Owned by Sandy Taylor and Pam Favorite.

This smiling Rottweiler is the noted Ch. Rodsden's Ultima v d Harque, by Ch. Rodsden's Ikon v d Harque ex Ch. Dina v Schloss Rietheim, C.D. Ron and Sandy Taylor, owners, Cynthiana, KY.

been imported by Mrs. Klem and was the Winners Bitch at the 1973 Colonial Rottweiler Club Specialty and Best of Opposite Sex at the Medallion Rottweiler Club 1976 Specialty. She has several champion offspring, among them the Taylors' Champion Rodsden's Ultima v d Harque sired by Champion Rodsden's Ikon v d Harque.

Although the Taylors consider Dina their foundation brood bitch, Ultima is the mainstay of their breeding program. She has produced Champion Sanron Juggernaut v d Harque and Champion Sanron's Josie v d Harque along with several others that are pointed.

SRIGO

Kennels such as "Srigo," which is owned by Ms. Felicia Luburich and situated in East Brunswick, New Jersey, are the type that truly become the background of the breed to which the Fancy can point with pride and which can be depended on to produce more and better Rottweiler quality with each succeeding generation. Ms. Luburich holds a well deserved position of deep respect throughout the Working Dog Fancy. Long before I was particularly interested in Rottweilers or had "discovered" their magnificence as a breed, I had known of "Srigo" and of this lady with such a talent for breeding quality. Now that I have become personally acquainted with her, I can, even more thoroughly, appreciate her dedication to the breed, her steady, enthusiastic desire to produce superior Rottweilers in each succeeding generation, and the true merit of her contribution to Rottweilers generally.

Felicia says, as she starts to record Srigo's history, "How far back does one go in a doggy history? To 'Blackie', owned by Aunt Rose in Pennsylvania? To 'Sparky', given by Daddy and disposed of by Mama? Or to the product of the first litter? Each in turn has an effect, no matter how unconscious or subliminal, on one's doggy career. Mama was always snatching me from the jaws of one dog or another, and at one time I narrowly missed having to undergo the dreaded series of rabies shots." Thus, one sees that right from earliest childhood Felicia had a true deep love of dogs, which provides the motivating force behind the success which has been hers.

In 1948, when Felicia was twelve years old, the first litter on which she was listed as breeder was born. This was a Doberman litter. The first "high class purebred" was another Doberman, named Nora, acquired from a well known breeder in New Jersey when Felicia was eighteen. Later in the 1950s she personally whelped a litter for the first time, again a Dobe. During those years Felicia read everything about dogs on which she could lay her hands. Fortunately, the Rottweiler was mentioned in one of those books!

In 1955 Felicia joined the Colonial Rottweiler Club and the Allgemeiner Deutsche Rottweiler Klub (ADRK). She wanted and waited for a grown bitch, which she acquired in 1955, Reidstadt's Helissend.

Her second bitch, Missy v Stahl, came to her in 1961, following two previous owners, and later became a Champion, despite a huge scar on her leg from a bad heartworm treatment. Helissend's first litter of only one puppy went to her previous owner. Afterwards she produced only one litter of two puppies, which became Champion Srigo's Bernard v Dervis and Srigro's Bernice v Heller. The latter broke her foot after having won a major. Bernice left no descendants. Bernard sired the "F" and "G" litters.

Champion Srigo's Diensta produced the "F" litter. It included Champion Srigo's Faxonia and two other excellent bitches, one of which was killed by a car. The other was re-sold to a cattle breeder who "had no sympathy for dog breeders and would not show or breed her."

The "G" litter contained Champion Srigo's Garret v Zaghin and Champion Srigo's Garner v Zaghin. Garret left produce, but Ms. Luburich did not keep any of them. Garner produced two litters. Of these, from the "S" litter came Champion Srigo's Spruce v Kurtz that was Winners Dog at the Colonial Rottweiler Club Specialty the day he was fourteen months old. He was the youngest entry there outside of the puppy classes. At this same Specialty, judged by Earle Adair, Best of Breed was Champion Srigo's Garret, winning the honor from the Veterans Class, bred, owned and handled by Felicia! Best of Opposite Sex was Champion Srigo's Madchen v Kurtz. The interesting sidelight on this is that Madchen and Spruce were out of the same bitch, Champion Srigo's Econnie v Lorac, C.D., with Spruce sired by the litter brother of the Best of Breed dog. With the Winners Bitch being a German import, the consistency of Mr. Adair's judging could not have been higher.

The "C" litter consisted of two bitches, a repeat of the "A" litter's breeding, by Champion Dervis v Weyershof and Champion Missy v Stahl. The "A" litter had produced only Champion Srigo's Amai v Missle, that although bred six times produced a total of one dead puppy. The "C" litter more than made up for the earlier disappointment, as it included Champion Srigo's Creshenda v Missle and Srigo's Constance v Missle that in her one litter, by Champion Arno v Kafluzu, produced four dogs and four bitches which included Champion Srigo's Econnie v Lorac, C.D., Champion Srigo's Eshenda v Lorac, and Champion Srigo's Missle Again. The latter three bitches completely dominated the impor-

Ch. Srigo's Garret v Zaghin, Best of Breed, Colonial Rottweiler Club Specialty from the Veterans Dog Class. **Below:** Ch. Srigo's Madchen v Kurtz with her handler-breeder, Felicia Luburich, taking Best of Opposite Sex at Westminster under Judge Haworth Hoch. Madchen belongs to Lucille and Donald Kurtz.

tant shows while they were in the ring. This came as a pleasant surprise to Felicia who says, "at eight months they were so 'puppy awful' at the one show where they were entered that they stayed home after that until the following Westminster." There Eshenda was Winners Bitch and Best of Opposite Sex over 'specials', and Econnie was Reserve Winners Bitch; after Felicia had returned to the bench to get her, she had been so certain that they wouldn't beat the Open Bitch that she had not even kept Econnie at the ringside should she be needed to compete for Reserve, since both had been in the American-bred Class. But, as she says, "the judge knew better." At the Colonial Rottweiler Club, Econnie was Winners Bitch and Eshenda was Reserve. Subsequently Econnie was Best of Opposite Sex at the Colonial Rottweiler Club Specialty three times! Later in the year, Econnie had a Group Two under Alva Rosenberg, who is quoted as saying that there was "not a Rottweiler alive that he had seen that he would put up over her." Herr Berger also admired her very highly, remembering her six years later when he gave her daughter, Champion Srigo's Machen v Kurtz, Best of Breed at the Baltimore show.

The "D" litter, by Champion Arno v Kafluzu from Champion Missy v Stahl, contained Champion Darla v Missle that was barren, and Champion Srigo's Diensta v Missle, that became the grand-dam of Champion Srigo's Watch My Smoke.

In speaking of Arno, Felicia says, "Now there was a dog and a half. He was always BIGGER than life. I acquired him from Gladys Swenson because no one could manage him. It took me six months, and at nearly six years of age he accepted me, but only after I had gingerly entered him at dog shows and acquired a championship title on him. At his very first point show in his whole life, the Colonial Rottweiler Club Specialty, he was Best of Breed under Major Godsol over several Champions and professional handlers, shown on a loose lead with no 'stacking'. And his daughter was Winners Bitch and Best of Opposite Sex!"

About this same period an imported son of Champion Harras v Sofienbusch joined the Rotts at Srigo Kennels. This was Casper v d Lowehau. He weighed seventy-five pounds when he arrived in the United States as a fully grown dog. With time Felicia took him to his championship, and bred three of her best bitches to him. She says, "On the whole, the temperaments of his puppies were too intense and sharp, particularly the males, but also some of the

Ch. Srigo's Opportunity and How, by Ch. Srigo's Garner v Zaghin ex Srigo's Honeybun. Bred and owned by Felicia Luburich, East Brunswick, NJ.

bitches. And it passed through to the next generation. When his daughters were bred to sharp dogs, the resulting progeny were a liability. I therefore sold him feeling that dogs not manageable in a household are not the essence of the Rottweiler for all practical purposes."

From Casper's "H" litter came Srigo's Hester von dem Walde that was Reserve Winners Bitch at the Colonial Specialty before her untimely death, and Srigo's Honeybun that became the dam of the very impressive Champion Srigo's Opportunity And How (that was sired by Champion Srigo's Garner v Zaghin) and also of the handsome Champion Srigo's Viking Spirit, whose name was inspired by Felicia's trip to northern Europe shortly after attending the second International Federation for Rottweiler Friends meeting in Holland.

The next Srigo litter of real importance was the "M" litter which contained Champion Srigo's Merno v Kurtz and the incomparable Champion Srigo's Madchen v Kurtz. Felicia never bred anything to Merno, and Madchen only produced two litters, the "X" and "Z". She was an exhibitors' and breeders' dream come true, being by the gorgeous German Bundessieger and American Champion Erno v Wellesweiler out of Champion Srigo's Econnie v Lorac, C.D. Starting her show career at eight months, Madchen was, until her death, either Best of Breed or Best of Opposite Sex 90 percent of the time, and out of the ribbons only once. At her initial Colonial Rottweiler Club Specialty she was first in her Puppy Class. The following year she took Winners Bitch and Best of Opposite Sex under Peter Knoop. The next year she took Best of Opposite Sex under Robert Wills, and in the subsequent year Best of Breed under Eleanor Evers. This was the only time she was shown that year owing to maternal duties. She was not entered the next year, either, as she was bred again. Then she returned a year after that in the Veterans Class from which she won Best of Opposite Sex to Champion Srigo's Viking Spirit's Best of Breed under noted Rottweiler authority Barbara Hoard Dillon.

Champion Srigo's Opportunity and How won the Veteran Dog Class that same day. He had been sold as a puppy and reacquired at almost five years of age. He came out at Boardwalk Kennel Club, his first show ever, under Donald Booxbaum, who took him from the Bred-by Exhibitor Class to Best of Breed over three "specials." At his next two shows, he was Winners Dog for another "major" under Mr. Paterson at Philadelphia, then the following day Reserve to his half brother, Viking. The following summer, Viking went on the New England Circuit, fresh from a Group fourth his first time out as a "special." He was Best of Breed at all but one show on the Circuit.

Viking sired only two litters. From the second of these, out of Champion Srigo's Xclusive v Kurtz , came Champion Srigo's Big Opportunity and Champion Srigo's Billet Doux.

"Stamp" was a litter sister to Srigo's Big Girls Don't Cry, the latter a very lovely bitch that had won second in the Sweepstakes to a bitch that went on to outstanding wins and records. "Boo Hoo" was injured in a playing accident and never recovered. So "Stamp" was re-acquired, having been sold, and in her first litter produced four Champions and became the Top Producing Bitch in the Working Group for 1979. "Stamp" finished her championship from the Bred-by Classes, being Winners Bitch at Westminster, Philadelphia, and Framingham, three of the most prestigious shows for Rotts on the East Coast.

In the "P" litter, an excellent bitch, Srigo's Paint Your Wagon, had ten points including both majors in five shows when her owner reneged on showing her. She had been Winners Bitch at Westminster and Philadelphia where both judges voluntarily commented on her beauty. She was never bred, like so many of Felicia's really good ones.

The "Q" litter, of one dog and five bitches, produced Champion Srigo's Quindle v Kurtz. The "R" litter produced Srigo's Reflection of Cheer, out of Srigo's Honeybun, that was best puppy at the

The exquisite and typical Rottweiler bitch, Ch. Srigo's Paint Your Wagon, by Ch. Srigo's Garret v Zaghin ex Srigo's Anabel v Missle. Winners Bitch at Westminster Kennel Club. Judge, Muriel Freeman. Handler, Felicia Luburich.

Colonial Rottweiler Club Specialty Match. "Her owner claimed, at a later date when I wanted her bred, that she had run away," notes Felicia.

The "T" litter combination of a daughter of Champion Casper v d Lowehau and Champion Srigo's Garret v Zaghin resulted in males much too sharp, so the other bitches were not bred.

The "U" litter contained only one puppy that was sold.

The "V" litter produced Viking Spirit and another lovely dog that, despite some splendid wins, was not finished.

The "W" litter's Champion Srigo's Watch My Smoke was another of the type breeders dream about. She was the American Rottweiler Club Top Winning Bitch for 1973 and produced one litter of two puppies. Her litter brother was Reserve Winners Dog from the 6-9 Month Class at the Colonial Rottweiler Club his first time in the show ring.

Above left: Ch. Srigo's Watch My Smoke here is winning first prize in the Puppy Bitch Class, 9—12 Months, at the Medallion Rottweiler Club Specialty, Aug. 4, 1973. Felicia Luburich, owner handler. **Right:** Ch. Srigo's Xclusive v Kurtz, first in the Puppy Bitch Class at the Colonial and Medallion Club's Specialty Shows. Felicia Luburich breeder, owner handler. **Below:** Ch. Srigo's Elyssian Fields, by Ch. Jack v Emstal, C.D., from Ch. Srigo's Xclusive v Kurtz. Owners, Pat Rinero and Srigo Kennels, Spotswood, NJ.

Probably one of the most keenly anticipated litters ever born at Srigo was that from Champion Srigo's Madchen v Kurtz by Troll v Hook. Troll was brought in from Colorado by Dorothea Gruenerwald at the time of the Colonial Rottweiler Club Specialty specifically to be bred to Madchen. She was bred on Friday and on Sunday, the night on which she took Best of Breed at the Specialty, and subsequently whelped Felicia's "X" litter, consisting of two dogs and three bitches.

Felicia kept all of the puppies until they had reached six months of age, then placed the two males as pets—one with the owner of his grand-dam's brother, the other with her kennel girl. The three bitches became Champion Srigo's Xclaim v Kurtz, co-owned with Betsy Orgler, that whelped only one litter of all males, Champion Srigo's Xclusive v Kurtz and Champion Srigo's Xquisite v Kurtz. The latter two remained with Felicia. At the next Colonial Specialty, Xclaim went into the Bred-by Exhibitor Class at eight months, already having a major to her credit, and took Winners Bitch for five points, while Srigo's Xclusive v Kurtz was first in the Puppy Bitch Class. At the Medallion Rottweiler Club Specialty shortly thereafter, Xclusive again took the Puppy Bitch Class. Xquisite was Best Novice and Xclaim first in Bred-by Exhibitor and Reserve Winners Bitch. Xclaim finished to her title shortly afterwards, Xclusive the following January and Xquisite in April. Thus Madchen had three champions in her first litter. At about that time she was bred for the second one, on this occasion to Champion Lyn Mar Acres Arras v Kinta, from which she whelped four dogs and four bitches. Again Felicia kept them all until six months of age, except for one bitch which developed a cowlick on her neck and she was placed as a pet. Three bitches and two males Felicia considered to have great potential, so they were either kept or placed each in a show home. Both Srigo's Zephre and Srigo's Zinger had points from the puppy classes, as did Srigo's Zeitgeist that had nine points with both majors from the Puppy Class at eight months. Srigo's Zarras had thirteen points with both majors at ten months, in two weeks, from Bred-by Exhibitor. He finished in just two more shows. Srigo's Zoom's career got off to a late start, but once she had entered competition, she finished in nine shows.

Champion Jack v Emstal and Champion Srigo's Xclusive v Kurtz, who had become a very steady producer of quality, gave Felicia Champion Srigo's Elyssian Fields, another breeder's

Ch. Srigo's Zigger v
Kurtz, C.D.

dream! This one eclipsed Felicia's fondest hopes, winning her title after an exciting career in the puppy classes to become a champion at twelve months and twelve days of age. She also garnered Best Puppy in Match during the summer under Janet Marshall at the Colonial Rottweiler Club Match and would have gone to California for the American Rottweiler Club National had there been anyone to whom Felicia could have entrusted the kennel at that time.

The "F" litter by Champion Kokas K's Degan v Durga, C.D., T.D., O.F.A., that Felicia had started on his show and breeding career, produced Champion Srigo's Flim Flam Man, owner-handled, Champion Srigo's Front Runner, American and Canadian Champion Srigo's Flight of the Eagle, American and Canadian C.D., O.F.A., now a Best in Show winner and always owner-handled by Mr. Art Rihel. Eagle has been a steady winner from the beginning, in the Top Ten for the past two years, with his best years still ahead of him. Felicia feels that he could even outshine his show career as a stud and is planning to breed to him every suitable bitch that she owns.

One of the girls from Srigo's "F" litter. **Below:** Srigo's Front Runner, winner of two "majors" in two days. Owned by Felicia Luburich, Srigo Kennels.

Travel can be tiresome! Am. Can. Ch. Srigo's Flight of the Eagle rests his head on the seat-back and wonders how much longer the trip to the show will be. The Arthur L. Rikels owns this gorgeous Best in Show winning dog. **Below left:** Ch. Srigo's I Am Invincible showing off the ideal head and front that have helped make it so! Felicia Luburich, breeder-owner-handler. **Below right:** Srigo's Johnny Come Lately in El Salvador, Central America, with his young owner, Miss Siemans.

In the "H" litter, Heaven Only Knows was Best Puppy at the Colonial Rottweiler Match with Srigo's I Am Invincible Best Opposite. She later won a five point major and has been sold to a fancier in California.

Srigo's Heart of Gold has seven points and Felicia has kept ownership of her. Her first litter, by Champion Srigo's Zarras v Kurtz, O.F.A., is promising.

From the "I" litter of Felicia's favorite bitch, Champion Srigo's Zoom v Kurtz, C.D. sired by Champion Kokas K's Degan v Burge, C.D., T.D., O.F.A., came two dogs and two bitches, delivered on the 58th day. It was well worth the nightly loss of sleep for tube feeding these puppies, as they included Srigo's Imitation of Life, Srigo's I Am Invincible, and Srigo's Incredible Is the Word. Imitation of Life was Best in Match over the adults at only four and a half months at the American Rottweiler Club Specialty Match in Atlanta, while her dam, Champion Srigo's Zoom v Kurtz, took Highest Score in Obedience. What a day! The following spring, Srigo's I Am Invincible was first and Srigo's Incredible Is The Word was second in the 12-18 Month Class of the Colonial Rottweiler Club Specialty Sweepstakes, "Vinny" going on to Best in Sweepstakes. Incredible took two majors when he came out in Open Class, then developed a lung growth and died. In Felicia's heart, he is second only to his dam as a personality.

The "J" litter produced Bermudian Champion Srigo's The Jig Is Up, Reserve Winners Dog at the 1980 Colonial Specialty. Srigo's Joy To The World was second in the 12-18 Month Bitch Sweepstakes at Colonial, plus first in Bred-by Exhibitor at the Medallion Specialty under Herr Berger and at the American Rottweiler Club Specialty Match in North Carolina. Herr Berger, incidentally, certainly admired Champion Srigo's Madchen v Kurtz and Champion Srigo's Viking Spirit on other occasions when judging over here, since he gave each of them Best of Breed while officiating at point shows on the East Coast. Herr Berger is the present Chief Breed Warden in Germany.

Elyssian Fields had a litter by Zarras while Felicia was in Europe for the fourth International Friends of the Rottweiler meeting, and she feels that negligence and apathy caused their death. She repeated the breeding at the first opportunity, which is the "O" litter: Srigo's Only By Magic, owned by W. Gray and H. Weaver, Srigo's Of Thee I Sing and Srigo's On With the Show, the latter two still owned by Felicia.

As we write this, Felicia Luburich is looking forward to her "T" and "U" litters, from Eagle and Srigo's On With the Show and from Champion Srigo's Zarras and Srigo's Joy To The World. She has Eagle's first litter now and a singleton from Champion Srigo's Xclusive, which brings this resume up to date and covers twenty-five years' interest in and devotion to the Rottweiler breed.

The words of a breeder as successful as Felicia Luburich are well worth attention, so we conclude this kennel story, as did she, with the following observations.

"Breeding and raising dogs as an intellectual pursuit, i.e. to enhance the breed and carry it forward into the following generations in such a way that they bring prestige and respect to the Rottweiler is a difficult, expensive, all-consuming, heart-breaking effort. High points come along, but the day-to-day routine is very taxing. Not the faint of heart or 'easy buck' person appearing far too frequently nowadays due to the sudden public discovery of the Rottweiler's attributes, will benefit the breed. Or those maintaining a non-selective hit-or-miss type breeding. The attributes which make those who know the breed love, respect and admire it are possessed only because the Europeans who have developed the breed only used for breeding purposes those specimens that came up to a rigid selection level of size, type, color, movement, temperament, trainability, protectiveness, character and athletic ability necessary to insure that their produce would inherit enough of the desirable qualities to develop into the so very worthwhile individual we who are familiar with the well-bred Rottweiler know him to be.

"Everyone has a particular type of dog and way of doing things. Considering that from the very beginning my intent was never to breed dogs for the purpose of merchandising them, it was unfortunate that in the beginning I was not able to keep any of the puppies I bred, but sold them with agreements that they be shown and returned to me for at least one litter, if worthy of it. This proved eminently unsatisfactory, since almost everyone reneged on their written contracts. Although several people lived up to part of their agreements, the person who has been my one constant and steadfast supporter over the years has been Lucille Kurtz. Without question or stinting of time, and expending every effort, she made it possible for me to breed Rottweilers. Without her I would have *no* Rottweilers of my own continuous breeding. To her I take off my hat and will forever be in her debt.

Srigo's Incredible Is the Word; dam, Ch. Srigo's Zoom v Kurtz, CD. **Below:** Srigo's Heaven Only Knows took five points at eight months by going Winners from the Bred-by-Exhibitor Class. Bred and handled by Felicia Luburich.

"All the Rottweiler puppies carrying the Srigo name have been bred by me whelped by me mostly or under my direct supervision. I do not buy, re-sell or broker puppies for anyone, applying my kennel name to them and thus collecting kudos for dogs that have only passed through my hands, and for which I am not directly responsible from start to finish. I am now into my seventh generation of my own breeding on both sides of a pedigree, continuing the excellence it has been my good fortune and pleasure to have had with me since 1955. The Rottweiler!

"Now I keep all puppies until I feel I can assess their potential, which usually means after the permanent teeth have erupted. At that time I start selling. If I feel it will not bring great credit to the breed in the show ring or the whelping box, I sell it without American Kennel Club registration until it has been rendered incapable of reproducing. The remainder I either keep or sell in co-ownership until all parts of the contract have been fulfilled. This has insured that a greater percentage of my efforts on behalf of the Rottweiler are bearing fruit and not being wasted on the one hand, or improperly used on the other, for breeding by any commercial outfit that might seek to commercialize on my good name from stock which, although far above being cull quality, still should not be bred. Particularly by people who have no real knowledge of or interest other than commercial in the breed."

Srigo's Nobody Does It Better, out of Ch. Srigo's Zinger v Kurtz, CD, OFA.

Rottweilers love
Winter! Here is Am.,
Can. Ch. Rodsden's
Ander v h Brabant, CD,
enjoying his favorite
time of year. Sherri
Page, owner, Somer-
ville, OH.

TOBANT

Sherri Page, owner of the Tobant Rottweilers, became involved with the breed during the early 1970s, when she started in obedience which, as she says, is a "must" for this breed, since there is nothing worse than an ill-behaved, ill-mannered large dog. She put a C.D. and a C.D.X. on her first two Rottweilers.

Then she purchased Ander, now American and Canadian Champion Rodsden's Ander V H Brabant, and went into conformation showing. Ander was owner-handled to his championship in both the United States and Canada and was handled by Tom Glassford to some Working Group placements. Ander placed in the Top Ten Rottweilers for 1977, the year he retired from showing, and is described by his owner as "one of the pleasantest Rotts you'll ever meet." He was personality tested by Finnish and German judges at the Medallion Rottweiler Club, where he scored 2+ out of a possible 3+. Ander's sire and dam, CACIB Champion Falco V H Brabantpark, an importation from Holland, and Champion Rodsden's Lady Luck C.D. are both Top Producers in this breed, and Ander is well on his way toward joining them, with eight champions to his credit, although he has been used sparingly at stud.

At seven years of age, Ander made the final cut at the Medallion Rottweiler Club Specialty, having won the Veteran's Dog Class and becoming one of the three dogs still under consideration at the very end.

The dogs at Tobant all live in the house as family members, which is the way Rottweilers prefer it.

Above: Eight-week-old Rottweiler babies, by Am., Can. Ch. Rodsden's Ander v h Brabant ex Ch. Edwards Brandy Caroline, belonging to Sherri Page. **Below:** Southwood's Faline of Tobant at four months old winning the first Tri-State Rottweiler Club Match Show, August 1980. Sherri Page, owner.

TOBAR

Tobar Rottweilers were founded during 1977 with the purchase of two Rottweiler puppies from the Midwest. Today these puppies are Champion Tobar's Colonel Crunch and Tobar's Ruffian (eight points including both majors). Crunch and Ruffian have been shown sparingly and both have produced beautifully for their owners, Barbara Baris and Thomas J. Condon of Oxford, Connecticut.

But the real story behind Tobar was the acquisition of a "pet quality" Rottweiler named Erich bred by Pauline Radkowski but sold years before Tobar Kennels were established.

Tom Condon and Barbara Baris found Erich in the New Haven dog pound one freezing cold winter day. His original owners had divorced and he was given to a friend who also ran this pound. Tom and Barbara tried to acquire him at that time, but were unsuccessful. A year later the phone rang. "If you are still interested in Adolf" (which they had named him) "a purchase agreement can be worked out." They very definitely were still interested, and promptly purchased the dog. No papers, just a promise of papers when they were located. At that time Tom and Barbara still had not the slightest idea of the breeding or background of this animal.

When the papers did come through, as Barbara says, "We almost died. His name was Erich von Paulus, and he was then nearly six years old."

But the best was yet to come. Erich was sired by Champion Lyn Mar Acres Arras Von Kinta out of Champion Amsel Von Andan, C.D. His pedigree reads like "Who's Who in Rottweilers."

At once the new owners had Erich's hips x-rayed and obtained an O.F.A. number on him, after which he was turned over to a professional handler and became Champion Erich von Paulus almost overnight.

Since then Erich has produced several litters, all still young, and is shown only very sparingly. At seven years of age he is living at home with the other Rotties, as well as cats and horses. He was not discovered until he had reached five years of age, having been the cast-off of two broken marriages. As Barbara Baris puts it, "Thank God we were the lucky ones to discover this gorgeous animal."

Although Erich himself is not yet a "pillar of the breed," his sire and dam very definitely are in that category. From all indications, Erich should carry on in the family tradition.

Rottweiler charm personified by an eight-week-old Argus von Kruse. From the von der Kruse Kennels in Michigan.

VON DER KRUSE

Alan Kruse first became aware of Rottweilers when he was eleven years old, at which time his father brought one home when he returned from World War II. This dog had been purchased in Germany while the senior Mr. Kruse was stationed there at the Nuremberg Trials.

So lasting an impression did this dog make that Alan Kruse decided to own one himself. Subsequently in 1968 he made the purchase of Ehrenwach's Ansgar. In 1973 he purchased a second Rottweiler, and with that one began his interest in showing. Champion Juno von Gruenerwald completed the title at thirteen months of age, and since then Champion Olga von Gruenerwald has been added to the family.

Now Alan Kruse and his wife, Karen, have started seriously to breed these dogs and are becoming more enthusiastic by the moment. They have a home-bred bitch with both "majors" in her first two shows and a male, Christo von Kruse, with seven points. Although actively breeding only since the late 1970s, the Kruses are producing some excellent young stock backed by the finest bloodlines. We predict that this will become an important kennel in the breed's future history.

Von Der Kruse's Fearless Odis at five months of age. Sired by Ch. Astro vom Chrisstenbrod from Anja von Kruse. From the Von Der Kruse Rottweilers belonging to Alan and Karen Kruse. **Below:** Just testing! Two baby Rottweilers trying out the water. These adorable eight-week-old puppies belong to Von Der Kruse Rottweilers, and are by Ch. Bethel Farms Apollo ex Ch. Olga von Gruenerwald.

Ch. Von Gailingen's Dassie Did It and Von Gailingen's Dark Delight, CD.

VON GAILINGEN

The Von Gailingen Rottweilers belong to Catherine M. Thompson of Freehold, New Jersey, whose kennel slogan is "puppies with a future." Judging by her success as a breeder, there can be no doubt of this fact, as Mrs. Thompson's Rottweilers have distinguished themselves by producing exceptional quality right from the beginning.

Cathy Thompson's family always had dogs, Toy Manchester Terriers as house pets and Irish Water Spaniels as hunting dogs. A good deal of her youth was spent training and showing horses, which she still raises and shows occasionally. Then in 1969 she purchased her first Rottweiler, a breed in which she had been interested for several years. This first Rottweiler was owner-handled by Mrs. Thompson to her bench championship and her Companion Dog title. Her name was Champion Natascha Von Hohenreissach, C.D. She was by Champion Fago Von Hohenreissach, C.D., from a German import, Catja V Friedrichsberg.

Champion Natascha was bred to the German import Champion Dux Von Hungerbuhl SchH I, Ro-234. This was her only litter, and the pups all sold quickly. Then, says Cathy Thompson, "seven months later I was privileged to buy back one of the bitch puppies, Anka Von Gailingen."

Anka promptly took over as the pimary brood bitch and show gal, doing both in an entirely admirable manner. She was the Top Producing Bitch, *Kennel Review* System, for the breed in 1977, and now has had four litters by three different studs, all of which were from the same male line: two grandsons and a son of Champion Ferdinand Dachsweil. Like her dam, Natascha, had been before her, Anka was owner-handled to her championship, which she scored in a spectacular manner, including a five point major at Baltimore (Maryland Kennel Club) where she was Winners Bitch, Best of Winners and Best of Opposite Sex over specials under the German judge F. Berger, Head Breed Warden for ADRK (German Rottweiler Club). She was Winners Bitch at Westminster under Peggy Adamson for another point, took a five point major under Robert Wills at Tidewater Kennel Club and finished the next day with four points at Virginia Kennel Club under Robert Salomon—all of this from the Bred-by Exhibitor Class.

Like mother, like daughter! Ch. Natascha V Hohenreissach, CD and Ch. Anka V Gailingen, both belonging to Catherine M. Thompson.

Opposite:
Above: Ch. Von Gailingen's Welkerhaus Cia, RO 1241-T, a Top Producer and a Top Ten Rottweiler. By Ch. Igor v Schauer, RO-235, a Top Producing Sire, from Ch. Anka Von Gailingen, RO 522, a Top Producing Dam. Owned by Catherine M. Thompson, Freehold, NJ. **Below:** V. Gailingen's Dassie Did It, first in the 9-12 Month Puppy Bitch Class, American Rottweiler club National Specialty Match. Sired by Ch. Srigo's Zarras v Kurtz. Owned by Cathy Thompson.

253

On a beautiful autumn day, Von Gailingen's Derring Do explores a bit. Eight weeks old, the pup is owned by Catherine M. Thompson.

Ten weeks old and gorgeous! Von Gailingen's Elfin Magic by Ch. Srigo's Zarras v Kurtz, RO 791 from Ch. Anka Von Gailingen, RO 522. Owned by B. White and C. Thompson.

Littermates of Anka in the Von Gailingen "A" litter included Champion Axel Von Gailingen, C.D., Ro-527, a dog; Alfie Von Gailingen, C.D., a dog; Ampa Von Gailingen, Ro-529, a bitch that had major points when she was struck by a car, and Afra Von Gailingen, Ro-567, a bitch that has produced champions.

Anka was dam of the Von Gailingen "B" litter, sired by the Ferdinand grandson Champion Hintz Von Michelburg, Ro-524, Top Producer in 1977 and 1978, by Champion Lyn Mar Acres Atlas V Kinta from Hylamar's Heidi. Included in it were Champion Blitz Von Gailingen, Ro-934-T, who made the Top Ten; Champion Brannsen Von Gailingen, Ro-955; Champion Bokar Von Gailingen, C.D. and Barr Von Gailingen, with points. These four are all dogs.

The "C" litter also was courtesy of Anka. She was bred to the Ferdinand son Champion Igor Von Schauer, also a Top Producer. This time she produced Champion Von Gailingen's Chancellor, Ro-1246, a dog; Champion Von Gailingen's Carry on, Ro-1260; Champion Von Gailingen's Welkerhaus Cia, Ro-1241-T, a Group placing bitch, a Top Ten winner, and a Top Producer with six champions as this is written; Von Gailingen's Commandant, Ro-1345, a dog with major points and Von Gailingen's Witzend Caper, Ro-1265, a bitch with major points.

The third and fourth litters from Anka are the Von Gailingens' "D" and "E" litters, both by Champion Srigo's Zarras V Kurtz, Ro-791, son of Champion Lyn Mar Acres Arras V Kinta. Heading the "D" list is Champion Von Gailingen's Dassie Did It, a bitch with two legs on her C.D. and certified in tracking; Von Gailingen's Dark Delight, C.D., a bitch that has points and is certified in tracking; Von Gailingen's Decidedly, C.D., a bitch with a leg in Open; Von Gailingen's Determined, who made quite a hit at the 1980 American Rottweiler Club Match. Dassie and Dark Delight have been first in the Brace Class at the Colonial Rottweiler Club Specialty in 1979 and 1980, and at the American Rottweiler Club Specialty in 1980.

The "E" litter is now just one year old. Based on the past performance of Anka's progeny, we feel certain that Catherine Thompson has more exciting winners among them.

An eight-week-old puppy belonging to Alan and Karen Kruse of Von der Kruse Rottweilers, Howell, MI, by Ch. Fritz von Der Haus Roy from Anja von Kruse. **Below:** Ch. Hannalore von Gruenerwald, by Troll vom Hook ex Ch. Eloise von Gruenerwald. This producer of two champions belongs to Dorothea Gruenerwald.

Am., Bda. Ch. Adler von Andan, CD, pictured in 1973 winning one of his many Best of Breed for Mrs. Benjamin Tilghman, handled by Joy Brewster, under Judge Arnold Woolfe. Adler became a Best in Show winner in Bermuda and was one of the Top Ten Dogs in the American Rottweiler Club ratings for 1975 and 1976. A member of the Medallion Rottweiler Club Hall of Fame, Andan also won Best Stud Dog and Best Veteran at the Colonial Rottweiler Club Specialty in 1977.

A twelve-week-old puppy by Ch. Srigo's Zarras V Kurtz ex Ch. Anka V Gailingen, belonging to Catherine Thompson, Freehold, NJ.

Opposite:
Above: Ch. Srigo's Madchen v Kurtz winning Best of Breed at the Colonial Rottweiler Specialty. Felicia Luburich proudly handled the magnificent bitch to this honor. **Below:** Ch. Srigo's Zarras v Kurtz, OFA Best of Breed at nine months from Bred-by-Exhibitor Class. From Champion Srigo's Madchen v Kurtz. Felicia Luburich breeder, owner, handler.

259

One of the great bitches of the Rottweiler world, Ch. Amsel Von Andan, CD, owned by Pauline Rakowski, Middletown, NJ. This is the dam of nine Champions, including Best in Show dog, Ch. Donnaj Vt. Yankee of Paulus, CDX.

Opposite:
Ch. Borgvaale Black Gardenia became a champion in fewer than 10 shows, handled by Sid Lamont for Martin Regan of Ridgefield Park, NJ. This typey bitch is registered in both the U.S. and Great Britain, and boasts some of the best international bloodlines in her pedigree. Her dam is English Ch. Borgvaale Bonita, sired by English Ch. Chesara Akillis, imported to Great Britain from Sweden. A great-grandfather on her dam's side also was a Nordic champion, and a great-grandmother was a champion imported from Holland.

261

Ch. Eloise von Gruenerwald, by Ch. Nick vom Silahopp from Ch. Lorelei, produced six champions for her owner, Dorothea Gruenerwald.

VON GRUENERWALD

The "von Gruenerwald" name in Rottweilers proves once again that a small kennel can have impact on a breed. Bill and Dorothea Gruenerwald's first Rottweiler, Abingdon Aphrodite, carried the prefix of the well known Miniature Schnauzer kennel founded by Mona Meiners in the Chicago area. Acquired in 1959, "Aphra" was a member of the family, living in a high-rise apartment during the winters and chasing cattle and treeing porcupines in the mountains of Colorado in the summer. She was not bred until over five years of age. Happily, the stud chosen by the Gruenerwalds was the German import BS Champion Harras vom Sofienbusch, SchH I. Harras had been a Bundessieger in 1961 and 1962.

On the sixty-ninth day, a one puppy litter was delivered by Caesarian section. Lorelei, the first American-bred daughter of Harras, was to become the Gruenerwald foundation bitch, typifying all of the hoped-for qualities in the breed: size, excellent topline, correct temperament, fluid movement and sound hips (OFA Ro-8).

Above: Note the lovely head and expression of Troll vom Hook owned by Dorothea Gruenerwald. **Below:** The very handsome dog, Ch. Nick vom Silahopp, snapped informally. Photo, courtesy of Dorothea Gruenerwald.

Ch. Northwinds Just Blew In, CD, at 15 months. Jessica Nichols, owner, Burnside, NC.

Opposite:
Above: A moment's pause along the way! Catherine Thompson in the cart, her homebred Rottweilers, Van Gailingen Dark Delight, CD, and Ch. Von Gailingen's Dassie Did It "taking five." **Below left:** Ch. Olga von Gruenerwald, by Ch. Donar v d Neckarstrom ex Ch. Jenni von Gruenerwald, pictured with friends. Alan and Karen Kruse, owners, Howell, MI. **Below right:** Ch. El Torro von Stolzenfels, owned by the Jack P. Ellmans, August, MI.

Ch. Jennie von Gruenerwald shown going Winners Bitch and Best of Opposite Sex under Judge Barbara Dillon at ten months of age at the Southern Colorado Kennel Club Dog Show. Owned by Dorothea Gruenerwald. **Below:** Ch. Goliath von Gruenerwald, owned by Robert and Marie Hayutin, handled by Sally Terroux, shown going Best of Breed at Southern Colorado Kennel Club, June 1974, under judge, Barbara Hoard Dillon.

A lovely headstudy of the German import, Ch. Gina vom Ingenhof, CD, the producer of two champions. Dorothea Gruenerwald, owner.

Champion Lorelei finished in five shows, going Best of Winners under judge Derek Rayne for five points over twenty-seven class dogs in the largest entry of Rottweilers to have assembled at any show in California up until that time. Then a month later, she went Best of Winners for another five points at Chicago International over seventeen class dogs under judge Phil Marsh. The third major quickly followed, in Colorado, under the late Marie Meyer. Lorelei was handled to these splendid wins by a family friend, Miss Ann Maurer.

In 1965 Champion Lorelei was bred to Champion Nick vom Silahopp, a German import belonging to the Gruenerwalds. "Nicky" was sired by Bundessieger (1963) Blitz vom Schloss Westerwinkel, SchH III; thus, the breeding was three quarters German bloodlines. Their first litter of eight produced four champions, three males that were almost look-alikes and one bitch. These were Champion Cache von Gruenerwald, Champion Conrad von Gruenerwald, Champion Colin von Gruenerwald and

Ch. Freeger's Ingela, CDX, RO 141, Top Producing Dam, *Kennel Review*, 1975, 1976. Ingela is a member of the Medallion Rottweiler Club's Hall of Fame. X-rayed at the age of 7½ years, she received an "excellent" rating from the OFA. Owned by Mrs. Margareta McIntyre, Gatstuberget's Rottweilers, Enumclaw, WA.

Opposite:
The lovely Ch. Der Catlin's Cologne v.d. Oder finishing her title under Ernest Loeb at the Atlanta Kennel Club Show, April, 1979. Cologne is co-owned by Keith and Pat Marston and her breeder, Susan Catlin.

BEST OF
OPPOSITE SEX

KENNESAW
KENNEL CLUB SHOW
OCT 27 1979
PHOTOS BY D ALVERSON

Champion Carla von Gruenerwald. Nick and Lorelei's progeny were noted for heavy bone and impressively large heads. Two repeat breedings in 1967 and in 1969 produced Champion Drusus von Gruenerwald and Champion Eloise von Gruenerwald. Bred to outside bitches, Champion Nick vom Silahopp sired an additional six champions.

Champion Cache von Gruenerwald was used at stud only once, but produced in this litter two outstanding males, Champion Rich von Rickthofen, C.D.X., and American and Canadian Champion Ivan von Gruenerwald.

The introduction in 1971 of the then five year old Troll vom Hook, a German import co-owned by the Gruenerwalds with Barbara Hoard Dillon, into the von Gruenerwald breeding program carried on the qualities of heavy bone and good heads. Champion Eloise von Gruenerwald, shown to her championship by Miss Ann Maurer, was twice bred to Troll. Their first litter produced Champion Fate's Chance von Gruenerwald. Their second litter, in 1972, produced two sisters, Champion Hannalore von Gruenerwald and Champion Happy von Gruenerwald. Eloise was then bred for the third and last time to Champion Dieter vom Konigsberg, C.D., a German import, and this proved to be her most outstanding litter. Out of five puppies, three became champions. They were Champion Juno von Gruenerwald, Champion Jenni von Gruenerwald and Champion Jiggs von Gruenerwald, C.D.X. One became an obedience titled dog, Jaeger von Gruenerwald, C.D.

Troll vom Hook was also bred to a grandaughter of Nick and Lorelei, Alexis von Kongslien. A litter of four males produced two champions: Champion Goliath von Gruenerwald and American and Canadian Champion Grimm von Gruenerwald. A third male was pointed. Bred to outside bitches, Troll sired an additional six champions and was named a 1974 Top Producer by *Kennel Review*. Despite the fact that, when acquired, Troll was past his prime for conformation competition, his contribution to the breed was evident in his breeding value.

In 1974, Champion Goliath von Gruenerwald was bred to a German import bitch leased to von Gruenerwald, Gina vom Ingenhof. The litter produced Champion Maxa Bear von Gruenerwald, C.D., and Champion Marlee Bear von Gruenerwald, the latter becoming in later years the dam of two Working Group winners. Gina later went on to win her championship and obedience titles when owned by Andrea Vrana.

Ch. Druseus von Gruenerwald, by C. Nick v Silahopp ex Ch. Lorelei, winning under Robert Waters. Owners, Jean Goshorn and Walter Roher.

Trenton Kennel Club, 1977, Colonial Rottweiler Club Specialty. From left are: Amsel von Andan, CD, handled by Walter Kuberski, winning Best Brood Bitch; her son, Am., Can. Ch. Donnaj Vt. Yankee of Paulus, CDX,

handled by owner, Jan Marshall and Amsel's daughter, Am., Bda. Ch. Andan Indy Pendence v Paulus, Yank's littermate, handled by Clayton P. Fell, Jr. Amsel and Indy are owned by Mrs. Benjamin C. Tilghman.

In 1976, Champion Hannalore von Gruenerwald was bred to Champion Starkrest's Polo-R. Their first litter of only two bitches produced Champion Noralei v Gruenerwald and Neela Namora von Gruenerwald, C.D. A repeat breeding produced Champion Pfeffer von Gruenerwald. Also in 1976, Champion Jenni von Gruenerwald was bred to a Dutch import, Champion Donar vom Neckarstroom. This litter arrived on July 4th 1976, the United States' Bi-Centennial, and produced Champion Olga von Gruener- wald. Unfortunately this was to be Jenni's only litter, as she was later spayed.

Von Gruenerwald's most recent champion as this book is writ- ten is Champion Ukiah von Gruenerwald, sired by Olaf von Gruenerwald from Running D's Heather, a grandaughter of Champion Cache von Gruenerwald.

Their latest litter, whelped November 11th 1979, was sired by Champion Centurion's Che Von Der Barr from Champion Noralei von Gruenerwald. Mrs. Gruenerwald says of these puppies, "This litter, at ten months of age, seems exceptionally promising. But then, each litter along the way *should* seem promising and should be an improvement of the breed and not merely monetary. By re- taining the best bitch from exceptional litters and breeding to the best stud available at the time 'von Gruenerwald' is proud to have produced four generations of champion dams."

All von Gruenerwald puppies are home raised, and none leave the "nest" until eight to ten weeks of age. Each pup is carefully evaluated at seven and a half weeks of age by Dorothea Gruener- wald and Ann Maurer, and a record is retained for future reference. Some line-breeding has been done, but no in-breeding.

Dorothea Gruenerwald has personally handled six of her own dogs to their championships. She gives generously of her time in many ways to furthering the best interests of her breed. She is a past president of the American Rottweiler Club (1975-1977) and currently is editor-publisher of their bi-monthly newsletter, ARK. She is a regular contributor to several dog magazines, including the *American Kennel Gazette - Pure Bred Dogs.* Over the years she has shown her dogs in many states, helping to teach the public to recognize the breed.

In 1972, the von Gruenerwald Kennel was represented at the In- ternational Friends of Rottweilers Conference in Holland and in 1975 at the conference in Finland. She notes that most European breeders have quite small kennels, numbering not even as many as 20 individual Rottweilers in most cases.

Olga von Blaine, age six weeks and weighing in at seven lbs. By Duchess von Gruenerwald from Heintz von Leezucht of C.J. Whelped October 21, 1970. Photo, courtesy of Dorothy Gruenerwald. **Below:** An eight-week-old von Gruenerwald puppy contemplates the future. Photo, courtesy of Dorothy Gruenerwald.

Ch. Muffins Special Spaatz, owned by Dr. Otto and Emilie Jungschaffer and Jean Goshorn who is handling, pictured completing the title at Beverly Hills Kennel Club, June 25, 1972, under Judge Larry Downey.

Opposite:
Radio Ranch Gypsy v Notara with owner-handler
Vina Bechard and co-owner breeder Pamela Weller,
takes Best in Sweepstakes under Judge E. Lauria at
a Colonial Rottweiler Club Specialty.

FIRST

ASHBEY PHOTO

277

An excellent example of correct type and quality in a Rottweiler bitch. This is Ch. Liberty Bell Von Paulus belonging to Pauline Rakowski who is owner-handling.

VON PAULUS

A kennel that has had some very special impact on the Rottweiler world is that known as Von Paulus, which belongs to Mrs. Pauline L. Rakowski and is in Middletown, New Jersey.

Mrs. Rakowski has the distinction of owning a famous bitch, Champion Amsel Von Andan, C.D., which she purchased as a six-week-old puppy from her breeder, Anna Tilghman. In three litters Amsel produced nine bench Champions, the most famous of which are Champion Donnaj Vt. Yankee of Paulus, C.D.X., and Champion Andan Indy Pendence Von Paulus, which over the past three years as this book is written (during 1980) have been a Top Winning Dog and a Top Winning Bitch among the leading show Rottweilers in the United States. Yankee, as noted elsewhere in this book, is a Best in Show winner and a three time Best of Breed Winner at the Colonial Rottweiler Club Specialty Show.

In addition to these, Amsel's noted progeny also include Champion Frick Von Paulus, C.D., Champion Liberty Bell Von Paulus, Champion Trajan Imp Von Paulus, C.D., Champion Shana Tova Von Paulus, C.D., Champion Arrow Ranch Bridget Von Paulus, Champion Baron Thor of Braeburn, Champion Andan Vesta Von Paulus and additionally, the highly successful Oskar Von Paulus, U.D.

Lornalei von Gruenerwald, an eight-month-old bitch, practicing for the show ring. Dorothea Gruenerwald, owner, Colorado Springs, CO.
Below: Ch. Juno von Gruenerwald shown going Winners Bitch for a 5 point major under judge Howard Tyler. Dorothea Gruenerwald, owner, Colorado Springs, CO.

BEST OF OPPOSITE SEX

Above: And a Doberman Pinscher friend, too, with whom to share the latest gossip. Mary Jo Duguay's Rottweiler, Jo Mar's Preiss of Von Rimar. **Below:** When introductions are properly handled, there is no reason why a Rottweiler cannot adapt to other breeds within the family! Jo Mar's Preiss of Von Rimar, illustrates this fact as she plays with two of the Jo Mar Beagles also owned by Mrs. Duguay.

Opposite:
Ch. Lyn-Mar Acres Chesarras v Amri, by Ch. Lyn-Mar Acres Arras v Kinta ex Plaisance Irma (imported from England). Owned by Margaret S. Walton, handled here by Alan Levine, winning Best of Breed at the Union County Kennel Club in 1978 under the late Mrs. Winifred Heckmann, judge.

BEST OF BREED
UNION COUNTY
KENNEL CLUB, INC.
KLEIN   MAY 26, 1978

281

VON STOLZENFELS

Jack P. Ellman and Dr. Evelyn M. Ellman are owners of von Stolzenfels, a Rottweiler kennel in Augusta, Michigan, which was established on the finest German bloodlines. Evelyn Ellman says, "I have been associated with Rottweilers since a very tender age. When I was a baby our Astor, harnessed to a cart would take me to the city park and pull the cart round and 'round the pond, which was home to the swans, much to my delight. When the church bells chimed vespers he would know it was time to return me home for lunch. I sincerely believe that Astor and I were better known to the people of Schwabach, my home town, than the local mayor. Unfortunately, the extreme food shortage during World War II (my father was an insurance executive, not a farmer) forced us to place our Rottweilers with those who could afford to feed them. I renewed my interest and enthusiasm for the breed following my marriage when I had moved to a home which I felt had something to offer to a breed which loves nature and is in need of daily long walks. We live on an old farm with 270 fenced acres of woodland, ponds and stream, and nobody appreciates this more than our Rottweilers."

It was bound to happen, following her closeness with the breed as a child in Germany, that Dr. Ellman would grow up to become an important owner of these noble dogs! Her first Rottweiler in the U.S.A. was Nello von Silahop, C.D., that was fully trained in Schutzhund work at a time when the meaning of the word was hardly known here. He was a son of the German Bundessieger Blitz vom Schloss Westerwinkel SchH I and Queen von der Solitude, and traced his ancestry back to one of the all time "greats," Bundessieger Igor von Kohlwald. Sadly, the Ellmans lost this dog to an unfortunate accident when a drunken man trespassing on their property saw the dog, mistook him for a deer and shot him. This dog always will continue to live in the hearts and memory of his owners, for they considered him to be the most exceptionally courageous, intelligent, loyal and protective dog they have ever known. Each Christmas Eve they light a candle on his grave.

The next additions to von Stolzenfels from Germany were two bitches, daughters of Bundessieger 1968 and '69 Igor vom Hause Henseler SchH II and Donka vom Schultenhof SchH II. To the Ellmans' disappointment, they tell us, these both turned out to

Dr. Evelyn M. Ellman and Nancy Morrison co-own this winner, Ch. Erda von Stolzenfels. **Below:** Cooling off! Two six-month-old Rottweilers enjoying wading. From Jack and Evelyn Ellman's von Stolzenfels kennel.

Ch. Rodsden's Ander, CD, RO 2131, at 27 months. Ander finished with four majors, beginning with Best of Winners at 15 months at the Medallion Rottweiler Club 1979 Specialty judged by Breed Warden Ebers. Sired by Am., Can. Ch. Trollegen's Frodo, CD, RO 1021 ex Ch. Rodsden's Red Pepper v h Walor, RO 877; bred by James DeFrancisco and R.F. Klem, he belongs to Anthony and Harriet Stockanes, Urbana, IL.

Opposite:
Ch. Muffins Rough Rommel winning Best of Breed over 11 specials at the San Francisco Cow Palace, Golden Gate Kennel Club show, judged by the British authority, Stanley Dangerfield. "Rough" belongs to his breeder, Jo Gorman, Studio City, CA.

The great Ch. Cosi vom Steigstrassle resting on her laurels after a busy day. Cosi belongs to the Jack Ellmans of Augusta, MI.

have hip dysplasia, so they became just pets rather than part of their owners' breeding program. One of them, Christel, recently died at a ripe old age. The other, Freya, is twelve years old.

To avoid any possibility of further hip dysplasia problems, the Ellmans decided that next time they would purchase a mature, fully developed bitch rather than a youngster. Thus it was that Cosi vom Steigstrassle, rated Sg. 1, came to them, and it was she who founded the von Stolzenfels strain. Still going strong, she points with pride to her winning progeny! Among these are Champion Czarina von Stolzenfels, C.D., an outstanding bitch that was Best of Opposite Sex in 1978 at the Medallion Rottweiler Club Specialty under judge Robert Moore; she repeated her win in 1979 at the largest Rottweiler Specialty, the Medallion Rottweiler Club Jubilee Show, where the judge was the German Breed Warden Heinz Eberz. Cosi also produced Champion Imor von Stolzenfels, who recently completed his title in just seven weeks under five different judges, twice taking Best of Breed from the classes. As this book is written, Imor is starting out as a "special." The Ellmans have high hopes for his career, as he has been highly praised by judges and other Rottweiler authorities.

Champion Erda von Stolzenfels is a Cosi daughter. She quickly became a champion and in her first litter produced the exciting puppy Ferro von Stolzenfels.

Centa von Stolzenfels, also from Cosi, achieved her American and Canadian tracking degrees at just over two years old.

Champion Gandalf von Stolzenfels is from Cosi and sired by Champion Centurian's Che v.d. Barr. He has done well on the way to his title, winning at prestigious shows under noted judges.

Then there is Champion El Torro von Stolzenfels, by Champion Rodsden's Ikon v.d. Harque C.D. He is now working on his C.D. and has made his presence felt in Variety Group competition in the conformation classes, too.

With her progeny having thus distinguished themselves to date and a number of younger ones on the way to what will it is hoped be equally auspicious careers, Cosi is almost certain to go down in history as one of the breed's outstanding producers. Irina von Stolzenfels, Ebony von Stolzenfels-Alpental and Etzel von Stolzenfels are three more of her younsters now in the ring, working on their titles.

Champion Czarina von Stolzenfels is carrying on in her dam's pawprints as a fine producer and, like Cosi, has some top progeny in the rings, including Champion Heiko von Ammerberg, C.D., and Luna von Stolzenfels C.D. It is interesting to note that, as a show bitch, Czarina was Number 7 for 1978 in the American Rottweiler Club Rating System, and again in 1979. Her sire is Champion Kavon Mr. Murphy, Am., Can. C.D., and *Dog World* Award Winner for Obedience.

The Ellmans have another splendid imported bitch that has contributed well to their kennel. She is Gunda von Ingenhof, C.D. and she is the dam of Champion Bandetta von Stolzenfels, C.D.X., Bruiser von Stolzenfels, T.D., Champion Darra Michaela von Stolzenfels and Champion Dolf Fuller von Stolzenfels. Bandetta finished her C.D. at ten months her championship at 22 months, and her C.D.X. at just over two years. She is by Adrian von Daemmerwald, Youthbest Germany 73, SchH I owned by Rottweiler Judge I. Lyons. Champion Bruiser is a full brother to Bandetta.

Champion Dolf Fuller and Champion Darra Michaela are brother and sister by Champion Kavon Mr. Murphy, mentioned above. Dolf became a champion at 18 months, his sister Darra at

Above: Kava and Maxwell like to back pack with the Willmarths, as can be gathered from these photos. **Below:** Rottweilers make great companions! Kava von Stolzenfels at ten months, stops for a rest during a hiking trip with her master. The Willmarths and Kava live in Kalamazoo, MI.

Opposite:
Type and quality make this headstudy an outstanding one. The subject, Ch. Graudstark's Luger. The owners, Mark and Pat Schwartz. The photographer, Alton Anderson.

Well depicting the beauty and intelligence of this breed, Ch. Bandetta von Stolzenfels, CDX, has brought many good wins both in conformation and in obedience competition to owners, Gerald and Kay Watson, Louisiana.

Opposite:
Above left: Ed and Bonnie Kuhlman own this adorable Rottweiler puppy, photographed at four weeks of age. Ebony von Stolzenfels-Alpental was bred by Dr. Evelyn Ellman. **Above right:** Jack and Evelyn Ellman's first imported Rottweiler, their beloved Nello vom Sillahop CD, at five months of age. A son of the Bundesseiger 1963 Blitz vom Schloss Westerwinkel ex Queen v.d. Solitude. **Below:** This pretty baby grew up to become Centa von Stolzenfels, CD, pictured at nine weeks old. From the kennels of Jack and Dr. Evelyn Ellman.

Tom and Marion Sallen of Tarpon Springs, FL, co-own this famed Rottweiler bitch, Ch. Radio Ranch's Christmas Spirit. Here, Mr. Sallen handles her to one of her numerous Best of Breed victories, this time at Roanoke Kennel Club 1980, under Judge J. Council Parker. Christmas Spirit made history at the Thronateeska Kennel Club Dog Show, October 1980, by becoming the first owner-handled Rottweiler bitch to win a Working Group in the United States.

Opposite:
Ch. Erdelied Astraea, CD, at eight weeks old. "Star" is owned by Ms. C.L. Rawlings, Coral Gables, FL. Photo by M.P. Gross.

A four-month-old Kalua von Stolzenfels is looking very pensive here. Owners are David and Gloria Eaton.

Opposite:
Above: One of the cutest puppy pictures we've seen! These five-week-old baby Rottweilers belong to noted European judge, Gerd Hyden, who officiated in the U.S. at an important Specialty, and left this picture with Dr. Evelyn Ellman as a souvenir. Note the pup on the far left. **Below left:** A handsome front view of Ch. El Torro von Stolzenfels. Owners are Noah and Bonnie Creech. **Below right:** Ch. El Torro von Stolzenfels, a splendid example of the fine Rottweilers raised at Dr. Evelyn Ellman's kennel, is owned by Noah and Bonnie Creech from Indiana.

Ch. Panamint Anytime Anywhere, CD, TD, owned by Barbara Dillon.

Opposite:
Harry Z. Isaacs has sent us this photograph of the
beautiful and well known dog, Erno vom Ingenhof, a
splendid example of the desired type and quality.

A boy and his dog! David Dorner had been wishing long and hard for a Rottweiler when his Dad presented him with Jason Bear von Stolzenfels, a puppy purchased from Jack and Dr. Evelyn Ellman. Not even six months old, Bubba and Dave worked the dog's way through kindergarten obedience training to conformation competition, with Bubba coming home several times a first place winner.

15 months, both with four majors. Darra has also been busy in the whelping box. Her progeny by Champion Centurians Che v.d. Barr include Kundri von Stolzenfels, C.D., Kondor von Stolzenfels and Kugar von Stolzenfels, all with championship points. She is, as well, the dam of Kava von Stolzenfels who gained her C.D. at just over a year old.

The Ellmans are strictly hobby breeders who strive for quality rather than quantity, quality that will be inherited through future generations, as evidenced by correct conformation, working ability, good hips and true Rottweiler temperament. They are proud that during 1979 all but two of their Rottweilers entered at specialty shows were in the ribbons, and feel that this record corroborates the fact that they are working hard to achieve their goals.

WITZEND

Judith Ann Coen, owner of the Witzend Rottweilers, is a professional handler, and therefore her own dogs must often remain in the background as she campaigns those belonging to clients. Nonetheless she has spent considerable time working with her Rottweilers, especially in obedience, where her dogs have made some fine records.

Judy's first Rottweiler was Am., Can. Champion Negus vom Hohenreissach, II, C.D.X., U.D. "Seigo" was a great friend and the first dog Judy trained and he did her proud, becoming the High Scoring Rottweiler, Schuman System, in Obedience for 1970 and 1971 both for the United States and Canada. He was also, to Judy's knowledge, the second Rott to win Highest Scoring Dog in Trial, All Breeds, which he did at Barrie in 1971. Judy believes that the first of the breed to accomplish this was back in the early 1960s.

Judy has very successfully campaigned, through most of his show career, Am., Can. Champion Bingo vom Hohenreissach for Darlene Adam of Winston-Salem, North Carolina. Bingo finished with five majors at 13 months old, won three Colonial Rottweiler Club Area Supported Shows and has two Group first along with other Group placements to his credit. Currently Judy has high hopes for her Witzend "I" litter, which is sired by Bingo out of Von Gailingen's Witzend Caper. One puppy in particular, Witzend Inside Information, is especially promising.

Am., Can. Champion Greta vom Hohenreissen, C.D., purchased as a puppy while Judy lived in Ohio, is now co-owned with Kristin M. Rugg. Judy actively trained and exhibited her prior to moving East (she now is in Baltimore, Maryland), but started to pursue her handling career when she reached Maryland, and so Greta remained at home. She did come out on National Capital weekend in 1975 to finish, "going Best of Opposite Sex over the top bitch out at that time." Having a light load going to Greater Philadelphia in 1977, Judy decided to take Greta along to try for her C.D. Despite a complete absence of work during the previous four years, she earned two legs on her Obedience Title that weekend. Soon after that she went to live with Kris Rudd, who had never been in the obedience ring before. At Philadelphia in 1978, Greta managed to take her very nervous handler through the class, and at seven years old completed her Companion Dog title!

An historic occasion in Rottweiler show history: Ch. Radio Ranch's Christmas Spirit becomes the first Rottweiler bitch to win Working Group owner-handled, and the second of her sex to have gained the Group blue ribbon in the United States. Thomas Sallen accepts the award for himself and co-owner, Becky Jones, at the Thronateeska Kennel Club Show on Oct. 18, 1980 from Judge J. D. Jones.

Opposite:
Ch. Donnaj Green Mountain Boy, by Ch. Donnaj Vt. Yankee of Paulus, CD, ex Ch. Northwinds Helga, bred by Jan Marshall. This fine young Rottweiler, whelped Dec. 18, 1977, started his campaign in the breed ring during 1980, and has become a powerful force among the country's leading Rottweilers. His owner, Anthony P. Attalla, has been active in the dog fancy for about 10 years, but this is his first Rottweiler and certainly Green Mountain Boy is getting him off to a splendid start in the breed. Ross Petruzzo, handler.

Ch. Srigo's Billet Doux, another winner from Srigo Kennels. **Below:** Am., Can. Ch. Rodsden's Ander V H Brabant, handled here by Tom Glassford for owner, Sherri Page, goes Best of Breed under Langdon Skarda en route to Working Group fourth at the Springfield Kennel Club 1977.

Above: Looking forward to a bright future at ten weeks old, this outstanding puppy grew up to become a Working Group winner for his owners, Wanda and Jim White. He is now Ch. Windmakers Arlo der Gremlin. **Below:** This handsome bitch, Ch. Fona v Konigsberg, belongs to the Woodland Kennels of Mrs. Karen Wakefield. Finished in 11 shows, her wins include two four-point majors and one five-point.

Wellesley, MA, the Ladies Dog Club Show, 1973. Mrs. Nicholas Demidoff judging. From left are: Am., Can. Ch. Rodsden's Kato von Donnaj, CDX, TD, first Rottweiler in the United States to go Best in Show, with owner, Jan Marshall; Amsel von Andan, CD, later a champion, with Walter Kuberski and on the right, Adler von Andan, CD, that became an

American and Bermudian champion with Carol Selze. Adler was the first and to date only Rottweiler to take an all breed Best in Show in Bermuda at the November event, which he did in 1975. Mrs. Benjamin C. Tilghman, Centreville, MD, breeder-owner of Amsel and Adler.

Am., Can. Ch. Negus V Hohenreissach II, Am., Can. UD. By Ch. Fago V Hohenreissach ex Catja v Friedrichsberg. Owned by Judith A. Coen. **Below:** Centa von Stolzenfels, with a friend, enjoying a blizzard at their Michigan home. Owned by the Jack Ellmans.

Ch. Sciroco's Ruffian belongs to Karen Wakefield and represents outstanding bloodlines. By Ch. Centurian's Che Von Der Bar, Top Winning Rottweiler for 1976, 77, and 78, from Srigo's Billet Doux.

WOODLAND ROTTWEILERS

Mrs. Karen Wakefield owns this small but select kennel, situated at Belfast, Tennessee. Here the first, and foundation, bitch is the handsome and well bred Champion Sciroco's Ruffian. Born in August 1977, Ruffian was sired by the Top Winning Rottweiler in the U.S.A. for 1976, '77 and '78, Champion Centurian's Che Von Der Barr, a son of Champion Northwind's Barras ex Champion Rodsden's Ericka Deidre Dahl, while her dam is Champion Srigo's Billet Doux, representing the finest of the Srigo strain.

Believing, very correctly, in the importance of outstanding bitches, Mrs. Wakefield concentrates on them in her kennel. Champion Fona v Konigsberg, a Champion Northwinds Barras granddaughter, is another one belonging to her. As this book is written, she recently has acquired another, a young bitch from Swedish bloodlines, not yet named as the registration is being processed. This one is a granddaughter of the World Champion Working Dog over a four-year period, so Mrs. Wakefield is pleased at the prospect of her arrival.

There is, however, along with these bitches a splendid 16-month-old dog, Armin vom Mayerhof, representing noted German bloodlines that soon will start out in the show ring here. We wish him success!

A striking young Rottweiler who completed his title at only 13 months of age is Ch. Radio Ranch's Weekend Warrior owned by Pam and Dale Kok and handled by Richard Yates.

Opposite:
Above: Ch. Rodsden's Kato v Donnaj, CDX, TD, pulling the milk cart, one of the jobs for which his ancestors were noted. Kato is America's first Best in Show winning Rottweiler and was one of a litter of five champions bred by Laura Cooney. Owner, Mrs. Donald S. Marshall, Woodstock, VT. **Below:** Jodie Lee Pearl, talented artist, has done this handsome drawing of a Rottweiler that is to be seen on a wide variety of leather goods ranging from key rings, purses, check book covers and in many other unique and useful forms. Jodie's work is displayed at major eastern dog shows in the New Jersey and New York areas.

## CHAPTER 12

Breed Standard of Perfection

APPROVED IN 1979 BY THE AMERICAN KENNEL CLUB

A Standard of Perfection is the guide by which we evaluate and judge members of a specific breed of dog. Based on the accepted Standard from the country of the breed's origin, these Standards are drawn up by a parent club for each breed, usually by a committee of experienced authorities selected for their knowledge and willing to undertake the task. Their work next is discussed, reviewed and eventually approved by the Board of Directors and general membership of the specialty club, then submitted to the American Kennel Club for final review, examination and eventual acceptance as the Standard for that breed. As the years pass, sometimes it is found desirable to review and revise or clarify a Standard in order for it to better serve its purpose. That is what has happened to the original Rottweiler Standard which has been in use here since 1935. Although it was a good one as far as it went, it seemed to be in need of expansion to make it more in line with the original Rottweiler Standards from Europe, those of the German Rottweiler Club (ADRK) and the Federation Cynologique Internationale (FCI). The following is the 1979 revision of the original American Kennel Club approved Rottweiler Standard. We feel that the revision has been a job well done.

General Appearance: The ideal Rottweiler is a large, robust and powerful dog, black with clearly defined rust markings. His compact build denotes great strength, agility and endurance. Males are characteristically larger, heavier boned and more masculine in appearance.

Ch. Challange Von Dansor owned by Olivia and Richard Dangler of Howell, NJ was finished at only 11 months old and claimed numerous breed wins and Group placements as a very young dog. Sidney Lamont is handling. Mr. Dangler, a police officer with the Long Branch, NJ, K-9 Unit, has trained "Charley" to police work, and the dog accompanies his master on rounds when not off on the show circuit.

Opposite:
The handsome Rottweiler, Kezia Heidenmauer from the first Panamint litter in 1952. Photo, courtesy Barbara Dillon.

Ch. Von Gailingen's Dassie Did It, by Ch. Srigo's Zarras V Kurtz, RO 791 from Ch. Anka Von Gailingen RO 522, taking Best of Winners from the Bred-by Exhibitor Class, Trenton Kennel Club, 1980, at the Colonial Rottweiler Club Specialty Show.

Opposite:
Am., Bda. Ch. Andan Indy Pendence v Paulus, OFA, RO 1002-T, finished her championship in September 1976 at 14 months of age. By Ch. Axel von Schwanenschlag from Ch. Amsel von Andan, CD. Indy was 44 times Best of Breed, 38 times Best of Opposite Sex, including Westminster 1978 and Colonial Rottweiler Club Specialty, 1979. Owned by Mrs. Benjamin C. Tilghman. She is pictured here taking Best of Breed at Rock Creed, 1976, over specials under Heywood Hartley.

BEST OF
BREED

GILBERT PHOTO

313

Ch. Srigo's Garret v Zaghin winning Best of Breed at Westchester during the early 1970s. Mrs. Bernard Freeman, judge. Felicia Luburich, breeder, owner.

Size: Males, 24″ to 27″. Females, 22″ to 25″. Proportion should always be considered rather than height alone. The length of the body, from the breast bone (Sternum) to the rear edge of the pelvis (Ischium) is slighly longer than the height of the dog at the withers; the most desirable proportion being as 10 to 9. Depth of chest should be fifty per cent of the height.

Serious Faults: Lack of proportion, undersize, oversize.

Head: Of medium length, broad between the ears; forehead line seen in profile is moderately arched. Cheekbones and stop well developed; length of muzzle should not exceed distance between stop and occiput. Skull is preferred dry; however, some wrinkling may occur when dog is alert.

Muzzle: Bridge is straight, broad at base with slight tapering towards tip. Nose is broad rather than round, with black nostrils.

Lips: Always black; corners tightly closed. Inner mouth pigment is dark. A pink mouth is to be penalized.

Teeth: 42 in number (20 upper and 22 lower); strong, correctly placed, meeting in a scissors bite, lower incisors touching inside of upper incisors.

Serious Faults: Any missing tooth, level bite.

Disqualifications: Undershot, overshot, four or more missing teeth.

Eyes: Of medium size, moderately deep set, almond shaped with well fitting lids. Iris of uniform color, from medium to dark brown, the darker shade always preferred.

Serious Faults: Yellow (bird of prey) eyes; eyes not of same color; eyes unequal in size or shape. Hairless lid.

Ears: Pendant, proportionately small, triangular in shape; set well apart and placed on skull so as to make it appear broader when the dog is alert. Ear terminates at approximate mid-cheek level. Correctly held, the inner edge will lie tightly against cheek.

Neck: Powerful, well muscled, moderately long with slight arch and without loose skin.

Body: Topline is firm and level, extending in straight line from withers to croup.

Brisket: Deep, reaching to elbow.

Chest: Roomy, broad with well pronounced forechest.

Ribs: Well sprung.

Loin: Short, deep and well muscled.

Croup: Broad, medium length, slightly sloping.

Tail: Normally carried in horizontal position, giving an impression of an elongation of top line. Carried slightly above horizontal when dog is excited. Some dogs are born without a tail, or a very short stub. Tail is normally docked short close to the body. The set of the tail is more important than length.

Forequarters: Shoulder blade long, well laid back at 45 degree angle. Elbows tight, well under body. Distance from withers to elbow and elbow to ground is equal.

Legs: Strongly developed with straight heavy bone. Not set closely together.

Pasterns: Strong, springy and almost perpendicular to ground.

Feet: Round, compact, well arched toes, turning neither in nor out. Pads thick and hard; nails short, strong and black. Dewclaws may be removed.

Eight weeks old, and surely facing a bright future, pictured here is Van Gailingen's Eureka, by Ch. Srigo's Zarras v Kurtz, RO 791 ex Ch. Anka Von Gailingen, RO 522. Owned by Catherine Thompson, Freehold, NJ.

Opposite:
Above left: A proud father's Christmas girl! Ch. Mc-Coy von Meadow (the father) is owned by Donna Wormser, Ocala, FL. **Above right:** An informal shot of a very correct and lovely head. Am., Can. Ch. Rodsden's Ander V H Brabant at 7½ years of age. Sherri Page, Tobant Kennels, owner. **Below:** A very handsome quartet! From left are: Ander, Major, Robin and Libby, from the Tobant Kennels of Sherri Page.

Ch. Panamint Pakt v Rheintal winning Best of Breed at the Del Sur Kennel Club May 16, 1976. Judge, Robert Wilson. Barbara Dillon, owner.

Hindquarters: Angulation of hindquarters balances that of forequarters.

Upper Thigh: Fairly long, broad and well muscled.

Stifle Joint: Moderately angulated.

Lower Thigh: Long, powerful, extensively muscled leading into a strong hock joint; metatarsus nearly perpendicular to ground. Viewed from rear, hind legs are straight and wide enough apart to fit in with a properly built body.

Feet: Somewhat longer than front feet, well arched toes turning neither in nor out. Dewclaws must be removed if present.

Coat: Outer coat is straight, coarse, dense, medium length, lying flat. Undercoat must be present on neck and thighs, but should not show through the outer coat. The Rottweiler should be exhibited in a natural condition without trimming, except to remove whiskers if desired.

Fault: Wavy coat.

Disqualification: Long coat.

Color: Always black with rust to mahogany markings. The borderline between black and rust should be clearly defined. The markings should be located as follows: a spot over each eye; on cheeks, as a strip around each side of the muzzle, but not on the bridge of nose; on throat; triangular mark on either side of breastbone; on forelegs from carpus downward to toes; on inside of rear legs showing down the front of stifle and broadening out in front of rear legs from hock to toes, but not completely eliminating black from back of legs; under tail. Black penciling markings on toes. The undercoat is gray or black.

Quantity and location of rust markings is important and should not exceed ten percent of body color. Insufficient or excessive markings should be penalized.

Serious Faults: Excessive markings; white markings any place on dog (a few white hairs do not constitute a marking); light colored markings.

Disqualifications: Any base color other than black; total absence of markings.

Gait: The Rottweiler is a trotter. The motion is harmonious, sure, powerful and unhindered, with a strong fore-reach and a powerful rear drive. Front and rear legs are thrown neither in nor out, as the imprint of hindfeet should touch that of forefeet. In a trot, the forequarters and hindquarters are mutually co-ordinated while the back remains firm; as speed is increased legs will converge under body towards a center line.

Character: The Rottweiler should possess a fearless expression with a self-assured aloofness that does not lend itself to immediate and indiscriminate friendships. He has an inherent desire to protect home and family, and is an intelligent dog of extreme hardness and adaptability with a strong willingness to work.

A judge shall dismiss from the ring any shy or vicious Rottweiler.

Shyness: A dog shall be judged fundamentally shy if, refusing to stand for examination it shrinks away from the judge; if it fears an approach from the rear; if it shies at sudden or unusual noises to a marked degree.

Ch. Panamint Saphir v Rheintal, CD, owned by Barbara Dillon.

Opposite:
Ch. Bergluft's Fee, by Ch. Radio Ranch Axel v
Notara ex Ch. Bergluft's Carla, bred, owned and
handled by Mrs. Dorit S. Rogers.

BEST OF OPP. SEX

MAHONING SHENANGO
KENNEL CLUB

KLEIN   AUG 5 1978

321

Ch. Lyn Mar Acres Ruffian v Amri, by Ch. Lyn-Mar Acres Arras v Kinta ex Plaisance Irma (English import), a truly quality Rottie. Winning Best of Breed Amri is here handled by Alan Levine. Owned by Mrs. Margaret S. Walton, Mt. Holly, NJ.

Viciousness: A dog that attacks or attempts to attack either the judge or the handler is definitely vicious. An aggressive or belligerent attitude towards other dogs shall not be deemed viciousness.

Faults: The foregoing is a description of the ideal Rottweiler. Any structural fault that detracts from the above-described working dog must be penalized to the extent of the deviation.

Disqualifications: Undershot, overshot, four or more missing teeth. Long coat. Any base color other than black. Total absence of markings.

EXPLANATION OF THE ROTTWEILER STANDARD

By Barbara Hoard Dillon

Any Standard is essentially a measuring stick which allows a judge to determine that one thing is greater or smaller than another. The breed Standard does not define a single ideal dog, but has to do rather with the ideal of the breed.

The Standard for the one-dog owner is only secondarily a breed Standard. His standard is an individual one, determined by his personal prejudices and special needs.

The genuine dog breeder is primarily interested in the breed and only secondarily in a single dog. The breeder wants to produce not one champion but an entire bloodline of champions. The breed Standard helps him to do this by setting the limits within which the ideal of the breed is to be produced.

Therefore, the breed Standard must be precise enough to say what shall not be considered ideal and it must be vague enough not to disqualify because of merely individual differences. Thus, the Standard to meet the demand for precision must list everything considered a fault, particularly disqualifying ones. It should be a stimulant and a guide to serious breeders and to conscientious judges.

General Appearance: This section gives one the first impressions of the breed as a whole, the "thing" that sets a Rottweiler apart from all others. It was redundant to add that females would be less masculine in appearance. That statement should be obvious.

Size: The height limitations were clearly defined and the fractions in the previous Standard were rounded off to the closest round number in accordance with the present German Standard. The most serious failure here would be the lack of proportion, no matter what the height. Less size is also more serious a problem than more height.

Head: The description in the Standard seems to be fairly clear as to the ideal type of head and proportions. The real problem came with the number of teeth! This one factor seemed to cause so much consternation among the membership of the American Rottweiler Club that it appeared for a time that the revision committee, which drew up the present Standard that became effec-

Ch. Imor von Stolzenfels finished with four majors, is pictured here winning under Kurt Mueller, handled by Jay Richardson for owners Jack and Dr. Evelyn Ellman. He is another of the title holders from Ch. Centurion's Che von der Barr and Ch. Cosi vom Steigstrassle.

Opposite:
Mali von Stolzenfels contemplating the future. Owned by the Jack Ellmans, in this photo Mali is 11 weeks old.

tive during 1979, would not be able to resolve it. It is preferred that the ideal Rottweiler have forty-two *correctly placed* teeth. The American Kennel Club set the policy for any disqualifications here by stating that it "could be for four or more missing teeth ONLY." It is not uncommon in certain lines to find the dogs having a set of double teeth. This could account for forty-three or forty-four teeth in total. But it could also account for forty-two teeth if the dog were also missing two normal teeth.

It was difficult for the revision committee to make the policy clear to the membership for some reason. The situation was complicated in a way by the fact that a number of local clubs had installed a code of ethics permitting the breeding of up to two missing teeth. Was it right to breed a possible genetic fault cumulative as it is, but wrong to show it?

The eye color yellow, as seen in most "birds of prey," is considered a serious fault and was carried into the American Standard from the present German Standard. It involves the quality of expression, which is definitely influenced by the level of eye color. Occasionally Rottweilers have been found to have eye of unequal shape or size, and sometimes one eye is not the same color as the other.

The ears must never be "rose" shaped (i.e. one in which the front or upper edge turns outward and back, exposing the burr). The Standard clearly defines the correct shape, size and position.

Neck: Obviously less than what is stated in the Standard is incorrect.

Body: From the withers to the croup the topline must be FIRM and LEVEL. A "roach," "dip" or soft topline is undesirable. A dog having any of these conditions should be penalized in accordance with the degree of the fault.

The "brisket" (chest in front of and between the forelegs) is deep and should reach clear to the elbow. The chest must include a well pronounced forechest that extends past the juncture of the upper arm and the shoulder blade. The ribs are well sprung (deep and slightly rounded) not flat (slab-sided) or barrel shaped.

The loin is short and deep with good muscle. It should *not* be tucked up in a fully mature dog, although one might find a *slight* tuck-up in an extremely young dog. Remember that the Standard is written to describe the ideal dog of full maturity. The croup (line from pelvis to set-on of tail) is slightly sloping. In a normal dog the pelvis setting should be of an angle approaching thirty degrees for optimum efficiency of motion. The "steep" croup causes the dog to trot with his rear end high and with a bobbing up and down action to his back. It also restricts the forward motion into a more upward motion and restricts the backward stroke of the hind limb, losing the follow-through necessary for a strong gait. Stronger forward thrust is achieved by setting the croup flat. However, this improvement in thrust is counteracted by a restricted forward reach which reduces the lifting power of the hindquarter. Consequently, though the drive may be strong, an excessive lifting load is placed on the forequarter and the dog soon tires up front. Hence, regardless of the stronger drive achieved, a flat croup is a fault because endurance thus is inhibited.

In the steep croup, the rear foot is well forward beneath the body and gives greater lifting capability to the rear quarter, beneficial to the dog with a poor forequarter. However, this results in the action of the back feet interfering with the motion of the front feet. Off lead the dog combats this by "crabbing" or "pacing." On lead he is forced to take high, short steps with the rear legs, resulting in a cyclic pumping action which wastes muscular energy and is not good movement. The ideal pelvis set means the dog is able to reach forward from behind sufficiently well to balance, not interfere with, the action of the forequarters.

Tail: The actual set of the tail is more important than the length at which it has been docked because the set-on determines the outline of the croup. The Rottweiler has been whelped without a tail or with a very short stub. Usually there is some deformity of the vertebrae when this happens. The ideal docked length would show about one or two vertebrae externally.

Forequarters: These are defined to consist of (1) the shoulder blade (scapula), (2) the upper arm (humerus), (3) forearm (radius and ulna), (4) pisiform and the seven bones of the pastern joint, (5) pastern (five metacarpals), and (6) toes (phalanges). This whole assembly is attached to the body solely by muscles and tendons. There is no skeletal connection as there is with the hindquarters. Before much meaning can be attached to the written description, however, it is essential that the function of the forequarters during motion be understood.

One function of the foreassembly is to absorb concussion. The second function is that of weight support. During one phase of mo-

Am., Bda. Ch. Andan Indy Pendence v Paulus, Best of Opposite Sex at the Colonial Rottweiler Club Specialty, 1979, in an entry of 176 with 51 specials. Mrs. Benjamin Tilghman, owner.

Opposite:
Mrs. Peggy Adamson is pictured here awarding Best of Breed at Huntington Valley, 1979, to Mrs. Benjamin Tilghman's Am., Bda. Ch. Andan Indy Pendence v Paulus.

BEST OF
BREED

HUNTINGDON VALLEY
KENNEL CLUB

JUNE 1979

ASHBEY

329

At 16 months of age, Ch. Bergluft's Carla finishes her title with her fourth major. John Patterson, judge; Mrs. Dorit S. Rogers, owner.

tion, practically the entire weight of the dog is supported by the forequarter. A third function is that of lifting and applying forward thrust to the body. Two additional functions performed by the foreassembly, not evident while viewing the side gait, are propelling on turns and combatting lateral displacement, which is caused by off-center force from rear quarter drive.

The Standard calls for shoulder blades which are long and obliquely angled. The need for long blades is related to the length of muscle which they can support. The mobility and strength of a muscle is proportioned to its length and cross-sectional area respectively. A longer blade, which is generally accompanied by greater width, permits the attachment of longer and thicker shoulder muscles. It is apparent that the longest possible blade must be well angled. Any lesser angle results in a shorter blade with less muscle and less lifting power. Further evidence confirming the foregoing is that a well angled blade permits the greatest reach of the forequarter. Functionally, the amount of reach in the forequarter is directly coupled with the rear quarter angulation which provides the push to the dog's movement. A right angle between the upper arm and the shoulder blade is specified because this angle, supplemented with equal length of shoulder blade and upper arm, establishes the conformation which provides the longest length and hence the greatest distance through which the front assembly supports and propels the body forward during a given stride.

If we were to apply the laws of mechanics, we would find that the strongest support is given by a straight column of bones with the center of support directly under the center of the shoulder blade. If the shoulder blade were pushed out from the rib cage by heavy muscles beneath the blade, the bone structure would take the form of "loaded shoulders" with the effect of breaking the straight column of bones, forcing the joint between the shoulder blade and upper arm inward and the elbows out. Additionally, the supporting center pad of the foot is shifted somewhat from below the center of the blade and the dog must exert muscular energy to counteract the resulting unbalanced forces. Of course, the foregoing comments are based on the assumption that the dog has the correct well-sprung but not barrel shaped rib structure, the latter already mentioned as undesirable.

The Standard calls for straight bone in the legs. We should now understand this request in view of the comments regarding the straight column of bone for structural strength.

Our attention now turns to the pastern angulation, which in accordance with the Standard should be almost perpendicular. The objective behind this specification is that it enables the dog having correct placement of the shoulder blade and upper arm to place his front paw directly under the center of his shoulder blade. The center of the shoulder blade is essentially the point of axis around which the shoulder blade rotates. With the foot pad positioned directly below the axis of rotation, the force supporting the body acts through the center point; thus there is no tendency for the blade to rotate when the forequarter is in the weight supporting or static position and no need for the dog to expend muscular energy to counteract such rotation. Moderately sloping pasterns are nearly always associated with good fronts, the

This is the first Canadian-bred Rottweiler to win Best in Show, all breeds, in Canada. Can. Ch. Rintelna the Dragoon owned by Pat Johnson and Jim Schwartz of Winnipeg, also went Best of Breed at the Canadian Rottweiler Club Specialty Show under noted breeder-judge, Mrs. Bernard Freeman.

Opposite:
Scoring another of his frequent victories, Am., Can. Ch. Srigo's Flight of the Eagle, Am., Can. CD, and Canadian all breed Best in Show winner belongs to the Arthur Rikels of Butler, PA. He was bred by Felicia Luburich of Srigo Kennels.

333

reason being that they are part of the bone assembly which receives and cushions impact from the ground. A pastern with a slight bend has spring and resilience. Straight or "steep" pasterns take impact with the ground "head on," jarring the entire front assembly of the dog.

The dewclaws may be removed from the front legs if you wish. They are never removed in Europe, and to date it has not been stated in the Standard here that they are to be removed, though removal is practiced by a number of breeders.

Hindquarters: The hindquarters are defined to consist of those parts of the body known as pelvis, croup, upper thigh, lower thigh, stifle joint, hock joint, os calcis, metatarsus, toes and tail bones.

The pelvis forms the foundation of the hindquarters. Its position and the relative position of the tail bones (coccygeal bones), shape the croup. Connected to the pelvis by a ball and socket type joint is the upper thigh bone or the femur. The upper thigh bone joins at the stifle joint to two bones called the tibia and fibula. These are collectively referred to as either the lower thigh bone or the stifle bone.

The hock is formed from five metatarsal bones, four of which are active. The connection between the hock and the lower thigh bone is technically called the tarsus, but for simplicity we refer to it as the hock joint. The hock joint is a complicated arrangement of seven bones, the most significant being the relatively large bone having the name 'os calcis." Frequently the tip of the os calcis is called the point of the hock. The toes, or phalanges, complete the hindquarter.

The task of the hindquarter is to provide the power or thrust which propels the dog forward while gaiting. Consequently unlike the forequarter, the hindquarter is rigidly attached to the other parts of the body through the essentially immobile joint called the sacroiliac joint. This positive union of the pelvis with the spinal column assures that the drive generated by the hind legs is converted without mechanical loss to forward locomotion of the dog. The functions of the hindquarters are (1) absorbing concussion, (2) providing lift through powerful rearing muscles and (3) generating forward thrust by extending powerfully and rapidly. It is strongly emphasized that the most efficient conformation is sought, for there are any number of structures which will function for locomotion. In fact some will perform certain functions better than the ideal structure for short periods of time. However, this

Headstudy of Olaf von Gruenerwald, sired by the Dutch import, Ch. Donar v.d. Neckarstroom ex Ch. Jenni von Gruenerwald. Photo, courtesy of Dorothea Gruenerwald.

better performance either requires a large expenditure of muscular energy or disrupts the balance of the dog resulting in other parts of the body being overworked. In both cases the dog soon tires, and consequently cannot gait continuously for extended periods of time as the service or working dog must.

Gait: All of the above explanations have been aimed at the fact that the Rottweiler is a trotter, a dog that was required to move at a trot for extended periods of time over rough terrain. He was required to be agile as he kept the stubborn hogs or cattle together on the way to market. He needed all of his energy for work. It was important not to break down on the road. Those dogs not capable of doing the necessary work for extended periods over the sometimes very long treks were not kept or used for breeding. By this method, the owners implanted an inbred ability to herd, guard, etc, without training, by concentration on the dog's abilities, physical as well as mental.

It should also be noted that upon occasion a Rottweiler is born with double dewclaws and/or very heavy dewclaws. The dewclaws on the rear feet are always removed. However, the dog with double dewclaws, or such very heavy dewclaws as to suggest

Am., Dutch, and Belg. Ch. Oscar Van Het Brabant-park, OFA RO 1428, Good, owned by Mrs. Clara Hurley and Michael S. Grossman, was the first Rottweiler to have gone Best in Show in California, July 15, 1979. His show career was a fabulous one during his short lifetime. Born Oct. 2, 1973, his death on Oct. 28, 1979, was a sad and tragic loss for the entire breed as well as for his owners. In addition to the Best in Show wins, his record includes four Working Group firsts, five Working Group seconds, four Working Group thirds and seven Working Group fourths in addition to 54 Best of Breed wins. He was handled by Corky Vroom.

a fifth toe, will develop a twist in the bones of the metatarsal area. This causes the rear feet to turn out and the hocks to move extremely close to one another. This is a condition that should be eliminated by breeding it out. It is a hindrance to gaiting cleanly and smoothly, as the dog is not able to move without excessive energy loss nor with the mobility of the dog born without dewclawsor with dewclaws that are very small. A dog with the conditions described should be considered inferior to his counterparts in the show ring, and one should use such a dog for breeding with extreme care, if at all.

Color: The Rottweiler is *always* black with rust to mahogany markings. It is important to emphasize this. The dogs with light straw colorings on their markings are not desirable next to darker red markings. The dog *without* markings is to be disqualified, and the dog with some missing markings should be penalized to a degree. The markings are specifically placed and patterned on the dog. They should not extend beyond those locations, nor should they be missing in some areas. The base color is *always* black. There are examples of other colors reported in the breed, and these are specifically disqualified from the show ring, and should be prevented from any breeding. The black dog is always prone to "sunburn." Careful attention to the amount of light and some good conditioning will eliminate this problem.

A *few* white hairs do not constitute a marking. However, any white markings on the body should be penalized and are highly undesirable in the Rottweiler.

Character: The Rottweiler carries a certain aloofness that shows up in his expression and attitude. He is a dog of extreme self-assurance, fearlessness and he tends to pick his own friends on his own terms. He was bred to protect his charges (home, livestock, master, etc), many times doing so instinctively and without actual training. There has never been room in the breed for the shy or vicious dog, neither trait being desirable. While the Rottweiler may be somewhat stubborn, it really amounts to the fact that he is not a submissive dog. He possesses an extremely high work level and desire to please. The old instincts are still very much alive in that he still carries the herding ability inherent in the breed. Thus you may find him lagging in obedience work. It is also not uncommon for the Rottweiler to allow someone into his territory, but very likely they will not be permitted to leave it without help!

American, Dutch and Luxembourg Ch. Quanto Van Het Brabantpark, OFA, RO 1935 T-Excellent. Owned by Mrs. Clara Hurley and Michael S. Grossman, Powderhorn-Wencrest Rottweilers. This younger brother of the late American, Dutch and Belgian Ch. Oscar Van Het Brabantpark has done exceedingly well in the short time he has been in the U.S.A. The pedigrees of Quanto and Oscar are identical and their progeny in this country, while still young (just for over a year for the oldest) are following in the footsteps of their European brothers and sisters.

All of the preceding explanations are for the adult Rottweiler. The idea in judging is to seek and find that one dog coming closest to this ideal description.

Faults involving balance, proportion or soundness of the Rottweiler should lower the dog's value as a contender in the show ring, due to the fact that these are weaknesses which interfere with working ability. A well balanced, well proportioned, sound moving Rottweiler is what judges should be seeking in the show ring—a dog that is thus well equipped to perform, capably and without breaking down, the duties for which the breed was originally intended.

In Germany, tremendous emphasis is placed upon the dog's ability to move correctly without breaking down and also to correct formation of the teeth and mouth. Rottweiler owners have frequently been heard to lament the fact that these essential features do not always receive the careful attention that they deserve from the many multiple breed judges officiating in the United States.

BEST OF
BREED

ASHBEY PHOTO

Ch. Radio Ranch's X-per-tease is owned by Tom and Marion Sallen, Tarpon Springs, FL. Handled by Tom Glassford, she is piling up an impressive list of wins in the Ohio area as this book is being written.

Opposite:
Am., Bda. Ch. Andan Indy Pendence v Paulus owned by Mrs. Benjamin C. Tilghman. Indy was Number One Rottweiler Bitch in America, winning the American Rottweiler Club Award for that honor in 1977; Number Ten Rottweiler in breed competition *(Kennel Review system)* in 1978 and Number One Rottweiler Bitch plus a member of the Medallion Rottweiler Club Hall of Fame, 1979.

CHAPTER 13

Owning A Rottweiler

Rottweilers are very special dogs. For that reason they are not automatically suitable for every owner or for every type of household or situation. If your ownership of a member of this breed is to be successful, it is necessary that you give great thought and consideration to the demands that will be made on you, and to whether they will fit into your scheme of living. This should be done *prior* to your decision regarding ownership of the breed; otherwise you may find yourself with an unhappy if not disastrous situation on your hands.

If you have very little time to spend with a dog, it is unlikely that your association would work out well if that dog is a Rottweiler, for a number of reasons. First of all, Rottweilers are a loyal devoted breed noted for strong attachments and devotion. This makes them natural protectors, but it also makes them demanding of your time and attention. They like being with you, some even to the extent of following you from place to place, dogging your footsteps, so to speak. They enjoy the companionship of their loved ones and thrive best in a situation that permits it.

Rottweilers are large and extremely powerful dogs—due to their muscular development a great deal stronger than one might judge from their size. A fully grown one can easily knock a person to the ground; thus they are unsuitable for the elderly or infirm or for young children, unless reared with the child from puppyhood.

Ch. Srigo's Elyssian Fields taking Reserve Winners Bitch from the 6-9 Month Puppy Class at a Colonial Rottweiler Club Specialty, Mrs. McIntyre, judge; owned and handled by Felicia Luburich.

Opposite:
A promising eight-week-old male puppy bred by von Gruenerwald Kennels.

343

Ch. Radio Ranch's Christmas Spirit, taking Best of Opposite Sex under Judge Council Parker with owner-handler Tom Sallen. Christmas Spirit was Winners Bitch and Best of Winners at the Colonial Rottweiler Club Specialty, Number Two Rottweiler Bitch, and Number One Owner-Handled for 1979.

Opposite:
Here's looking at you! Alton Anderson's front view of Ch. Graudstark's Luger, a Best of Breed and Group placement winner. Truly a handsome devil, this dog wins many friends for the Rottweiler breed. Owners, Mark and Pat Schwartz, West Nyack, NY.

Because they are so large, so strong and so powerful, it is absolutely essential that a Rottweiler be trained carefully and well to obey your commands from puppyhood, usually starting at or before six months of age. Your Rottweiler *must* be reliably obedient, making it possible for you to keep the dog under control of your voice at all times in every situation. Here too, a Rottweiler owner must spend time with the dog.

Since they are big dogs, Rottweilers need exercise in ratio to their size. An outdoor fenced area is seldom sufficient to provide this, and to be kept properly and in condition, your dog should be walked on lead at least once daily for a reasonable distance (not just fifty yards down the street and home). This, too, places demands on your time.

The rewards are great, however. If you are willing and able to put the required effort into it and want a dog "for the pleasure of its company," you could not possibly find a better, more loyal, more devoted breed than this one!

All Rottweilers are aggressive to some degree, particularly where their own property and territory are concerned. They quickly develop a strong sense of "territorial rights," feeling the defense of this area or place to be their duty. This is one of the reasons they are regarded so highly as guard dogs. It is also one of the things you must realize and be prepared to deal with when you make a Rottweiler a member of your family.

Rottweilers are not quick to bite without provocation. However, through hundreds of generations they have worked as guard dogs. This instinct must be carefully channelled if problems are to be avoided. Being cornered by one of these dogs—in your absence—will soon put you out-of-bounds with gardeners, delivery men or the letter carrier. Careful obedience training from puppyhood on is a must, as we have stated. Regular visitors to your home or property should be "introduced" to the dog under your watchful eye, and the dog should be sufficiently familiar with these people to regard them as friends. The American Rottweiler Club in its pamphlet *Introducing the Rottweiler* notes, "Your Rottweiler must be carefully schooled to accept your friends into your home, but physical contact or roughhousing should be approached carefully until the dog realizes it's all in fun." It goes on to caution that "people expected to be in contact with the dog during your absence should be thoroughly familiar with it!" Good advice on both counts!

Above: Whose move next? Playful friends belonging to Mary Jo Duguay are her Rottweiler, Jo Mar's Preis of Von Dimar, and one of her champion Beagles. **Below:** Roomeo vom Heidenmoor from Finland. Photo, courtesy of Barbara Dillon.

Co-owners Mary Brennan, handling, and Susan C. Catlin, breeder, smile their pleasure as the puppy, Trollknoll's VC Domino, goes Winners Bitch from the Puppy Class under Judge Donald Booxbaum.

Opposite:
Am., Can. Ch. Northwinds Kaiser of Mallam, jointly owned by Jessica Nichols and Joyce de Vries, was Number One Rottweiler in Canada for 1978, where he piled up an impressive total of 13 times Best of Breed during 15 ring appearances. He was twice Best of Opposite Sex, once Group IV, and finished his Canadian championship at 15 months winning the Working Group under Leslie Kodner, the first Rott to win a Working Group owner-handled. Sold by Art Newman to Joyce Nichols August, 1979, Kai also is Schutzhund trained, but has never been trialed.

S. I. K.C.
JUNE 22, 1980

BEST OF
BREED

A BUSHMAN PHOTO

349

Ch. Srigo's Xclusive v Kurtz, still another in the long series of important Rottweilers from the Srigo Kennels of Ms. Felicia Luburich at East Brunswick, NJ.

Opposite:
Above: This is Noel P. Jones, Jr., son of the noted professional handler, back in 1947 with his Rottweiler, Kris. **Below:** Jo Mar's Preis Von Dimar has other friends, too. For example, the Mastiff, Jo Mar's Venus of Deer Run, also owned by Mary Jo Duguay.

Above: A family portrait from Sherri Page's Tobant Kennels. From left are: Am., Can. Ch. Rodsden's Ander V H Brabant, Ch. Assy von Lohauser, Southwood's Beauregarde, Southwood's Ciona of Tobant, and Southwood's Faline of Tobant. Left: An informally posed photo showing what one looks for in an excellent Rottweiler. Note shoulder placement, hindquarters, topline, head and neck, all of the quality that adds up to a winner. This is Srigo's Imitation of Life, belonging to Felicia Luburich.

As in most breeds, the Rottweiler's attitude toward children varies with the individual dog. Many love them and would protect them with their lives. Others resent the rough handling sometimes inflicted on dogs or puppies by a child's not realizing the hurt it is causing the pet. The danger with a Rottweiler is not that it is less patient with children than other breeds, rather that because of its size and strength it can inflict greater damage should the situation become unendurable for the animal.

Again as with any breed, a Rottweiler will tolerate the introduction of another pet into your home, depending on the individual temperament and the manner in which the introduction is handled. It is, of course, easier with puppies than with mature dogs and usually easier with bitches than with the males.

We hope that we have succeeded in alerting you to the fact that in taking on a Rottweiler you are taking on a *responsibility*. This is *not* a breed that you can acquire, then neglect and forget about. You will have very serious problems if you approach Rottweiler ownership with that attitude.

If you are the person for this breed, you have a very pleasant and satisfying relationship ahead of you. A properly reared, properly trained Rottweiler who enjoys the interest, time and attention to which such a dog is entitled will be a canine companion, protector and friend upon whom you can depend and who will be a source of comfort and joy. Rottweilers are natural clowns in temperament, ranging from being affectionate to almost everyone to the more reserved and stand-offish one-man (or woman) dog. They should be alert but calm. Remember, socialization is the key word influencing your Rottweiler's temperament. The more time these dogs spend sharing your life, the better adjusted, happier and more satisfactory companions they will become.

Rottweilers are exceedingly companionable dogs and should be welcomed as family members, not shut off by themselves. If you acquire a Rottweiler, do so with this thought in mind. To be allowed to share his or her owner's life and activities is the ideal circumstance for members of this breed; it is this sort of situation which will bring out the best in the breed, allowing for development of intelligence, steady good temperament and the protective instinct. A Rottweiler that has been obedience trained and receives loving attention from an owner who truly enjoys the dog can make a canine friend second to none!

CHAPTER 14

Ask The Person Who Owns A Rottweiler

What better way to learn about the personality and character of a breed than by discussing it with an owner of one? We may not always get an unbiased opinion, as I have noticed that the majority of folks owned by Rottweilers are pretty well "gone" on them. But that fact, too, speaks for itself. You just don't get all that carried away with enthusiasm unless the breed you have chosen is a worthy one!

Two Rott fanciers, Bob and Kay Willmarth, own their own business, a gas station-car wash, at Kalamazoo, Michigan. When they bought their puppy, it was as a companion; as such they did not like leaving it at home alone when they went to work. So Kava von Stolzenfels has grown up doing what Rottweilers like best—enjoying the companionship of their humans!

Kay, who had never before thought of becoming involved with obedience training, began training her new puppy at eight weeks old. By the time she had reached fifteen weeks, Kava had learned to sit, down, heel, and finish. At nine months, Kay decided to enter her puppy in her first Fun Match in sub-novice and novice. The puppy finished first in sub-novice with a score of 197 and first in novice with a score of 199½ and brought home a trophy for the highest score in the match! This was certainly exciting for her owner-handler and not all that unusual. Rottweilers seem to have a natural instinct for obedience, and you will note that many do distinguish themselves in this field.

Ch. Noralei von Gruenerwald taking Best of Breed under Judge Joe Gregory. By Ch. Starkrest's Polo -R ex Ch. Eloise von Gruenerwald. Owned and bred by Dorothea Gruenerwald.

Opposite:
Kava von Stolzenfels, CD, looking over her gate.
Kava belongs to Kay Willmarth, Kalamazoo,
Michigan.

A day at the beach. Nello von Stolzenfels and Irina von Stolzenfels owned and photographed by Jan Wahl. Nello is 27 months old here, Irina seven months.

Kay next decided that Kava was ready for the real thing, so off they started to three shows, Toledo, Kalamazoo and Lansing. In Toledo the puppy beat 23 dogs for the first prize ribbon with a score of 194 (the winner's score was 196). In Lansing she competed against sixty dogs and came in second with a score 194, this time the winner beating her out by only one half point! and at sixteen months of age, Kava, completely trained and handled by her owner, had gained her Companion Dog title. Training her to jump was surprisingly easy, as was training her to take and retrieve the dumb-bell. But when you consider the training to which her ancestors were undoubtedly accustomed in Germany, it becomes obvious that Kava was merely reverting to the instinct that has come down through heredity.

As I write this, Kava, at less than two years old, is now ready to go for her C.D.X. and is already trained for her Utility Dog trials as well. In a week's time Kay had taught her glove retrieving and hand signal jumping. Kava has been rated Number Six Rottweiler in the Nation for Novice Obedience during 1979 by the American Rottweiler Club, with a combined score of 193.8 in three Novice showings.

At the service station, Kava stands guard in the hallway alongside the front salesroom. Here she works for a living, too, guarding her owners against trouble. Kay says, "I don't believe she has ever made an error in judging our customers' character, and she has growled when necessary."

Kava also is no exception to the early custom of using Rottweilers to guard their owner's money. For more than a year now she has accompanied Kay daily to the bank, and upon arrival jumps up resting her paws in the teller's window. When the money has been safely counted, she takes the bag in her mouth and carries it back with her to the station. Shades of the Rottweiler Butcher Dogs carrying their master's money bag tied to the collar! Kay says, "At times I feel a little left out when I walk into the bank. All the tellers say 'Hi, Kava' and ignore me."

Bob and Kay love to camp, so last year when Kava was nine months old they took her for a two-week trip to Lake Superior at the Pictured Rocks in Michigan's Upper Peninsula. They hiked at least five miles daily with Kava leading the way. It was here that Kava discovered one of her greatest loves, swimming. Once in the water, it is almost impossible to get her out, and, like most Rottweilers, she has no fear of the biggest waves and will even put her head under water.

Now Kava has learned about backpacking, and from the moment the pack went on her back, she obviously has loved it. Kay says, "It made her feel so important, carrying the pack for us. She was obviously bursting with pride and seemed to know that she could not play when wearing it. The first day we backpacked nine miles, and the second an additional seven. At the end of each day, she would finish off her dinner, attend to some personal matters, then walk to the entrance of the tent to be let in to go to bed." Where could anyone find a more diverse and interesting companion?

Then we have some comments from Linda Griswold, a Rottweiler breeder. She, too, speaks of the versatility of these animals and gives the following examples.

Her Champion Ravenwood Black Gold, C.D., pulls more than his weight on a Northern dog sled team. This is a real labor of love for "Luggie." Just try to run the team without him! Summer is fun, too. For "Luggie," going to the beach is among his favorite sports. His sire, Champion Pondutt Von Schweitzer, C.D., proves that the early herding instinct of the breed still remains intact. He

Ch. Srigo's Zarras v Kurtz with breeder-co-owner Felicia Luburich. **Below:** When good friends get together! Ms. C.L. Rawlings has photographed this very familiar scene at her home. The Rottweilers (l. to r.) are Star and Stazia. The Cockatiel is Alfalfa.

Ch. Dervis v Weyershof, a charcoal headstudy by the son of Gladys Swenson. **Below:** A 9½-month-old Rottweiler surrounded by friends! Photo courtesy, Barbara Dillon.

Ch. Srigo's Big Opportunity during August of 1976 out for a country stroll. Felicia Luburich, breeder-owner. **Below:** This handsome Rottweiler is Baron Von Essig, owned by Robert Yarnall and handled by Alan Levine.

This is Northwinds Kondor in Autumn 1978 playing with his favorite toy—an airplane tire! Kondor belongs to Barbara and Dale Miles, Franklin, TN. **Below:** Playing tug of war! Ch. Pondutt Von Schweitzer, CD, (right) and Ravenwood Nightmare, CD. Both owned by Linda Griswold, Ravenwood Kennels, Michigan City, IN.

is always eager to round up and bring in a herd of quarter horses. Another of the Griswold Rotts, Dagna, has been known to spend entire afternoons herding geese.

Mrs. Griswold's Ravenwood Kennel Obedience Drill Team gives demonstrations and participates in area parades. The team is comprised of Black Gold, Pondutt, Champion Ravenwood Nightmare, C.D., and Luna von Stolzenfels (soon to become a champion). This highly praised team has been a hit at every appearance. Their excellent temperament and perfect manners make them good ambassadors for their entire breed.

Dorothea Gruenerwald, who has owned Rottweilers over a couple of decades or so, observes that Rottweilers, generally, do not thrive in a kennel environment, and some reproductive problems in the breed have been thought to be the result of such confinement. Rottweilers are extremely intelligent and imaginative dogs and need the stimulus of learning situations whether this be through obedience, tracking, or simply engaging in a continuing owner-dog relationship. When they are deprived of this, Mrs. Gruenerwald points out, their behavior pattern suffers. They can then become mischievous, destructive or depressed.

Rottweilers are loyal and devoted to one another as well as to their owners. Among our photographs is one of the "von Gruenerwald brothers," two males from the first litter raised at this kennel, which Mrs. Gruenerwald decided to keep. These grew up to become Champion Cache von Gruenerwald and Carder von Gruenerwald, who was known as 'Turk'. These two large males were always compatible, even when they had been separated for a two year period. They were excellent watchdogs, enjoyed swimming together in beaver pools and the backyard pool and posing for pictures. They even shared a mutual dislike of their sire! Both brothers reached eleven years of age, then died within two weeks of one another.

We have a wide assortment of glowing letters about what great friends and companions Rottweilers can be, to the extent that we feel this truly is a dog of tremendous merit. I do not know of any breed with such strong instincts to carry on in the tradition of its ancestors, for as you have read, it is those things for which their breed was created originally that are the occupations which Rottweilers today enter with greatest efficiency!

Another individual show dog of which we must tell you is Champion Challange Von Dansor, who spends his weekends at dog

"The Brothers Gruenerwald" taken at nine years of age, Turk (left) and Ch. Cache von Gruenerwald. Dorothea Gruenerwald, owner.

shows, winning high awards. During the week, however, he works, even as you and I. His master, Mr. Dangler, is a police officer with the Long Branch, New Jersey, K-9 Unit, who has trained "Charley" for police work. And "Charley" is very much on the job, accompanying his master on his rounds when not in the show ring.

Our good friend Robert J. Moore, noted judge of many breeds, including all Terriers and all Working dogs, has owned a wide assortment of breeds over the years. But now he has a Rottweiler! Says Bob: "He is the smartest dog that we have ever owned and is the most perfect watch dog and guard that we have had. He is most protective of our family and property. He loves a ball to play with and, sits up and begs like a ridiculous little dog. His acts of intelligence are too many to enumerate, but he could never be replaced in our love." This Rottweiler is Southwood's Tribune, known to his friends as "Tarkus." He was whelped on January 1st 1975, bred by Linda W. Howard, and is a son of Champion Falco v h Brabantpark from Champion Southwood's Ave.

Well, as I said in the beginning—if you want to learn about Rottweiler personality, ask someone who owns one.

CHAPTER 15

Selecting Your Rottweiler

Once you have made the decision that the Rottweiler is to become the breed of dog for you, the next important step for you is to begin your education on selection of exactly the right Rottweiler to satisfy your needs. Do you prefer to start out with a puppy or with a grown dog? Would you prefer a male or a female? And what type of dog do you wish; for show or as a pet and companion? A decision should be reached about these matters before contacting breeders, in order for you to describe your requirements accurately and to help them to offer you something suitable. Remember, with any breed of dog, or for that matter with any major purchase, the more care and forethought you invest when planning, the greater the satisfaction and pleasure you are likely to derive.

Referring to a dog as a "major investment" possibly may seem strange to you. It is an accurate description, however. In the case of a Rottweiler, not only is a sizeable sum of money involved, but also you are assuming responsibility for a living creature, taking on all the moral obligations this involves. Assuming that everything will go well, the dog you purchase will be a member of your family for perhaps about ten years, sharing your home, your daily life, your interests. Whether these years will be happy and enjoyable for you as they should be or filled with irritation and frustration or terminated because of disappointment and dissatisfaction depends largely on the knowledge and intelligence that goes into the start of the relationship.

Pictured here at five months of age, Von Gailingen's Dark Delight is owned by Catherine Thompson, Von Gailingen Kennels.

Opposite:
Ch. Freeger's Ingela, CDX, RO 141, Top Producing Dam, *Kennel Review*, 1975, 1976, Ingela is a member of the Medallion Rottweiler Club's Hall of Fame. X-rayed at the age of 7½ years, she received an "excellent" rating from the OFA. Owned by Mrs. Margareta McIntyre, Gatstuberget's Rottweilers, Enumclaw, WA.

Certain ground rules apply to the purchase of a dog regardless of your intentions for its future. Foremost among these rules is the fact that no matter what your plans are for your dog, you must get it from a reputable source where you can be sure the puppy's health and well being are of primary concern. This can be either a conscientious pet shop dealer who is known to you or a private breeder.

Rottweilers, which are not as numerous as certain other breeds, are not always found in pet shops. Since sources for first-rate Rottweiler litters are less easy to come by than some other breeds whose size makes them more amenable to apartment and city living as well as more rural life styles, they seem to be carried less frequently by pet shops. Wishing to bring only top-quality puppy stock to their customers, truly reputable shop owners would rather not carry Rotties at all than carry those of questionable lineage.

Additionally, the nature of pet shops is such that location in fairly well populated areas is most advantageous to them. Under such circumstances, many have to deal with somewhat limited space. Rottweiler pups, being larger than pups of many other breeds, require a large amount of space to be comfortable and cannot be well housed in restricted circumstances. Most pet shops prefer to deal in smaller livestock and in a wide range of equipment for your pets. However, the reputable pet shop dealer with whom you are familiar is an excellent contact to put you in touch with a breeder who can either sell you a puppy himself or recommend to you another breeder who has puppies.

Breeders are usually conscientious people who raise dogs as part of a breeding program and sell only their surplus stock. They do not breed dogs for the specific purpose of sale.

By contrast, when you buy from a breeder, you are getting a dog that has been the result of parents very carefully selected for both conformation and temperament. The majority of breeders raise dogs for show or for the improvement of the breed, one way or another. A specialist of this sort wants to raise better dogs, and since it is seldom possible to keep all the pups from every litter, fine young stock thus becomes available for sale. Puppies with flaws which in no way affect their strength or future health are sold as pets. Such flaws may include bad bites (mouths in which the teeth do not meet correctly according to the Breed Standard) or several missing teeth, large white spots on the chest or belly,

Just see the excellence, balance, substance and overall quality of this magnificent dog! Ch. Srigo's Viking Spirit bred and owned by Felicia Luburich, East Brunswick, NJ.

long or curly coats, or monorchidism—faults which render them useless for the show ring but certainly not as pets, guard dogs or family companions. In many cases these faults are hardly noticed by the layman and would bother no one other than a knowledgeable judge of the breed. In buying a dog of this type from a reliable breeder, you are getting all the advantages of good bloodlines with proper temperament, careful rearing and the happy well adjusted environment in which puppies, in order to be of sound temperament as adults, need to start life.

If you are looking for a show dog, everything I have said about buying from a breeder applies with great emphasis. Show-type puppies are bred from show-type dogs of proven producing lines and are the result of serious thought and planning. They do not just happen, and they are not likely to crop up in commercially raised litters.

Throughout the pages of this book you will learn the names and locations of dozens of conscientious and reliable Rottweiler

Robert G. Yarnall of Kimbertal Kennels is the owner of Ch. Iris vom Bruckertor, being handled here to Best of Opposite at the Penobscot Kennel Club Show under Haworth Hoch by Alan Levine.

Opposite:
Above: Such a proud mother! Ch. Anka V Gailingen with her four-week-old puppies by Ch. Igor v Schauer. Catherine M. Thompson, owner. **Below:** Wouldn't you dearly love to own a baby like these? Rottweiler puppies from the Blue Meadow Kennels of Donna and Bob Wormser.

breeders. We have included also a list of Rottweiler Clubs that gladly will assist you in locating reputable breeders with puppies or young stock available for sale. Should it happen that no one has puppies ready to go at the moment you inquire, it would be far wiser for you to place your name on the waiting list and see what becomes available when a new litter arrives than to be impatient and rush off to buy somewhere less desirable. After all, you do not want to repent at leisure! And we do not want you to become a disappointed Rottweiler owner (or a former one) due to having made a bad choice.

Another source of listings of recognized Rottweiler breeders is the American Kennel Club, 51 Madison Avenue, New York N.Y., 10010. A note or phone call to them will bring you the names of breeders you can contact.

The moment you even start thinking of purchasing a Rottweiler, it makes sense to look at, observe and study as many members of the breed as possible prior to taking the step. Acquaint yourself with correct type, soundness and beauty before making any commitments. Since you are reading this book, you have already started on that route. Now add to your learning opportunities by visiting some dog shows if you can. Even if you are not looking for a show dog, it never hurts to become aware of how such a dog appears and behaves. Perhaps there you will meet some breeders from your area whom you can visit and with whom you can discuss the breed.

If this is to be your first Rottweiler and you wish it as a family dog to join your household, your wisest choice would be a bitch, for several reasons. The females are smaller in size, calmer in disposition and therefore easier for a novice to train. They are extremely loyal and make devoted companions. They are more likely to be gentle with children and other pets. They often make neater housedogs, and they are equal to the males in working ability and intelligence. The principal objection to having a bitch, in the eyes of some pet owners, is the periodic coming "in season." There are sprays and chlorophyll tablets available in these modern times that can cut down on the nuisance of visiting canine swains stampeding your front door. Of course I advocate having bitches spayed that will not be used for show or breeding. And even these should be spayed when their careers in competition or in the whelping box have come to a close. Bitches that have been spayed remain in better health when they become older.

A five-week-old Rott puppy owned by Frank W. Aube.

This operation eliminates almost entirely the possibility of breast cancer. Then too, in this way you avoid the messiness and spotting of rugs and furniture which can be considerable with a member of a large breed and annoying in a household companion.

To many, however, a dog (male) is preferable, for the males do seem somehow to be more strongly endowed with breed character and of course are physically stronger and more robust. But do consider the advantages and disadvantages both ways prior to deciding.

If you are buying a Rottweiler as a pet, a puppy is preferable as you can teach it the ways of your own household, accustom it to your schedule and start its training earlier. Two months is an ideal age at which to introduce the puppy into your home or as soon thereafter as possible. Older puppies may have already established habits of which you will not approve and which you may find difficult to change. Besides, puppies are such fun that it is great to enjoy every possible moment of the growing up process!

When you are ready to buy, make appointments with as many Rottweiler breeders as you have been able to locate in your area for the purpose of visiting their kennels, discussing the breed with them and seeing their dogs. This is a marvelous learning experience, and you will find that the majority of breeders are willing, even happy to spend time with you, *if you have arranged the visit in advance.* Kennel owners are busy people with full schedules so do be considerate about this courtesy and make that telephone call before you appear.

If you have a choice of more than one kennel where you can go and see the dogs and puppies, do take advantage of the opportunity rather than just buy the first puppy you see and like. You may return to your first choice, but will do so with greater satisfaction and authority if you have seen the others that are available too. When you look at pet puppies be aware that the one you should buy looks sturdy and big boned, bright eyed and alert, with an inquisitive, friendly attitude. The puppy's coat should look clean and glossy. Do not buy a puppy that seems listless or dull, or one that is strangely hyperactive. Do not buy a puppy that looks half sick, or one where the surroundings are dirty and ill kept. The condition of the premises where the puppies are raised is of importance as you want a pup that is free of parasites.

One of the advantages of buying at a kennel you can visit is that you are afforded the opportunity of seeing at least the dam of the puppies and possibly also the sire if he, too, belongs to the breeder. Be sure to note the temperament, looking especially for any indication of emotional instability which might reflect in the puppies as they mature.

If there are no Rottweiler breeders within your travelling range or you have not cared for what you have seen on your visits, do not hesitate to contact others who are recommended to you even if the kennels are at a distance and to purchase from one of them if you are favorably impressed with what is offered. The shipping of dogs is done with regularity nowadays, has become a recognized practice, and is reasonably safe, so this should not present a problem. If you are contacting a well known recognized breeder, the puppy should be described and represented to you fairly. Breeders of this caliber want you to be satisfied, both for the puppy's sake and for yours. They take pride in their kennel's reputation, and they make every effort to see that their customers are pleased. In this way you are deprived of seeing your dog's parents, but even so you can buy with confidence when dealing with a specialized breeder.

Everything we have said about careful selection of your pet puppy and the place where it should be purchased applies when you start out to select a show dog or foundation stock for a breeding kennel. You look for everything I have mentioned already, to begin with, but on a far more sophisticated basis, with many more factors to be taken into consideration. The Standard of the Rottweiler Breed should become your guide, and it is essential that you know and understand not only the words of this Standard but also their application to the actual dogs before you are in a position to make a wise selection. Even then, if this is your first venture with a show-type Rottweiler, listen well and heed the advice of the breeder. If you have clearly and honestly stated your ambitions and plans for the dog, you will find that breeders will co-operate by offering you something with which you should be successful.

There are several different degrees of show dog quality. There are dogs that should become top flight winners which can be campaigned for "specials" (Best of Breed competition) and with which you can strive for Working Group placements. There are dogs of championship quality, which should gain their titles for you but do not have that little extra something to make them "specials" potential. There are too, dogs that perhaps may never finish to championship, but which should do a bit of winning for you in the classes—blue ribbon here and there, perhaps Winners or Reserve occasionally, but probably nothing too spectacular. Obviously the hardest and the most expensive to obtain are those in the first category, the truly top grade dogs. These are never plentiful as they are what most breeders are aiming to produce for their own kennels and with which they are loath to part.

A dog of championship quality is easier to find and less expensive although it still will bring a good price. The least difficult to obtain is a fair show dog that may do a bit for you in the classes.

Obviously if you want a show dog, you must be aware of and in the habit of attending dog shows. Now this becomes a type of schooling rather than just a pleasant occupation. Much can be learned at the Rottweiler ringside if one truly concentrates on what one sees. Become acquainted with the various winning exhibitors. Watch the judging thoughtfully. Try to understand what it is that causes some dogs to win and others to lose. Note carefully the attributes of the dogs, deciding for yourself which ones you like, giving particular attention to temperament as well as conformation, and close your ears to the ringside "know-it-alls" who have only derogatory remarks to make about each one and every thing that happens inside the ring. You need to develop independent thinking at this stage and should not be influenced by the often entirely uneducated comment of the ringside spoil-sports. Especially make careful note which exhibitors are campaigning winning homebreds, not just an occasional successful "star," but a series of consistent quality dogs. All this takes time and patience, but this is the time to "make haste slowly" as mistakes can be expensive.

As you make inquiries among various breeders regarding the purchase of a show dog or show prospect, keep these things in mind: Show prospect puppies are less expensive than fully mature show dogs. The reason for this is that, with a puppy, there is the element of chance and one never can be absolutely certain how the puppy will develop, while a mature dog stands before you as the finished product, all set to step out and win.

There is always a risk factor involved with the purchase of a supposedly show-type puppy. Sometimes all goes well, but many a swan has turned into an ugly duckling as time passes; it is far less likely that the opposite will occur! So weigh this well and balance all the odds before you decide whether a puppy or a mature dog would be your better buy. There are times when one actually has no choice in the decision if no mature show dogs are available for sale. Then one must either wait awhile or gamble on a puppy, but please *be aware that gambling is what you are doing!*

If you do take a show prospect puppy, be guided by the breeder's advice in choosing from among what is offered. The person used to working with a bloodline has the best chance of being correct in predicting how its puppies will develop. Do not trust your own guess on this, but rely on the experience of the breeder. Bear in mind that there is no way to predict whether or not a puppy may develop hip dysplasia or other serious problems by the time it has reached two years of age. One simply cannot tell!

Some breeders will give you a guarantee on show prospect puppies delivered at about eight weeks old should the puppy develop hip dysplasia, bite problems, less than full dentition, sight or hearing problems, congenital heart disease or too long a coat.

Ch. Panamint Elke v Hohenwald, Barbara Dillon, owner, Panamint Kennels.

Others will guarantee part of the foregoing. Some give no guarantee at all. If a guarantee is issued to you, be certain that it is in writing or it may prove to be invalid. Guarantees range from replacement of the dog or refund of the money paid to a partial refund of the difference between the price the breeder charges for a pet-type puppy and a show prospect. In the latter event, the return of the papers is demanded if the refund is made.

Although initially more expensive, a grown show dog in the long run often proves to be the far better bargain. Here you buy what you see, thus avoiding any element of chance, and the dog is unlikely to change in appearance beyond weight or condition when the matters become your responsibility. Another advantage, if you are a novice and about to become an exhibitor, is that a grown show dog usually has been trained for the ring; thus an inexperienced handler will find such a dog easier to manage.

If you plan to have your dog campaigned by a professional handler, let the handler help you locate and select a future winner. Through their numerous clients, handlers usually have access to a variety of interesting show dogs, and the usual arrangement is that the handler buys the dog and re-sells it to you for the price paid, at the same time making the agreement with you that the dog shall be campaigned by this handler throughout the dog's career.

If the foundation of a future kennel is what you have in mind as you contemplate getting into Rottweilers, concentrate on one or two really excellent bitches—not necessarily top show bitches, but those representing the finest producing Rottweiler bloodlines and which have, along with their parents, been O.F.A. Certified as free of hip dysplasia. A proven matron which has already produced show-type puppies is, of course, the ideal answer here but, as with a mature show dog, is more difficult to obtain and more expensive, since no one really wants to part with so valuable an asset. You just might strike it lucky, though, in which case you will be off to a flying start. If you do not find such a matron available, do the next best thing. Select a young bitch of outstanding background representing a noted producing strain, one that is herself of decent type and free of glaring faults.

Great attention should be paid to the background of the bitch from which you intend to breed. If they are not already known to you, find out all you can about the temperament, character and conformation of the sire and dam. A person just starting out is

Ch. Radio Ranch's Kilroy is Here, owned by Radio Ranch Rottweilers, Chesapeake, VA.

wise to concentrate on a fine collection of bitches and to raise a few litters sired by leading *producing* sires. The practice of buying a stud dog then breeding everything you have to that dog does not always work out. Better to take advantage of the splendid available stud dogs for the first few litters.

In summation, if you want a "family dog," best buy it young and raise it to the habits of your household and best buy a bitch. If you are buying a show dog, the nearer it is to being fully mature, the better; generally the dogs gain greater recognition in the show ring than the bitches. If foundation stock for a kennel is the goal, bitches are better and proven matrons from top producing bloodlines ideal.

Now as to price: you should expect to pay a respectable sum for a healthy pet Rottweiler puppy. Pet puppies are not for breeding, as they generally have genetic faults which the conscientious breeder does not wish to have reproduced. The breeder will usually require that such puppies be neutered prior to releasing the registration papers to the purchaser, unless the dog had reached sufficient maturity before leaving the kennel for the surgery to have been previously performed. As already stated, these faults in no way affect the health of these dogs or their appearance except in the eyes of a judge or other expert on the breed.

Prices for show quality Rottweilers range between one and one-half times to more than double the prices paid for pet puppies depending on the maturity, quality, possible show record and producing record of the individual dog or bitch. The price of a successful show campaigner, or the producer of champion progeny, if available at all for purchase, can well run into four figures.

377

Ch. Srigo's Xquisite v Kurtz bred and owned by Felicia Luburich, brings home the honors with a "clean sweep" under judge Stanley Hanson.

Ch. Srigo's Opportunity And How goes Best of Breed at a recent kennel club show. Felicia Luburich, owner-breeder.

When you buy a pure-bred dog which you are told is eligible for American Kennel Club registration, you must be given an A.K.C. application form that has been properly filled in by the seller. You must then complete this application and submit it, along with the necessary registration fee, to the American Kennel Club. You will, in return, receive an A.K.C. registration certificate four to six weeks later in the mail. In some cases the breeder may already have registered the puppy or dog you are buying. Then you will receive a registration certificate at the time of purchase; this must be signed on the back by both of you and used to transfer the registered dog into your name. *Never* accept a verbal promise that the registration application will follow and never pay for a dog until you are certain that you are getting the registration in exchange. The seller should provide you with a pedigree of at least three generations of your puppy or dog, which should be delivered at the time of purchase.

CHAPTER 16

Preparing For Your Rottweiler Puppy's Arrival

T he moment the decision has been reached that you are going to bring home a Rottweiler puppy is not one second too soon to start planning. The new family member will find the transition easier if you have things ready upon its arrival at your home.

The first things you should have ready are a bed for the puppy, (in my opinion, preferably a crate), a fenced in area outdoors in which it can be safely placed, a sturdy drinking bowl and feeding dish both of unbreakable material, a lead and the correct size collar to fit the puppy *now*.

One of the safest playthings for a puppy are raw, beef leg bones. Avoid plastics, rubber toys, things with squeakers, poultry, lamb, veal or pork bones. Leather toys are generally permissible, but nylon bones, especially those with natural meat and bone fractions are probably the most complete, safe and economical answer to the chewing need. Dogs cannot break them or bite off sizeable chunks; hence, they are completely safe and being longer lasting than other things offered for the purpose, they are economical. Hard chewing raises little bristle-like projections on the surface of the nylon bones to provide effective interim tooth cleaning and vigorous gum massage, much the same way your tooth brush does for you. Nylabone is such a nylon chew product that is highly recommended by veterinarians as a safe, healthy bone chew that can't splinter or chip.

We're having fun, Mom. These are two of Catherine Thompson's seven-week-old baby Rottweilers.
Opposite:
Seven-week-old puppies by Ch. Donar v.d.
Neckarstroom ex Ch. Jenni von Gruenerwald. Owned
by Dorothea Gruenerwald.

At seven weeks of age is Terry and Betty O'Brien's Loki von Stolzenfels.

There should be comfortable bedding for the crate, such as an old blanket or, in warmer weather, a piece (remnant) of rug or carpet which can be easily and inexpensively replaced.

To elaborate a bit: I recommend a crate in preference to a pen or just a bed for several reasons. First, the crate can be left both securely closed or open. Thus when you wish the puppy to remain there at night or when you are away from the house, he can be closed in safely. When you are home and wish him free, then just leave the crate door open. As the puppy matures, you will probably leave the crate door open more often. You will notice that your dog, who grows to love its crate, will very likely return there for a nap, in preference to a chair or sofa. Crates are a good place for a dog to be away from home, too. In a car the crated dog is prevented from running off in panic should an accident occur, getting hit by another car or becoming lost in the excitement. On a plane, a crate, of course, is a "must." At motels it is often required that dogs be crated if permitted in the rooms. There again, familiarity with being in his crate is helpful to the dog.

"I'll bring it!" says Nadia von Stolzenfels, an eleven-week-old puppy at the Ellmans' von Stolzenfels Kennels. **Below:** Nadia von Stolzenfels at eleven weeks. Jack and Dr. Evelyn Ellman, owners.

On the subject of crates, the kind I recommend as best are the wooden ones with removable side panels for more ventilation in hot weather. These are sturdy, draft free in the winter, and provide sufficient air circulation in summer. Wire crates give no protection against cold or drafts. Aluminum crates can become burning hot in the summer and very cold in winter. When you choose the puppy's crate be certain that it is one that will not be outgrown or cramp the fully matured dog. Get one with plenty of size for its comfort. After all, it is a lifetime investment for the dog, so cost should not be spared for this purchase.

Sharing importance with the puppy's crate is the fenced in yard, and this, too, should be provided prior to bringing the pup home, not afterwards when perhaps an unfortunate toilet accident may have taken place!

There are various types of fences which can be adapted for the purpose, but I think it is pretty generally agreed that the best and safest for a Rottweiler is a fence six feet high around as large an area as you can provide. There should be shade in the fenced area for warm weather. Either wooden stockade fencing or chain link is fine; the former keeps the dog out of the neighbors' sight and from watching what is going on outside. While a lone dog might become bored being confined this way, stockade fencing is preferable. The chain link fence permits the dog to watch around the neighborhood, but it also gives the neighbors access to the dog; trespassing children may stick their fingers through, roaming dogs may start the pup barking and other such annoyances may occur. I suppose it depends on where you are located which type of fencing will work best. If you are well out in the country with a certain amount of privacy anyway, the chain link is great. If you have close neighbors or are in a more suburban neighborhood, do give serious thought to the advantages of the stockade fence. As an extra precaution against a dog digging under the fence, an edging of cinder blocks set tight against the inside bottom of the fence is useful. If there is an outside gate, provide a lock and key and strong fastening for it, so that it cannot be opened in your absence and a dog let out. The ultimate in convenience, of course, is to have a door that can be used for direct access from the house to the fenced area so that the dog can go in and out to the run by itself. This is not always possible, but if your home is arranged so that it can be done, take advantage of the convenience thus afforded.

Only eight weeks old and already posing like a winner! Ch. Von Gail-ingen's Chancellor owned by Catherine Thompson.

Too many changes at one time can be difficult for a puppy. Therefore, try to keep it on the food and schedule to which it is accustomed for at least the first few days following arrival in your home. Find out ahead of time from the breeder what the puppies are fed, how frequently and at what times. Then get a supply of the same food together with any supplements that have been used and recommended and have them there when the puppy comes home.

One more important thing that should precede the puppy's arrival at your home is the selection of a veterinarian. If the breeder is from your own area, ask for recommendations. If you have friends who are dog owners, question them regarding their opinions and experiences with the local vets. Choose someone with whom several of your friends have been successful, contact this veterinarian regarding your puppy and make an appointment to have the puppy checked out the day you bring it home. Be sure to obtain the puppy's health record from the breeder, with information on shots, worming, etc.

With these things attended to, you are all set to go and ready to introduce your new puppy to his new home.

CHAPTER 17

Bringing The Puppy Home

Remember, as exciting as it is for you, the puppy's move from the place of its birth to your home can be a traumatic experience for it. It will miss its mother and littermates and will perhaps be slightly frightened at the new surroundings. Everything should be planned to make the transition as smooth as possible and to give the puppy confidence that something pleasant is actually taking place.

Never bring a puppy home on a holiday. There just is too much going on, with people and gifts and excitement. If the puppy is commemorating an "occasion," plan that its arrival will take place a few days before or a few days after the big day, when there will be peace and quiet and you can give the newcomer your undivided attention to making it feel at home. Try not to bring the puppy home in the evening. Early morning is the ideal time, as then it will have the chance to become acquainted and get the "feel" of the place before dark and bedtime. You will all have a more peaceful night that way I am sure. Allow the puppy to investigate under your watchful eye. If you already have a pet in the household, keep careful watch that things go smoothly and that the relationship starts off on a friendly footing, or you may quickly have a problem. Much of the future attitude between the pets will depend on what happens that first day, so be alerted to what is taking place with the puppy and allow your other activities to slide a bit behind schedule for that one day.

Thinking about the future is Can. Ch. Kyladie Starmaster Antares when 12 weeks old. Kyladie Kennels, Mr. Aime and Mrs. Adele Brosseau, owners, Alberta, Canada.

Opposite:
An eight week old male puppy of von Gruenerwald breeding.

A boy and his dog, the latter being Krieger von Stolzenfels. Owned by the Jack Ellmans, Augusta, MI.

If you have a child, here again it is important that the relationship start out well. It is hoped you will have had a talk with the youngster ahead of time about puppies in general and Rottweilers in particular, so that it is understood that the puppy is not to be teased, hurt, mauled or overly rough-housed. Gentleness from your child toward the puppy should reflect in the dog's attitude toward the child as they both mature. And never permit your children's playmates free rein with the puppy as I have frequently seen happen: mauling, playing and teasing until the puppy turns on them in self-defense. As a responsible adult, you are obligated to see that your puppy's relationship with children is pleasant.

A bit of good advice is not to start out by spoiling your puppy. Put it in its bed at night and *leave it there,* even if it cries or whimpers. Moving the pup into your bed for "just this once" is only going to make matters worse, for after that it will try twice as hard to make this a habit. Command, loudly and firmly, *"Quiet,"* if the puppy fusses. It will quickly get the idea. Establish the rules of your household right from the beginning. Strike a routine and, as far as you can, stick to it. The puppy will learn more quickly this way, and everyone will be happier as the result.

A six-week-old puppy from the von Gruenerwald Kennels.

SOCIALIZING AND TRAINING
YOUR ROTTWEILER PUPPY

Socialization and training of your new puppy should begin the very day you bring it to your home. Never address it without calling by its name, and you will be amazed at how quickly the puppy will learn and respond to the name you have selected! A short, simple name is the easiest to teach to catch the dog's attention most quickly. Avoid elaborate call names and *always* use the same name when you address the dog; do not use a whole series of pet names as this will tend to cause confusion.

Call the puppy to you when it is awake and wandering about, using its name clearly. When the puppy comes to you, pet and make a big fuss over it. Thus, the sound of the name will be quickly associated with coming to you and with something pleasant happening.

Several hours after its arrival is not too soon to start accustoming the puppy to the feel of a light collar. It may hardly notice the collar, or it may struggle and try to rub the collar off its neck. Divert the pup's attention when this occurs, and it should quickly become accustomed to the feel of the collar. Next comes the leash. Attach it to the collar then take the puppy outside immediately where there will be interesting places to sniff and things to occupy its attention. Do not attempt to pull or lead; just follow along with the leash held slack. The puppy will probably react by struggling and attempting to work free at first, but in a few moments interest and curiosity should take precedence over resentment, and it quickly should forget to resist and start walking.

Once the puppy has seemingly forgotten the leash and is walking freely, attempt to guide it to follow you. When that has been accomplished, it should be taught to follow on the left at your side or heel. Of course this will not all be accomplished the very first day. Length of time will vary according to the puppy, but this should be done quite quickly, probably within several days.

As with most puppies, Rottweilers may chew gloves, shoes, slippers, or other such articles. If you see this starting take the article from the mouth, firmly and positively saying "NO" as you do so. If the pup resists, take your left hand and squeeze its lips against its teeth with your thumb and forefinger, again saying "NO." As the pressure starts to hurt, the puppy will probably

Rottweiler puppies at three months, dressed as Mouseketeers (Mickey Mouse Club shirts and ears). Owned by Catherine M. Thompson.

drop the object. The moment it releases the article to you the pup should be rewarded with a pat on the head and enthusiastic words of praise.

Never tease a puppy by reaching for the food dish while it is eating, nor permit anyone else to do so. This could lead to big problems, for while a tiny puppy on the defensive might strike you as funny, a fully mature Rottweiler doing likewise is *not*, and that is what could happen if the puppy is taught to defend its food. So let eating be peaceful, please. From just such little games very big problems can grow!

During the course of housetraining him, or her, you will need to take your puppy out frequently and at regular intervals: first thing in the morning, directly from the crate; immediately after meals; when the puppy wakes from a nap; or when you notice

Maxwell von Stolzenfels at ten weeks, who shares the Willmarths' household with Kava von Stolzenfels. **Below:** Five-weeks-old, future champion Axel Von Gailingen looks out at the world from a protected place. This pup later earned a companion dog title as well. Owned by Catherine Thompson.

A beautiful young Rottweiler in Finland. Whiskey photo courtesy of Barbara Dillon, Baring, WA. **Below:** Five-weeks-old and weighing in at eight pounds, this adorable Rottweiler puppy belongs to Frank Aube of Cranston, RI.

Fun playing in the snow! Kay Willmarth's Kava von Stolzenfels. **Below:** Ch. Juno von Gruenerwald, by Ch. Dieter vom Konigsberg ex Ch. Eloise von Gruenerwald. Picture taken at 12 months of age, one month before this splendid youngster became a champion. Owned by Alan and Karen Kruse, Howell, MI.

that the puppy is looking for a spot. Choose more or less the same place to take it each time, so the pattern will be established. If the pup does not relieve itself immediately, better not return it to the house as it will probably do so then. Stay outdoors with it until the act has been completed, then be lavish with praise for this good behavior. If you catch the young dog having an accident indoors, grab it firmly and rush it outside, saying sharply "NO" as you pick up the puppy. If you do not see the accident occur, there is little point in doing anything except to clean up the mess; once it has happened and been forgotten, the puppy will likely not even realize why you are scolding.

The puppy should be accustomed to spending a certain amount of time in its crate, even when you are home. Sometimes it will do this voluntarily, but if not it should be taught to do so. This is accomplished by leading the puppy over by its collar, gently pushing it inside and saying "down" or "stay." Whatever expression you use for each command, stick to it as repetition is the big thing in training. If at one time you say "sit," another "stay," and still another "down" all for the same action, you will soon confuse the puppy and make training doubly difficult. Select one term for each act and use it *only* for that.

As soon as it has had its immunization shots, take your puppy with you whenever and wherever possible. There is nothing that will build a strong, stable personality like socialization, and it is extremely important that you plan the time and energy necessary for its provision.

Take your Rottweiler puppy in the car so that it will learn to enjoy travelling this way and not suffer from motion sickness. Take the pup with you when you visit friends and relatives when you are sure they will not object and where there is not a house pet that may react. Take it to busy shopping centers and walk around with it on the leash even though dogs are now unwelcome in most stores. If someone admires the puppy (as often happens when we go walking with a puppy) let it be petted. Socialization of this type brings out the best in your puppy and helps it to grow up with a friendly outlook, liking the world and its inhabitants. The worst thing you can do for a puppy's personality is to shelter it too much. By keeping a puppy always at home, away from people and things that are different from its familiar surroundings, you may well be creating a personality problem for the mature dog that will be a cross for you to bear later on.

A typical Radio Ranch puppy, owned by Pamela Weller, Chesapeake, VA.

Make obedience training a game with your puppy when it is extremely young. Try to teach the meaning of "come," "stay," "sit," "down" and "heel" along with the meaning of "NO" even while the pup is still too young for formal obedience training classes. This procedure gives you a head start, and you will be pleased and proud to see how much in the way of good manners even a baby Rottweiler can pick up through gentle early lessons! These are intelligent dogs, adoring of their masters and anxious to please them, so take advantage of that fact right from the beginning.

Opposite:
Bda. Ch. Srigo's The Jig Is Up, clearly every inch a
winner, at six months old receives Best of Breed.
Carlton Wilkinson, owner.

CHAPTER 18

Pedigrees: Background of a Breeding Program

To anyone interested in the breeding of dogs, pedigrees are the basic tool with which this is successfully accomplished. It is not sufficient just to breed two nice looking dogs to one another, then sit back and await outstanding results. Chances are they will be disappointing, as there is no equal to a scientific approach in the breeding of dogs, if quality results are the ultimate goal.

We have selected for you pedigrees of dogs and bitches that either are themselves great producers or that come from consistently outstanding producing lines. Some of these dogs are so dominant that they have seemed to "click" with almost every strain or bloodline. Others for best results need to be carefully linebred. The study of breeding is a challenge and an exciting occupation.

Even if you have no plan to involve yourself in breeding, but just to own and love a dog or two, it is fun to trace the dog's pedigree back into earlier generations and thus learn the sort of dogs behind yours. Throughout this book you will find many pictures of dogs whose names you will find in these pedigrees, enabling you to trace not only the names in the background of your own dog, but also to see what the ancestors looked like, too.

A magnificent headstudy of Ch. Kuhlwald's Trakehner owned by Bergluft Rottweilers, Reg., Mrs. Dorit S. Rogers, Sewickley, PA.

Opposite:
Southwood's Tribune with his favorite lady, Mrs. Robert J. Moore.

CH. RODSDEN'S ZARRAS V BRABANT, RO-1167
Whelped: February 25, 1976
Breeders: Joan Klem and Marthajo Rademacher

Owner: Gwen Chaney (co-owner, P. G. Rademacher)
6N048 Old Homestead Road
St. Charles, Illinois 60174

CH. RODSDEN'S ZARRAS V BRABANT C.D., RO-1167
Whelped: February 25, 1976
Breeders: Joan Klem and Mathajo Rademacher

Owner: Gwen Chaney (co-owner, P.G. Rademacher)
6N048 Old Homestead Road
St. Charles, Illinois 60174

PARENTS	GRANDPARENTS	GREAT-GRANDPARENTS	GREAT-GREAT-GRANDPARENTS
SIRE: Ch. Rodsden's Axel v h Brabant WC643204 RO-582	Dutch Champion, Luxembourg Sieger & Am. Ch. Falco v h Brabantpark WC162229 HD Free, Utrecht, & RO-286	Bundessieger and World Sieger, Ch. Erno v Wellesweiler 39 499 SchH 1 RO-5	Int. Ch. & BS, Ch. Harras vom Sofienbusch 36 474 SchH 1
			Alke vom Gomaringen 37 398 SchH 2
		Dutch Ch. Burga v h Brabantpark 306489 HD Free, Utrecht	Fetz vom Oelberg 38 416 SchH 2 RO-25
			Dutch Ch. Rona v d Brantsberg NHSB 2111191
	Ch. Rodsden's Lady Luck, CD WB262642 RO-60	Ch. Falk v Kursaal WA 988601 SchH 1	Wotan v Filstalstrand 37 422 SchH 1
			BS & Schw. Sg., Assy v Zipfelbach 37 789 SchH 2
		Ch. Afra v Hasenacker, CD 38 822 SchH 1	Erno von Alt-Hornberg 34 923 SchH 1
			Indra v Sofienbusch 36 519
DAM: Ch. Oda v h Brabantpark, TD WC757853 RO-634	Gerlach v h Brabantpark 434982 HD Free, Utrecht	Moritz v Silahopp 324042 HD Free, Utrecht	Brutus v d Kurmark 38 519
			Queen v d Solitude 38 610
		Dutch Ch. Burga v h Brabantpark 306489 HD Free, Utrecht	Fetz vom Oelberg 38 416 SchH 2 RO-25
			Dutch Ch. Rona v d Brantsberg 211191
	Dutch Ch. Onsbessy v d Brantsberg JW'69, W.'70 456850 HD Free, Utrecht	Einar v h Brabantpark 390046 HD Free, Utrecht	Axel v Leitgraben 40 718 SchH 3
			Dutch Ch. Burga v h Brabantpark 306489 HD Free, Utrecht
		Capsones v h Brabantpark 339984 HD Free, Utrecht	Ajax v d Brantsberg 261967
			Dutch Ch. Rona v d Brantsberg 211191

The underscored names in this pedigree are either past Top Producers in our breed or
Producers of Merit, ARC system. Zarras' sire, Ch. Rodsden's Axel v h Brabant, is
well on his way to becoming a Top Producer.

DONNAJ

Pedigree of

CH. DONNAJ VT YANKEE OF PAULUS C.D.X. RO-964-T
Registered Name of Dog

Date Whelped ___ July 4, 1975 ___ Sex ___ · Male ___

Breeder ___ Pauline Rakowski ___ Address ___ Middletown, N.J. ___

Owner ___ Jan Marshall ___ Address ___ Woodstock, Vt. ___

WORKING ROTTWEILERS WITH BRAINS AND BEAUTY

PARENTS	GRANDPARENTS	GREAT-GRANDPARENTS	GREAT-GREAT-GRANDPARENTS
SIRE: Ch. Axel vom Schwanenschlag RO-166	Furst von der Villa Daheim, SchH 1	Axef v Simonskaul, SchH3	Kuno vom Weidbach, SchH 1
			Alli vom Elemenau, SchH 1
		Blanka v Itzelbach, SchH 1	Int. Ch. Lord v Blankenhorn SchH 2
			Flori vom Kanzachtal
	Cora Vom Grevingsberg	Quinn von der Schwarzwiese, SchH1	Eddi v d Hobertsberg
			Olli von der Schwarzwiese
		Britta von der Zuflucht	Quinto von der Solitude, SchH1
			Dolly von der Hardt
DAM: Ch. Amsel von Andan, C.D. RO-300	Am/Can. Ch. Rodsden's Kato v Donnaj, CDX, TD RO-37	Ch. Rodsden's Kluge v d Harque, C.D. RO-50	Int. Ch. & BS, Ch. Harras vom Sofienbusch, SchH 1
			Ch. Quelle v d Solitude, C.D.
		Ch. Franzi v Kursaal	Wotan vom Filstalstrand, SchH 1
			BS Assy vom Zipfelbach SchH 1
	Ehrenwache's Andernach RO-111	Fetz vom Oelberg, SchH 2 RO-25	Hektor von der Solitude
			Dora v d Brotzingergasse
		Rodsden's Ubermutig Karla, C.D.	Ch. Rodsden's Kluge v d Harque C.D. RO-50
			Ch. Afra v Hasenacker, SchH 1, C.D.

Certified Pedigree

VON STOLZENFELS
REGISTERED NAME OF DOG

BREED **Rottweiler**   DATE WHELPED   SEX

BREEDER Jack P. & Dr. Evelyn M. Ellman ADDRESS Rt. 1, Box 100-11, Augusta, Mi. 49012

OWNER   ADDRESS

GENERAL DESCRIPTION black with rust markings

			Int. Ch. & Bundessieger 1960-61-62 Harras vom Sofienbusch, Sch H 1	Arno v.d. Hammerpaote, SchH 3
				Afra aus den Mayen, SchH 2
		Ch. Rodsden's Kluge v.d. Harque, CD, RO-50	Ch. Quelle v.d. Solitude, CD	Droll v.d. Brötzingergasse SchH 2
				Fanny von der Solitude
	A/C Ch. Northwind's Barras, RO-75		Ch. Dervis vom Weyershof	Carlo von der Gathe, SchH 3
				Anka von Gänsebruch
		Can. Ch. Northwind's Tina	Katherina's Adorn of Town-view	Ch. Jaro vom Schleidenplatz
SIRE				Katharina of Townview
Ch. Centurion's Che von der Barr			Fetz v. Oelberg, SchH 2, RO-25	Hektor von der Solitude
REG. NO. WC 815172 RO-757				Dora v.d. Brötzingergasse
		Ch. Arco vom Dahl, CDX, SchH 3 RO-73	Assy vom Borsigplatz	Axel v.d. Kappernbergerheide, SchH
				Andra v. Schloss Westerwinkel
	Ch. Rodsden's Ericka Diedre Dahl, RO 157		Follow Me's Utz	Ch. Arras vom Stadthaus
				Cilli von Kaflunz
		Rafter M's Bandee, RO-109	Ch. Rodsden's Nuscha von der Rasse	Int. Ch. & BS 1960-61-62 Harras vom Sofienbusch, SchH 1
				Ch. Afra vom Hasenacker, CD SchH 1
			Droll v.d. Brötzingergasse SchH 2	Alex vom Glastal, SchH 1
				Asta v.d. Brötzingergasse SchH 2
		Quick v.d. Solitude, SchH 3, FH, Leistungssieger 1966, HD free, angekört	Fanny von der Solitude	Bodo von Laufenburg
	Bado vom Steigstrassle, SchH1 körfähig			Flora von Silahopp
			Arno vom Ilsenhof	Carlo v.d. Schildwach, SchH 3
				Blanka vom Schloss Staufenberg
		Dolli vom Schlossberg, SchH 1	Bella vom Ottenberg	Astor vom Löwen, SchH 2
DAM				Yonne v. Falkenstein-Schramberg
Ch. Cosi vom Steigstrassle, RO-495			Rowdy von der Mansarde	Mario von Echterdingen, SchH 1
REG. NO. WC 642451		Astor v. Kallenberg, SchH 2		Anamirl v.d. Welser Traunau SchH 3
			Cora von Winterbach	Droll v.d. Brötzingergasse SchH 2
	Lore vom Höllenstein			Kora von der Solitude
			Greif v. Schwabenbräu, SchH 2	Droll v.d. Brötzingergasse SchH 2
		Ella vom Kursaal		Pia von Echterdingen SchH 1
			Herta vom Kursaal, SchH 2	Arko vom Martinsberg, SchH 1
				Jutta vom Burgtobel

Certified Pedigree

SIRE

CH LYN-MAR ACRES ARRAS V KINTA RO-121
TOP PRODUCER 76, 77

- CH. FERDINAND V DACHSWEIL RO-61
  - CH. JARO V SCHLEIDENPLATZ
    - SGR ALF V D BURG HOHENSTEIN
    - SGRN ENKE V SCHLEIDENPLATZ
  - FOLLOW ME'S MICHELE
    - CH. ARRAS VOM STADTHAUS
    - CONNIE V SCHILDGREN
- RODSDEN'S GROSSKIND V HARRAS
  - CH. RODSDEN'S KLUGE V D HARQUE CD
    - BS/INTCH/CH HARRAS V SOFIENBUSCH SchH I
    - CH QUELLE V D SOLITUDE CD
  - BESSY V STUFFELKOPF
    - GRIMM V D HOBERTSBERG SchH I
    - ELLI V D FERNSTUCKSTUBE

CH SRIGO'S ZARRAS V KURTZ RO-791
REG. NO. WC-820345

- BS/INTCH/CH FERNO V WELLESWEILER SchH I RO-5
  - BS/WS/INTCH/CH HARRAS V SOFIENBUSCH SchH I
    - AROO V D HAMMERPARTE SchH I
    - AFRA AUS DEN MAYEN SchH I
  - ALKE V GOHARINGEN SchH II
    - CASTOR V SCHUSSENTAL SchH I
    - FLORA V BUTZENSEE
- CH. SRIGO'S MADCHEN V KURTZ
  TOP PRODUCER 75
  - CH ARNO V KAFLUZH
    - ALEX V GLASTAL SchH I
    - CILLA V D WANNE
  - CH SRIGO'S ECOONIE V LORAC CD
    - SRIGO'S CONSTANCE V MISSLE
      - CH DERUS V WEYERSHOF
      - CH MISSY V STAHL

DAM

CH. ANKA VON GAILINGEN RO-522
TOP PRODUCER 1977
REG. NO. TDC-341715

- CH. DUX VOM HUNGERBUHL SchH I RO-234
  TOP PRODUCER 74, 75, 76, 77
  - KUNO V BUTZENSEE SchH II
    - WOTAN V FILSTALSTRAND SchH I
      - CASTOR V SCHUSSENTAL SchH I
      - BELLA V REMSTAL
    - EDLE V DURBACH
      - INTCH NORD V BLANKENHORN SchH II
      - BONA V LOPODUNUM
  - BRITTA V SCHLOSSBERG
    - BS ALEX V LUDWIGSCHAFEN/SEE SchH II
      - CARLO V D SCHINDWACH SchH III
      - DAGA V REMSTAL
    - EVI V KANZACHTAL
      - BS/WS HEKTOR V BURGTOBEL SchH I
      - CITA V KANZACHTAL SchH II
- CH NATASCHA VOM HOHENREISSACH
  - CH FAGO V HOHENREISSACH
    - CH BINGO V D CHAUSEE
      - BS BLITZ V SCHLOSS WESTERWINKEL SchH II
      - QUANDA V HOHENREISSACH
    - MOLLSER OF RUNNING FOX FARM
      - CH. JARO V SCHLEIDENPLATZ
      - ARIAL OF MAPLE DELL
  - CATJA V FRIEDRICHSBERG
    - GRAF V KALTENTAL SchH I
      - INT CH NORD V BLANKENHORN SchH II
      - VENA V WEIDBACH
    - ASSI V D KASERNE SchH I
      - FETZ V DELBERG SchH II RO-25
      - KATI V FRANKENPLATZ

Still more "goodies" from Earle Adair at the Colonial Rottweiler Specialty for Srigo Kennels. Here Ch. Srigo's Spruce receives Winners Dog owner-handled by Felicia Luburich.

Saigo's "D" Litter

Reg. No. _____
Reg. No. _____

Sire Champion Arno v. Kafuzu
Reg. No. _____
Reg. No. _____

Dam Mismy v. Stahl
Reg. No. _____
Reg. No. _____

Breed Rottweiler
Whelped Sept 22, 1962
Sex _____
Weight 1045
Color. Black and rust
Owner Saigo Kennels 18 Oak Bridge, N.Y.

Alex vom Glastal Sch H I

Alec vom Weilgraben Sch H III

Cilla von der Manne

Hedeberlid's Fan (Danish Import)

Champion Fossus

Champion Valeria

Alex von Gottesbach Sch H I

Nella vom Jakobsbrunnen Sch H I

Christel von Burgtobel

Amny von Salamander Sch H I

Alex von Kongsoweg Sch H I

Nordpylena Fan

Asso v. Mittlebach

Traso v. Hohenzollern
Cita von Wisbachtal
Arno von Hohenheim Sch H I
Lanthippe v. Jacobsbrunnen Sch H I
Aleo v. Effringen Sch H I
Tony v. Hohenreisach
Aleo von Effringer Sch H I
Bora von Der Zaunheide
Xilu vom Kisnethblick
Arsa von Rutliweg
Clane vom Walbachtal Sch III
Lanthippe v. Jakobsbrunnen
Arno von Hohenheim Sch H I
Xenia v. Jakobsbrunnen Sch H I
Astor vom Hornberg
Vera v. Jakobsbrunnen Sch H I

Lord v. Kirkenbuck
Centa von Reichenboor
Arko v. Arbon
Ola v. Limmethlisk
Champion Bata
Rita
Champion Beta
Morco Moal
Nerro von Beshua Sch H I
Iris v. Jakobsbrunnen
Evo von Golburg
Ella von Gigelburg
Troff v. Hohenreisach
Dennis of Crestwood (by Erna)
Krfd
Dajua (by Erwin)

Champion Cita v. Ritliwg

Quitto vom Landhaus

Bills von Hohenreisach

Fox von Nurtingen

Genius von der Michelde Sch H I

Rita vom Jakobsbrunnen

IS/ Pluto von Jakobsbrunnen

Dora vom Hohen-Asperx

Morco Lesa

Champion Morco Nora

Atko vom Wolfbusch

Afra von der Lauterburg

Cuxja, Companion Dog Excellant
D.P.I.

Alex von Gottesbach Sch H II

i certify that this pedigree is true and correct to the best of my knowledge and belief.

PEDIGREE

Ch. Donar v d Neckerstroom

Sire: Basco Triomfactor	Cuno v Hause Kommatt	Juko v Kaltental, Sch.H.2
		Cilli v Luneberg
	Int. Ch. Facha Triomfactor Sch.H.I	Barry v d Neckerstroom
		Cita Triomfactor
Dam: Record Triomfactor	Barry v d Neckerstroom	Int. Ch. Harras v Sofienbusch
		Record v d Brantsberg
	Cita Triomfactor	Pipijn
		Ch. Nanja

PEDIGREE

WC815172
Individual Reg. No.

CH. CENTURION'S CHE VON DER BARR, RO-757

Registered Name of Dog

Date Whelped____January 24, 1974____ Sex__Male__

Breeder____Leslie Fulcher____ Address_1415 Longwood, Norfolk, Virginia_

Owner____Josef and Donna Hedl____ Address_758 Circle Dr., Roselle, Illinois_

PARENTS	GRANDPARENTS	GREAT-GRANDPARENTS	GREAT-GREAT-GRANDPARENTS
SIRE:	Ch. Rodsden's Kluge v d Harque, C.D. RO-50	Int. Ch. & BS, 1960-61-62, Ch. Harras vom Sofienbusch, SchH I	Arno v d Hammerpaote, SchH III
A/C Ch. Northwind's Barras WB49376			Afra aus den Mayen, SchH II
		Ch. Quelle von der Solitude, C.D.	Droll v d Brotzingergasse, SchH III
RO-75			Fanny v d Solitude
	Can. Ch. Northwind's Tina	Ch. Dervis v Weyershof	Carlo v d Gathe, SchH III
			Anka v Gansebruch
		Katherina's Adorn of Townview	Ch. Jaro v Schleidenplatz
			Katherina of Townview
DAM:	Ch. Arco vom Dahl, CDX, SchH III RO-73	Fetz vom Oelberg, SchH II RO-25	Hektor v d Solitude
Rodsden's Ericka Diedre Dahl WB703173			Dora v d Brotzingergasse
		Assy v Borsigplatz	Axel v d Kappenbergerheide, SchH II
RO-157			Andra v Schloss Westerwinkel
	Rafter M's Randee RO-109	Follow Me's Utz	Ch. Arras vom Stadthaus
			Cilli von Kafluzu
		Ch. Rodsden's Nuscha v d Rasse	Int. Ch. & BS, Ch. Harras vom Sofienbusch, SchH I
			Ch. Afra v Hasenacker, C.D. SchH I

407

412-264-4714

BERGLUFT ROTTWEILERS, reg.

PEDIGREE

NAME___Ch. Drossel vom Molzberg_____O.F.A.___RO-132___

A.K.C. REG. NO.___WB-113298_____SEX___Female___DATE WHELPED___November 22, 1967___

BREEDER_____Gretel Emerick, P. O. Box 4067, Tumwater, Washington___

SIRE				
SIRE		Hektor von der Solitude ADRK #36481	Bodo v d Laufenburg ADRK #33796	
	Fetz vom Oelberg SchH 2 ADRK #38416		Flora vom Silahopp ADRK #34127	
		Dora von der Brotzingergasse ADRK #35215	Alex v Glastal ADRK #31011 SchH 1	
			Asta v d Broetzinger-Gasse ADRK #32457 SchH 1	
Cuno vom Kronchen AKC #WA-960251		Brando von Niehorst SchH 3, PFP ADRK #35586	Astor vom Bucheneck ADRK #29695 SchH 3	
	Anka vom Siegerland SchH 2 ADRK #37838		Xanta von Gaisburg ADRK #30802	
		Aga v Castroper Busch SchH 3 ADRK #34760	Arko v Schmiedebrunnen ADRK #30090 SchH 3	
			Cora von Freudenberg ADRK #32568	
DAM		1959-1961 Grand Victor Ch. Emir v Kohlenhof SchH 1	Bobo v Dornberg	
	Victor		Ella v d Fleinerhoehe	
		Darla	Asso v Wittelsbach	
DoJean's Adventorous Miss AKC #WA-466562			Ch. Zola	
	Ch. Gessner's Brenna	Ch. Alf v d Kugellagerstadt	Amor v Sonnenhof	
			Pille v d Luisenhoehe	
		Ch. Cora aus der Lenbachstadt	Arko v Fichtenschlag	
			Blanka v Paarthal	

412-264-4714

BERGLUFT ROTTWEILERS, reg.

P. O. BOX 148, SEWICKLEY, PA. 15143

PEDIGREE

NAME   Ch. Kuhlwalds Little Iodine C.D.   O.F.A.   RO-58

A.K.C. REG. NO. WB-144332   SEX Female   DATE WHELPED December 25, 1967

BREEDER   Paul V. Harris, Box 312, Route #1, Dade City, Florida 33525

SIRE Bodo vom Stuffelkopf ADRK #40499 AKC #WA-765753 OFA #RO-28	Grimm von der Hobertsburg SchH-1 ADRK #37485	Axel von der Kappenbergerheide SchH-2 ADRK #34433	BS Igor vom Kohlwald ADRK #32149 SchH-1
			Dolli von der Immenruh ADRK #33221
		Biene von der Felsenquelle ADRK #35588	Jalk vom Kohlwald ADRK #33166 SchH-1
			Nelli von Hohen-Asperg ADRK #33296
	Elli von der Fruhstuckstube ADRK #36970	Amor vom Sonnehhof SchH-1 ADRK #34524	Dux vom Brunnen ADRK #29899
			Cilli vom Michelsberg ADRK #32858
		Kari Eulenspiegel ADRK #32814	Quitto vom Landhaus ADRK #30076
			Ena Eulenspiegel ADRK #29714 SchH-1
DAM Andra von der Vohsbeckshohe ADRK #40769 AKC #WA-769700	Fetz vom Oelberg SchH-2 ADRK #38416 AKC #WA-845097 OFA #RO-25	Hektor von der Solitude ADRK #36481	Bodo von der Laufenburg ADRK #33796
			Flora vom Silahopp ADRK #34127
		Dora von der Brotzingergasse ADRK #36215	Alex vom Glastal ADRK #31011 SchH-1
			Asta von der Brotzingergasse ADRK #32457 SchH-1
	Centa vom Pestalozzidorf SchH-1 ADRK #38538	LSg 1957 Castor von der Bokerauhle SchH-3 ADRK #34212	Jalk vom Kohlwald ADRK #33166 SchH-1
			Annette vom Brockskamp ADRK #33095
		Hota vom Goldenen Ritter SchH-1 ADRK #37064	Panther Eulenspiegel ADRK #33772 SchH-2
			Cilli vom goldenen Ritter ADRK #35227 SchH-1

CERTIFIED PEDIGREE

BREED _____

CALL NAME __ "R" luten

BREEDER _____

REG. NAME _____ A.K.C. REG. No. _____

COLOR AND/OR MARKINGS. _____

ADDRESS. _____

SEX _____

DATE WHELPED. _____

SELLER _____

Int. Ch., B.S., Ch. Harras vom Sofienbusch Sch H I
{
Champion Rodsden's Kluge v.d. Harque (Sire)
{
Arno von der Hammerpaote Sch H I (Sire)
{
B.S. Igor vom Kohlwald Sch H I (Sire)
Carin v. Zicksackhausen (Dam)

Afra au den Mayen Sch H I (Dam)
{
Arko vom Schmiedtbrunnen Sch H 3 (Sire)
Antje von der Immenruh (Dam)

Ch. Quelle v.d. Solitude (Dam)
{
Droll v.d. Brotzingergasse Sch H 2 (Sire)
{
Alex v. Glastal Sch H I (Sire)
Asta v.d. Brotzinggergasse Sch H I (Dam)

Fanny v.d. Solitude (Dam)
{
Bodo bon der Laufenburg (Sire)
Flora vom Silahopp (Dam)

Int. Ch., B.S., Ch. Harras v. Sofienbusch Sch H I (Sire)
{
Ch. Caspar v.d. Lowenau (Sire)
{
Arno von der Hammerpaote Sch H 3 (Sire)
Afra au den Mayen Sch H I (Dam)

Pedra v. Hohenreissach (Dam)
{
Lardo v. Jackbbsbrunnen Sch H 3 (Sire)
Diana vom Remstal Sch H I (Dam)

Srigo's Honeybun (Dam)
{
Ch. Arno v. Kafluzu (Sire)
{
Alex v. Glastal Sch H I (Sire)
Cilla von der Wanne (Dam)

Int. Ch. Srigo's Eshenda v. Lorac (Dam)
{
Srigo's Constance v. Missle (Dam)
{
Champion Dervis v. Wyershof (Sire)
Champion Missy v. Stazhl (Dam)

Top Winning Rottweiler in Canada 1966

I hereby certify that this Pedigree is true to the best of my knowledge _____ Signed

Am. Dutch and Belg. Ch. Oscar Van Het Brabantpark and Am. Dutch and Lux. Ch. Quanto Van Het Brabantpark. Bred by Mej. A. Huyskens in Holland. Owned by Mrs. Clara Hurley and Michael S. Grossman, U.S.A.

PARENTS	GRAND-PARENTS	GREAT-GRAND-PARENTS
		Brutus v.d. Kurmark
	Moritz v. Silahopp H.D. Free Utrecht	
		Queen v.d. Solitude
Gerlach v.h. Brabantpark H.D. Free Utrecht		Fetz v. Oelberg/I #RO-25 H.D. Free
	Ch. Burga v.h. Brabantpark H.D. Free Utrecht	
		Ch. Rona v.d. Brantsberg
		Axel v. Leitgraben/III
	Einar v.h. Brabantpark H.D. Free Utrecht	
		Ch. Burga v.h. Brabantpark H.D. Free Utrecht
Ch. Onsbessy v.d. Brantsberg H.D. Free Utrecht		Ajax v.d. Brantsberg
	Capsones v.h. Brabantpark H.D. Free Utrecht	
		Ch. Rona v.d. Brantsberg

(8)

BERGLUFT ROTTWEILERS, reg.

P. O. BOX 148, SEWICKLEY, PA. 15143

PEDIGREE

NAME **Ch. Berglufts Carla**   O.F.A. RO-538

A.K.C. REG. NO. **WC-379510**   SEX **Female**   DATE WHELPED **February 23, 1973**

BREEDER **Dorit S. Rogers**

OWNER: **Dorit S. Rogers, P.O. Box 148, Sewickley, Pennsylvania 15143**

SIRE Champion Axel vom Schwanenschlag ADRK #44778 AKC #WB-753207 OFA #RO-166	Furst von der Villa Daheim SchH 1 ADRK #42204	Axel vom Simonskaul SchH 3 39272	Kuno vom Weidbach 27176 SchH 1
			Alli vom Elmenau 37583 SchH 1
		Blanka vom Itzelbach SchH 1 39080	International Ch. Lord vom Blankenhorn SchH 2
			Flori vom Kanzachtal 36572
	Cora vom Grevingsberg ADRK #42691	Quinn von der Schwarzwiese SchH 1 39211	Eddi v d Hobertsburg 36930
			Olli v d Schwarzwiese 37669
		Britta von der Zuflucht 40127	Quinto v d Solitude 38609 SchH 1
			Dolly v d Hardt 36313
DAM Champion Drossel vom Molzberg AKC #WB-113298 OFA #RO-132	Cuno vom Kronchen AKC #WA-960251	Fetz vom Oelberg SchH 2 RO-28 WA-845097 38416	Hektor v d Solitude 36481
			Dora v d Brotzingergasse 35215
		Anka vom Siegerland SchH 2 ADRK #37838	Brando vom Niehorst 35586 PFP SchH 3
			Aga vom Castroper Busch 34760 SchH 3
	DoJean's Adventurous Miss AKC #WA-466562	Victor	1959-1961 Grand Victor Ch. Emir v Kohlenhof SchH 1
			Darla
		Champion Gessner's Brenna	Ch. Alf von der Kugellagerstadt
			Ch. Cora aus der Lenbachstadt

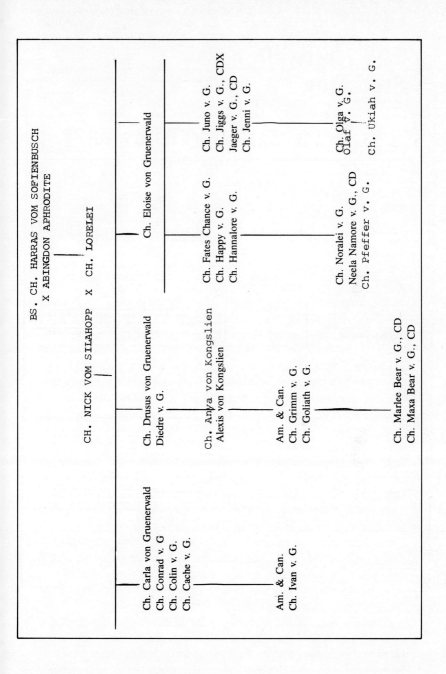

CHAPTER 19

The Rottweiler Stud Dog

Choosing the right stud dog to best complement your bitch is often very difficult. Two principal factors to be considered are the stud's conformation and his pedigree. Conformation is fairly obvious. You want a dog that is a good example of the breed according to the Standard. Understanding a pedigree is a bit more subtle, since this pedigree lists the ancestry of the dog and will also tell you the various bloodlines involved. If you are a novice in the breed, the correct interpretation of a pedigree may be difficult for you. Therefore I suggest that you study the pictures in this book, which include many of the famous dogs whose names you will find; then make an effort to discuss with some of the veteran more experienced fanciers the various dogs behind your proposed stud. Frequently these folks will be personally familiar with the dogs in question, can offer opinions on them and may have access to additional pictures it would benefit you to see.

It is very important that the stud's pedigree be harmonious with that of the bitches you plan to breed to him. Do not rush out to breed to the latest winner with no thought of whether or not he can produce true quality. Take time to check out the progeny of the dog or dogs you are considering.

Breeding dogs is not a money making operation. By the time you pay a stud fee, care for the bitch during gestation, whelp the litter and rear the puppies through shots, worming, etc., you will be fortunate to break even financially once the pups are sold.

Ch. Fate's Chance von Gruenerwald pictured going from the classes to Best of Breed, taking a 4 point major, at San Antonio Kennel Club. Dorothea Gruenerwald, Colorado Springs, CO, owner.

Opposite:
Xavier von Gruenerwald, photographed in July 1980 at eleven years of age. He is owned by Frank Aube, RI. A very handsome headstudy of a beautiful Rott-weiler!

Ch. McCoy von Meadow plays Santa Claus proudly for his five-week-old puppies at the Wormsers' Blue Meadow Kennel.

Your chances of so doing are better if you are breeding for a show quality litter, which will bring higher prices as the pups are sold as show prospects. Therefore your best investment is to use the best dog available regardless of the cost, as you should then wind up with more valuable puppies. Remember, it is as expensive to raise mediocre puppies as to raise top ones, and your chances of financial return are better with the latter, so breed to the best, most suitable dog you can find and do not quibble over the amount you are paying in stud fee. The only reason ever for breeding is to raise quality dogs!

You will have to decide which course you wish to follow when you breed your bitch, as there are three options. These are inbreeding, linebreeding and outcrossing.

Inbreeding is normally considered to be father to daughter, mother to son, brother to sister. Linebreeding is breeding a bitch to a dog belonging originally to the same family, being descended from the same ancestors, such as half-brother to half-sister, niece to uncle, cousin to cousin. Outcross breeding is breeding a dog and a bitch with no or few similar ancestors.

416

Each of these methods has its fans and detractors. I would say that linebreeding is probably the safest course, especially for the novice, who should leave the more sophisticated inbreeding to the very experienced long time breeders who know extremely well the line involved. Outcrossing is usually done when trying to bring in a specific feature, such as shorter backs, better movement, more correct head, etc.

It is every breeder's ambition to develop one's own strain, or bloodline. However, it must be realized that this will take time and at least several generations before you can claim the achievement. The safest bet in embarking on this plan is to select one or two bitches, the best you can buy, from which to breed. In the beginning you really have no need to own a stud dog. In the long run it is less expensive and better sense to pay a stud fee when you are ready to breed a bitch than to purchase a stud dog and to feed him all year. A stud dog does not win any popularity contests with owners of bitches to be bred until he becomes at least a champion, has been successfully "specialed" (i.e., shown as a champion in Best of Breed Only Competition) for awhile and has been at least modestly advertised—all of which adds up to quite a healthy expenditure.

The new breeder's wisest course toward eventual success in dogs, after starting out with one or two really well-bred good type bitches and breeding them to the most suitable studs, is to keep the best bitch puppy from the first several litters. Then you may want to consider keeping a stud dog. By this time your experiences will have developed to the point of enabling you to make a wise selection, either from one of your own litters or in the purchase of such a dog elsewhere.

When you do make the decision to acquire your own stud dog, the greatest care should be taken in his selection. He must be of stable temperament and the highest standard, as he may be responsible for siring many puppies each year. Ideally he should come from a line of excellent dogs on both sides of his pedigree, which in turn should come from good dogs of proven producing ability all the way through. This dog should have no outstanding faults in temperament or conformation and should be of the quality and type to hold his own in the top company of his breed. He should be in good health, virile and a keen stud dog, a proven sire able to transmit his correct qualities to his puppies. You should *never* use at stud an unsound dog or one with serious faults. Not

Ch. Kuhlwald's Trakehner, foundation stud at Bergluft, by Ch. Axel vom Schwanenschlag ex Champion Kuhlwald's Little Iodine, CD, taking Best of Breed at Butler County Kennel Club, May 25, 1974, under judge William Blessing. Mrs. Dorit S. Rogers, owner, Sewickley, PA.

Ch. Falco v h Brabantpark, RO 286, imported from Holland by Rodsden's Rottweilers, Joan R. Klem, owner. A Phillips System Top Producer, Falco has sired more than 20 U.S. champions, many with obedience titles. A member of the Medallion Rottweiler Club Hall of Fame, he holds the title Seiger in Belgium, Luxembourg and Holland.

all champions can pass along their good qualities, and occasionally you will find a truly great stud dog that never gained a championship title due to some unusual circumstance. Bear in mind that the bitch, too, plays her part in the quality of the litter. A stud dog cannot do it all himself, but there is no disputing the fact that a really *great* stud dog will reproduce quality with a wide range of bitches and bloodlines, not with just a few.

If you buy a stud dog, obviously he will not be a puppy but will be a grown, proven male with as many of the above-listed attributes as possible. He will be an expensive investment. But if you proceed toward his selection with study, care and forethought, he will prove an excellent one!

Perhaps you may be so fortunate as to find that a young male, which you have decided to keep from one of your homebred litters because he demonstrates tremendous potential as a show dog, will mature into a stud dog such as we have been discussing. In

419

this case he should be managed with care, for he is a valuable property that can contribute inestimably to your own kennel and to his breed.

Do not permit your young stud dog to be used until he is at least two years old. Then he should be bred to a mature, proven matron who is accustomed to being bred and who will make this first experience pleasant and easy for the stud. A young dog can be turned off breeding forever by a maiden bitch who fights and resists his advances. Never allow this to happen and remember always start out a stud dog with a bitch that is mature, has been bred previously and is of even temperament.

The first breeding should be performed in quiet surroundings with only you and one other person to hold the bitch. Do not make a circus out of this first time, as the experience will determine the dog's feeling about being bred in the future, and if he does not enjoy it or associates it with any unpleasantness, you may well have a problem with which to contend in the future.

Your young stud must permit help with the breeding, as later there will be bitches who will not be co-operative. If right at the beginning you are there assisting and praising him, he will accept and expect this.

Things to have handy before you introduce the dog and the bitch are K-Y jelly, which is the only lubricant that should be used, and either an old stocking or a length of gauze with which to tie the bitch's muzzle should it be necessary to keep her from biting you or the dog. Some bitches put up a fight while others do not.

At the time of the breeding, the stud fee becomes due, and it is expected that it will be paid immediately. Normally a return service is offered if the bitch misses or fails to whelp at least one puppy. Conditions of service are what the owner of the stud dog makes them, and there are no standard rules covering this. The stud fee is paid for the act, not for the result. If the bitch fails to conceive it is customary for the owner to offer a free service, *but this is a courtesy and not something to be considered a right.* Stud dog owners are always anxious to see their clients get good value and to have winning young stock by their dog in the show ring; therefore very few refuse to mate a bitch the second time. However, it is well for both parties to have the terms of the transaction clearly understood at the time of the breeding.

If the return service has been provided and the bitch has missed a second time, that is considered to be the end of the matter and

Ch. Panamint Biene v Hohenwald, one of the excellent Rottweilers imported by the Panamint Kennels of Barbara Dillon.

the owner would be expected to pay a further fee if it is felt that the bitch should be given a third chance with the same dog. The management of a stud dog and his visiting bitches is hard work, and a stud fee has usually been well earned when one service has been achieved, let alone by repeated visits with the same bitch.

Usually a litter is considered to be one live puppy. It is sensible to have a breeding certificate printed which both the owner of the stud dog and the owner of the bitch should sign. This should list in detail the conditions of the breeding as well as the dates of the mating. Also at this time the owner of the bitch should receive a copy of the stud dog's pedigree.

Sometimes arrangements other than cash are made for a breeding, such as the owner of the stud taking the pick of litter puppy. This should be noted on the breeding certificate, along with the following terms: at what age the owner of the sire will select the puppy, whether it is to be specifically of either sex or whether it is to be the puppy which the sire's owner considers to be the best at the time of selection.

The price of a stud fee varies according to circumstances. Usually, to prove a young stud dog his owner will permit the first breeding to be quite inexpensive. Then once a bitch has clearly turned out to be pregnant by him, the fee will rise as he is then a "proven" sire. The sire of champion quality puppies will likely bring a stud fee of at least the purchase price for a show type puppy. That is the usual "rule of thumb." Until at least one champion has finished by your stud dog, the fee will remain an amount equal to the price of any puppy. When his list of champions starts to grow, so does the stud fee and for the sire of consistent champions, litter after litter, the stud fee will rise accordingly.

Almost invariably the bitch must come to the stud dog to be bred. It is important, once you have selected the dog to whom you wish to breed her, that you contact the stud's owner immediately to discuss details. It is the stud owner's prerogative to refuse to breed any bitch deemed unsuitable for the stud dog; therefore the breeding behind your bitch or her pedigree should be submitted. Stud fee and method of payment should be discussed at this time and a decision reached on whether it will be payment in full at the time off mating or pick of litter. The stud owner should be told the approximate date on which the bitch should be ready for breeding (this varies in some cases as bitches do not always run exactly to cycle). It should also be decided whether the bitch will be brought

Am. Bda. Ch. Linguards
Scimatas is owned by Robert G.
Yarnall, Kimbertal Kennels, and
handled by Alan Levine.

to the stud personally by the owner or be shipped in by plane. If the latter, there may be an additional charge for the owner's time, gasoline and any road tolls involved on the round trip to the airport. The normal length of time for keeping your bitch is five days: the day of arrival, the day she is bred, one day in between, the day of the second breeding and the day she is shipped home. Generally this is included in the stud fee. If for some reason the bitch must remain a longer period, then her owner is charged board for this additional time at the normal boarding rate for the breed.

Another phone call must be made to the owner of the stud the day the bitch comes in season to finalize arrangements. I have known of cases where the bitch's owner has waited until the very last moment to advise the stud dog's owner that the bitch is close to being ready, only to find that the stud's owner is away on a circuit and cannot be reached in time. This could have been avoided, and suitable arrangements made, had the bitch's owner communicated at once that the bitch was "in."

It is essential that the owner of a dog offered at public stud have proper facilities for the care of visiting bitches. Nothing can be more heartbreaking than to have a bitch either misbred or, worse still, get away and become lost. There must be a safe place for her

Ch. Pfeffer von Gruenerwald, by Ch. Starkrest's Polo-R ex Ch. Hannelore von Gruenerwald, co-owned by Dorothea Gruenerwald and Frank W. Aube, was owner-handled to her title by Mr. Aube, with whom she is pictured winning at Providence County, 1979.

to be both housed and exercised, and the stud owner should be very certain of this before taking on the responsibility of other people's valuable bitches.

As already mentioned, breeding dogs is no road to riches and should not be entered into with that thought. It may seem that the stud fee you are paying, or charging, is astronomical when in actuality it is far from that. Consider all the time, effort and expense that goes into the making of a stud dog prior to anyone's being interested in using this dog. Once you have such a dog, guard his reputation carefully and do *not* permit him to be bred to just any bitch. Remember, it takes two to make the puppies, and inferior bitches are very unlikely to produce acceptable type and quality no matter how great the stud. You do not need a lot of second-rate puppies turning up with your dog listed as their sire; somehow, people always seem to feel the stud is at fault when a litter goes wrong. So guard your dog's reputation carefully, and remember that it is better to miss out on a stud fee than to risk producing puppies of which you will not be proud!

It is not necessary to describe the actual act of the mating here, as the experienced breeder already knows how and the novice should not undertake a first breeding merely from directions read in a book. Have a breeder or handler friend help you the first few times or, if that is impossible, discuss it with your veterinarian, who most likely will either handle the breeding with you personally or arrange for someone competent to take over.

If a complete "tie" is actually made, then only the one mating is absolutely necessary. However, especially with a maiden bitch or a bitch that has traveled a long, expensive distance, a second breeding, leaving a day in between, is good insurance.

Once the "tie" has been completed and they release, be sure that the male's penis goes completely back into its sheath. He should be allowed a drink of water, a short walk and then be put into his kennel or somewhere alone where he can settle down. Do not allow him to be with other dogs for awhile, as he will have the odor of the bitch still on him and, especially if there are other males, he could become involved in a fight.

The bitch, however, should not be permitted to relieve herself immediately or for at least an hour. In fact many people feel that she should be up-ended for several minutes to permit the sperm to travel further within. She should be crated and kept quiet for an hour in any case.

CHAPTER 20

The Rottweiler Brood Bitch

In a previous chapter we have discussed the selection and purchase of Rottweiler puppies; now we come to the subject of a bitch you plan to use for breeding. Remember, when you start out to make this important purchase, that the bitch you hope will become the foundation of your kennel must be of marvelous bloodlines, good temperament, excellent type and free of major faults or unsoundness. There is no such thing as a "bargain" brood bitch. If you are offered one, be extremely wary and bear in mind that you *must* have the best and that the price will be correctly in ratio to the quality.

Rottweiler people feel quite strongly that the only acceptable reason for breeding a litter is the ambition to produce calm, stable, sound and beautiful Rottweilers that are a credit to their breed and to their heritage—not because one wishes to make a cash profit on a mediocre litter.

No Rottweiler bitch should ever be bred until it has been ascertained that she has OFA Normal hip X rays, no serious or disqualifying faults and no radical departures from the Official Standard. The latter include undershot or markedly overshot bites, several or more missing teeth, ectropion or entropion, long coats, poor temperament in the form of shyness, nervousness or viciousness, or excessive white markings. The only type of bitch that should ever be bred is a good bitch.

Ch. Anka Von Gailingen, by Ch. Dux v Hungerbuhl, SchH I from Ch. Natascha V Hohenreissach, CD Anka was the Number 1 Top Producing Rottweiler Bitch in 1977, and is the dam of seven champions to date. Catherine M. Thompson, owner, Freehold, NJ.

Opposite:
Ch. Gandalf von Stolzenfels, by Ch. Centurion's Che von der Bar ex Ch. Cosi von Steigstrassle, owned by Dr. Evelyn M. Ellman was First Puppy at the 1978 Colonial Rottweiler Club Sweepstakes. He won the 6-9 month Puppy Class there and at the Medallion Rottweiler Club Specialty.

Rottweiler bitches should not be mated until their third season, by which time they should be two years of age or close to it and nearly fully mature. For at least several months prior to this time, you should be watching for that perfect mate for her, attending dog shows with this thought in mind. By now you will probably have become a member of a Rottweiler club and have developed the habit of attending meetings. Possibly this club issues a newsletter which you should be reading. Subscribe to all available breed magazines and an all-breed one or two also, as dogs in other areas thus far unknown to you might be more suitable for your bitch than those situated locally. Be sure to look for a stud dog that is strong in those features where your bitch is weak or lacking. Seek out this dog's progeny at the shows or in pictures, noting carefully whether or not he habitually passes along the features you need. Especially note if there is a similarity between the background of your bitch and those that have produced the progeny you admire.

If you will contact the owners of the stud dogs in which you are interested, they will furnish you with copies of their dogs' pedigrees, which you then can study in relation to that of your bitch. It might be well to discuss your plans with the breeder of your bitch or with other experienced fanciers with whom you are acquainted. You may not always get an entirely unbiased opinion, but discussion is a fine teacher. Listen to what each has to say, consider their comments; then you will be more qualified to reach a knowledgeable and intelligent decision of your own.

Once you are certain of the course you wish to follow, immediately contact the owner of the stud that is your first choice (as advised in the previous chapter) to see if this is agreeable. You will be asked about your bitch's health, soundness, temperament and freedom from serious faults. A copy of her pedigree may be requested, or it may be that a telephone discussion of her background will suffice. The owner of the stud may require that your bitch be tested for brucellosis, which should be done not more than a month before she is due to be bred.

Find out which airport will be used if you must ship the bitch, and also what airlines are available to that airport.

You will find that airlines also have special requirements on the acceptance of animals for shipping. These include weather limitations and types of crates. Weather limits have to do with extreme heat or extreme cold at the destination. The crate problem

Family portrait! This is Ch. Anka Von Gailingen (second from left), with her daughters sired by Ch. Srigo's Zarras V Kurtz. From left are: Von Gailingen's Dream Come True, Ch. Von Gailingen's Dassie Did It and Von Gailingen's Dark Delight, CD. All owned by Catherine M. Thompson, Freehold, NJ.

is a simple one as, if your own is not suitable (which quite possibly it may not be) most of the airlines have available crates which have been designed for the purpose and can be purchased at a fair price. This would be a good investment if you intend to ship fairly frequently. These crates are made of fiber-glass and are the safest type for shipping.

Normally you must notify the airline several days in advance to make a reservation, as they are able to accommodate only a certain number of dogs on each flight. Plan to ship the bitch on about her 8th or 9th day, but be careful to figure *not* to ship on a weekend. Airline schedules may vary then, and some freight offices do not open at all on these days; this means that your bitch may be delayed in reaching her destination. Whenever you can ship on a *direct* flight. Changing planes always carries a certain degree of risk; a dog may be overlooked or wrongly routed at the middle stop, so avoid weekend shipping whenever possible. The bitch must be accompanied by a health certificate obtained from your veterinarian before taking the animal to the airport. Usually it will be necessary to have the bitch there about two hours prior to flight time. Before finalizing arrangements, find out from the stud's owner at what time of day it will be most convenient to have her picked up promptly upon arrival.

If you plan to bring your bitch to the stud dog, it is best in the long run. Some people feel that the trauma of being shipped may cause the bitch to not conceive. Be sure to leave yourself sufficient leeway to assure that you arrive at the proper time for breeding, which is normally the 10th-14th day following the first signs of color. If you want the bitch bred twice, you must allow a day in between. Do not expect the stud owner to house you while you are there. Locate a nearby motel that accepts dogs and make that your headquarters.

Just prior to your bitch coming into season, you should take her for a visit to her veterinarian. She should be checked for worms and receive all necessary booster shots, including one for the new Parvo virus. The brucellosis test can be done then and her health certificate obtained for shipping if she will travel by air. If the bitch is slightly overweight, now is the time to get the excess weight off. She should be in good hard condition, neither overweight nor underweight, at the time of breeding.

Finally the day arrives when you notice the swelling of the vulva, and within a day or two color appears. Immediately phone the owner of the stud dog and settle on the day of shipping or make the appointment for you and the bitch to be there for the breeding. If you are shipping her, the stud fee check should be mailed *immediately,* leaving ample time for it to arrive when the bitch does and mating takes place. Be sure to call the airline for her reservation then, too.

Do not feed the bitch before shipping her. Be certain that she has had a drink of water and has been well exercised before closing her in the crate. Several layers of newspaper topped with some shredded newspaper will make a good bed and can be discarded when she arrives at her destination. Rugs and towels are not good as they may become soiled, necessitating that the stud owner launder them before the return trip. Remember, the bitch should be brought to the airport about two hours before flight time.

First in the Brood Bitch Class, Ch. Ishtar of C.J. (left) with Srigo's Where Eagles Dare. Felicia Luburich handling the dam.

If you plan to take the bitch by car, make certain that you will arrive at a convenient time of day. Do not appear late in the evening. If your arrival in town is not until then, get a good night's sleep and contact the stud owner the first thing in the morning. If possible leave children and relatives at home; they will only be in the way and possibly will not be welcomed by the stud owner. Most stud dog owners prefer not to have an audience on hand during the actual mating.

After the breeding has been accomplished, if you wish to sit and visit for awhile (and the stud owner has the time), return your bitch to the car and her crate. She should not be permitted to urinate for at least one hour following the mating. This is the time when you attend to the business part of the transaction. Pay the stud fee, at which time you should receive your breeding certificate and, if you do not have it already, a copy of the stud's pedigree. The owner of the stud dog does *not* sign or furnish a litter registration until after the puppies have been born.

When you have returned home, you may now settle down to planning for the puppies in happy anticipation of a wonderful litter. A word of caution! Remember that even though she has been bred, your bitch is still an interesting target for all male dogs. So guard her carefully for the next week or until you are certain that her season has entirely ended. This would be no time to have any unfortunate incidents with another dog!

Opposite:
Above: Ch. Pfeffer von Gruenerwald out for a walk with her kids who are four weeks of age. Owned by Dorothea Gruenerwald and Frank Aube. **Below:** An excellent producing bitch of several decades ago, Ch. Pomona, referred to in the Westminster comments, is owned by Mr. and Mrs. Stahl. Dam of Missy von Stahl and other important early Rottweiler champions that helped to establish the breed on the East Coast, her owners, the Stahls, did much to further the best interests of the breed in its early days. Through their von Stahl Kennel, they provided foundation stock for several important kennels.

CHAPTER 21

Gestation, Whelping and Caring For The Litter

Once the bitch has been bred and is back at home, keep an ever watchful eye so that no other male gets to her until at least the twenty-second day of her season. It will still be possible for an unwanted breeding to take place; this would be catastrophic. Remember that she actually can have two separate litters by two different dogs, so *take care!*

In all other ways she should be treated quite normally. It is not necessary for her to have any additives until she is at least four to five weeks pregnant; it is also unnecessary for her to have additional food. It is better not to overfeed the bitch this early, as the puppies do not strain her resources until the last stages of her pregnancy. A fat bitch is not an easy whelper.

Controlled exercise is good and necessary for the bitch. She should not be permitted to just lie around. At about seven weeks along, the exercise should be slowed down to several walks daily, preferably on leash.

At four to five weeks of the pregnancy, calcium may be added to the diet, and at seven weeks the one meal a day may be increased to two meals with some nutritional additives in each meal. Canned milk may be added to her meal at this time.

A week before she is due to whelp, your Rottweiler bitch should be introduced to her whelping box, so that she will have accustomed herself to it and feels at home there by the time the puppies arrive. She should be encouraged to sleep there, but permitted to come and go as she pleases.

Litter sisters at the age of 13 years are (left) Ch. Danka vom Molzberg and Ch. Drossel vom Molzberg. Owned by Bergluft Rottweilers, Reg.

Opposite:
Ch. Lorelei, dam of six champions in three litters. Owned by William and Dorothea Gruenerwald, Colorado Springs, CO.

The box should be sufficiently roomy for her to lie down and stretch out, but not too large or the pups will have too much room in which to roam and they may get chilled if they are too far from the mother. Be sure that there is a "pig rail" for the box, which will prevent the puppies from being crushed against the side of the box. The room where the box is placed, either in the home or in the kennel, should be free from drafts and should be kept at about 70 degrees Fahrenheit. In winter, it may be necessary to have an infra-red lamp over the whelping box, but guard against placing this too low or too close to the puppies.

Keep a big pile of newspapers near the box. You'll find that you never have enough when you have a litter, so start accumulating them ahead of time. Also keep handy a pile of clean towels, a pair of scissors and a bottle of alcohol. Have all of this ready at least a week before the bitch is due to whelp because you never know when she may start.

The day or night before she is due, the bitch will become restless, in and out of her box and in and out of the door. She may refuse food, and at this point her temperature will start to drop. She will begin to dig at and tear up the newspapers in her box, shiver and generally look uncomfortable. Only you should be with the bitch at this point. She does not need an audience. This is not a sideshow, and several people hovering around may upset the bitch so much that she will hurt the puppies. Stay nearby, but do not fuss over the bitch too much. Eventually she will settle down in her box and begin to pant and very shortly thereafter start to have contractions, and soon the puppy will begin to emerge, sliding out with the contractions. The mother immediately should open the sack, cut the cord and then clean up the puppy. She will also eat the placenta, which you should permit. Once the puppy is cleaned, it should be placed next to the bitch unless she is showing signs of having the next one immediately. The puppy will start looking for a nipple on which to nurse. You should make certain that it is able to latch on to it successfully.

If a puppy is a breech (i.e., born head first), then you must watch carefully to see that it is completely delivered as quickly as possible and the sack removed fast so that the puppy does not drown. Sometimes even a normally positioned birth will seem extremely slow in coming. Should this occur, you might take a clean towel and as the bitch contracts pull the puppy out, doing so gently and with care. If, once the puppy is delivered, it shows little

436

Mother and youngsters doing fine! Ch. Orlando von Ocala with her four-day-old puppies by Ch. McCoy von Meadow. Owned by Robert and Donna Wormser.

sign of life, take a rough (turkish) towel and rub quite briskly back and forth, massaging the chest. Continue this for about fifteen minutes, and be sure that the mouth is free from liquid. It may be necessary to try mouth-to-mouth breathing. This is done by pressing the puppy's jaws open and, using a finger, depressing the tongue, which may be stuck to the roof of the mouth. Then blow hard down the puppy's throat. Bubbles may pop out of its nose, but keep on blowing. Rub with the towel again across the chest and try artificial respiration, pressing the sides of the chest together slowly and rhythmically, in and out, in and out. Keep trying the one method or the other for at least fifteen minutes before giving up. You may be rewarded with a live puppy that otherwise would not have made it.

This puppy should not be put back with the mother immediately, as it must be kept warm. Put it in a cardboard box near a warm stove, or on a heating pad or, if it is the time of year for your heating system to be operating, near the radiator until the rest of the litter has been born. Then it can be put in with the others.

Srigo's Arieh of Ram Island, a pointed male from the first Srigo Rottweiler litter, with Garth Conover, son of the breeder, Felicia Luburich.

The bitch may go for an hour or better between puppies, which is fine, so long as she seems comfortable and is not straining or contracting. I would not allow her to remain unassisted for more than an hour if she does continue to contract. Now is the time to call your veterinarian, whom you should have alerted ahead of time of the possibility. He may want the bitch brought in so that he can examine her and perhaps give her a shot of pituitary extract. In some cases the veterinarian may find that a Caesarian operation is necessary if a puppy is lodged in some manner which makes normal delivery impossible. Sometimes this occurs due to size; sometimes it is just that the puppy is turned wrong. If the bitch does require a section, the puppies already born must be kept warm in their cardboard box with a heating pad under the box.

Once the section is done, get the bitch and the puppies home. Do not attempt to put the pups in with the bitch until she is at least fairly conscious as she may unknowingly hurt them, but do get them back as soon as possible, so they can start nursing.

If the mother lacks milk at this point, the puppies must be fed by hand, kept very warm and held to the mother's teats several times a day in order to stimulate and encourage the secretion of milk, which should start shortly.

Assuming that there is no problem and the bitch whelps naturally, you should insist that she go out to exercise, staying just long enough to make herself comfortable. She can be offered a bowl of milk and a biscuit, but then she should settle down with her family. Be sure to clean out the whelping box and change the newspapers so that she will have a fresh bed.

Actually, unless some problem occurs, there is little you must do now about the puppies until they become three to four weeks old. Keep the box cleaned and with new papers. When the pups are a couple of days old, towels should be tacked down to the bottom of the box so that the puppies will have traction when they move.

If the bitch has difficulties with her milk supply, or if you should be so unfortunate as to lose the bitch, then you must be prepared to either hand feed or tube feed the puppies if they are to survive. I prefer tube feeding as it is much faster and easier. If the bitch is available, it is best that she continue to clean and care for the puppies in normal fashion except for the supplementary food you will provide. But if anything has happened to prevent her from doing this, you must learn to gently rub the puppy's abdomen with wet cotton to make it urinate, and the rectum should be gently rubbed to open the bowels. This must be done after each feeding.

Newborn puppies must be fed every 2-3 hours around the clock. The puppies must be kept warm during this time. Have your veterinarian show you how to tube feed. Once learned, it is really very simple.

After a normal whelping, the bitch will require additional food to enable her to produce sufficient milk. She should be fed twice daily now, in addition to some canned milk several times during the day.

At two weeks old, you should clip the puppies' nails, as they are needle sharp at this stage and can hurt or damage the mother's teats and stomach as the pups hold on to nurse.

What could be more
adorable than a baby
Rottweiler? This one
belongs to Frank Aube,
and is five weeks old.
Below: Champion Pana-
mint Prise v Rheintal,
one of the handsome
Rottweilers imported by
Barbara Dillon.

WINNERS BITCH
CUDAHY K.C.
AUGUST 7, 1976
OLSON PHOTO

Between three to four weeks of age, weaning of the puppies should be started. A very small quantity of scraped raw beef may be offered a couple of times daily for the first few days. This is prepared by scraping off slices of beef with a spoon so that none of the gristle or tough membranous material is included. Then by the third day you can mix up ground puppy chow with warm water as directed on the package, offering it four times daily. By now the mother should be kept away from the puppies and out of the box for several hours at a time, until when the pups reach five weeks, she is left in with them only overnight. By the time they are six weeks old, the puppies should be entirely weaned, the mother checking on them only with occasional visits.

Most veterinarians recommend a temporary DHL (distemper, hepatitis, leptospirosis) shot when the puppies are six weeks of age. This remains effective for about two weeks. Then at eight weeks, the series of permanent shots begins for the DHL protection. It is also recommended, since the prevalence of the dreaded new Parvovirus, to discuss the advisability of having these shots, too, for your puppies. Each time the pups go in for shots you should bring stool samples to be checked for worms, even though the previous ones may have proved negative. Worms go through various stages of development and may be present although they do not appear positive in every check, so do not fail to keep after this.

The puppies should be fed four times daily until they are three months old. Then cut back to three feedings daily. By six months old, two meals daily are sufficient. Some people feed their dogs twice daily throughout their lifetime; others go to once a day when the puppy reaches a year of age.

The ideal time for puppies to go to new homes is between eight and twelve weeks. Be sure that they take with them to their future owners a diet list and schedule of the shots they have received and those they still will need. These should be included with the registration application and a copy of the pedigree.

CHAPTER 22

Showing Your Rottweiler

The showing of a dog can become a very exciting and absorbing hobby, depending on how seriously you attempt it and the extent of your goals. Obviously, no one enjoys an unsuccessful hobby. Therefore it is assumed that when you decide to show a dog, you are doing so for the purpose of winning.

The first step, of course, is to have purchased a puppy with this thought in mind. It is not too probable that the one you assured the breeder was to be "only a pet" can step into the ring and win for you. Maybe once out of every several hundred times this might happen, but the odds are more likely against it.

Once you have acquired your show prospect puppy, from that point forth everything should be geared towards making him a show dog. Careful attention to his diet is essential, but then that is true of every puppy that you want to grow up strong and healthy! You must not let him develop into a fat dog, nor do you want him overly thin. Never cut corners on the quality of food you give your dog. The best possible nourishment for a Rottweiler comes through a high grade, high protein prepared dry food, which is excellent for keeping teeth and gums healthy as well as for the total health of the dog. Modern fanciers have no idea how easy this has been made for them in this regard. This is actually a case of what is the simplest food to handle and the least expensive to provide being also the best. There are literally dozens of splendid com-

Ch. Srigo's Zoom v Kurtz, Felicia Luburich, breeder-owner-handler, taking Best of Opposite Sex from the Open Class under Mel Downing, Westminster 1976.

Opposite:
Ch. Srigo's Big Opportunity is baiting for the attention of the judge, Peggy Adamson, as the remainder of the class awaits its turn. Felicia Luburich breeder, owner handler. May 1978.

mercial dog foods available at your grocery store or super-market. If you have not had any specific recommendation from your veterinarian or the breeder of your puppy, read the labels, shop around a bit, try a few to see which the dog seems to enjoy most. These foods provide balanced, fortified nourishment and are actually far more useful to the dog than the old "home cooking" method. If you wish, you can add meat. Canned meat which is especially prepared for the purpose is considered by most to be preferable to meat fresh from the butcher as it, too, is fortified with all the things your dog needs most for correct nourishment. Any further suggestions on diet should be discussed with your veterinarian or with the person who bred your puppy and who is familiar with his background. Do not just buy the cheapest you can find. Provide one of the good products from a reputable company, and you will have the satisfaction of knowing that you are giving the dog the best.

Whether or not your puppy is to be a show dog, he should be well started on his obedience training by the time you are planning to take him to shows. To this you will need to add other lessons: gaiting properly on a show lead and standing "stacked" for the examination of the judge. If there are handling classes available in your area, it is more fun to join one and attend classes than just working it out for yourself at home. But should that prove impossible, watch carefully how others do it, then see if you can't master the procedure on your own.

The puppy should be taught to walk to your left side, sedately at your heel, neither forging ahead nor dragging behind. Additionally, he must learn to be "set up" or stacked to show his good conformation and permit the judge to examine him. The puppy must learn to have his teeth checked without showing resentment. Considerate judges permit the exhibitor to do it himself owing to the danger of the parvo virus, but some of the more old fashioned still consider that only they can accomplish their mission with their own two hands. The puppy must be prepared not to resent this, as it is something which he will have to contend with throughout his show career. Since counting teeth is a necessity owing to the breed disqualifications, the examination is more tedious for the Rottweiler than for the majority of breeds, so start at once, right from a few months old, to accustom him to the procedure. The first step is for you to learn the easiest way of doing it, which an experienced Rottweiler exhibitor can show you.

Above: An interesting picture of an exciting day. From left are: Ch. Srigo's Opportunity and How, owner-handled by Felicia Luburich to Best of Breed; Ch. Srigo's Xclusive v Kurtz, Winners Bitch; Ch. Koka's Degen v Burga, Winners Dog and Srigo's Zephre v Kurtz, Reserve Winners Bitch from the Puppy Class. **Below:** Ch. Srigo's Zinger v Kurtz, CD, OFA, owned by Felicia Luburich, East Brunswick, NJ.

Above: Ch. Marja Elka von Heidel, by Merrymore's Pastis ex Tara von Nadriches. Just six months old at her first show, Elka won Winners Bitch, Best of Winners and Best of Opposite Sex over "specials", receiving both her majors. She continued on to finish in short order with Best of Breed awards from the classes. As a "special" she has been Best of Breed many times, often over top male "specials" and Specialty winners. Owned by Jacqueline Puglise, Marja Kennels; handled exclusively by Ross Petruzzo, PHA. **Below:** Good Rottweilers retain their excellence over the years. At the age of 7½ Jim and Wanda White's Group Winning Ch. Windmakers Arlo der Gremlin shows that he still possesses the beauty that made him so successful in the ring.

446

Above: The prophetically named Srigo's I Am Invincible going Best in Sweepstakes at the Colonial Rottweiler Club, 1979. **Below:** Ch. McCoy Von Meadow finishing his championship with four majors at 13 months. Owned by Donna and Bob Wormser.

Above: Am., Can. Ch. Srigo's Flight of the Eagle, Am., Can. CD, owned by Mr. and Mrs. Arthur L. Rikel, pictured with the Rikel youngsters, his great friends. **Below:** Ch. Srigo's Madchen v Kurtz taking Winners Bitch and Best of Opposite Sex at the Colonial Rottweiler Club Specialty under Peter Knoop. Owned by Lucille and Donald Kurtz.

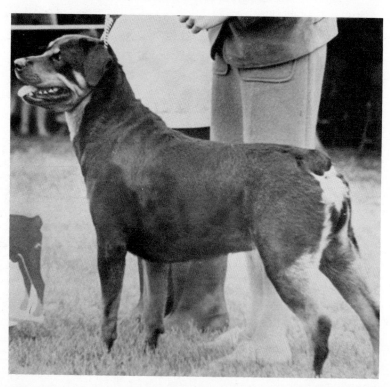

For a great deal of helpful advice, if you are planning a show career for your dog, I strongly recommend that you read my new book, *Successful Dog Show Exhibiting,* also from T.F.H. and available where you purchased this one.

Grooming a Rottweiler is really quite simple. There should be little in the way of trimming, the important part being that he present a clean, neat appearance. If you feel that bathing is a necessity, do it in a bath tub using a mild baby shampoo. Lather up well and rinse very thoroughly, as shampoo left in the coat can cause itching and present other problems. A drop of mineral oil in each eye before you start lathering is useful in preventing irritation from any lather that may come in contact with the eye. Have the water a comfortable, lukewarm temperature and use a good spray for wetting down and rinsing. Since Rottweilers love the water anyway, a bath can be made a pleasant procedure which they may well come to enjoy; this makes it easier for you too.

Toenails should be clipped or filed back. The teeth should be cleaned by your veterinarian if tartar accumulates. Of course, the puppy's preventive shots should be entirely up-to-date prior to your taking him where other puppies will assemble.

Match Shows are the ideal starting place for your dog's show career. These are regarded as more or less "practice sessions," where the judges are patient and your inexperienced youngster has the opportunity to get the feel of things. There are fun matches and more formal match shows, but none are on so "do-or-die" a level as the point shows. Attend as many of these as you can before you venture into the latter. To begin with, it is far less expensive, and why pay all those high-priced entry fees until the dog is ready and sufficiently well behaved to meet this more sophisticated competition?

When you do start out to the point shows, enter at first in the puppy classes, novice or American-bred so long as you need to get the dog adjusted and showing nicely. Importations can be entered only for Open, but if you have a puppy that was born in the United States of a mating that took place here, it will be to your advantage to take it slowly in some of the less filled classes than to get right in with all the professionals and mature dogs before you and your dog are ready.

CHAPTER 23

Obedience In The United States

W e cannot too strongly emphasize the fact that if your Rottweiler is to develop into a pleasant, well adjusted, manageable member of your family, some sort of obedience training is an absolute necessity. These dogs are just too strong and powerful to be permitted to have their own way, and one that is untrained can actually become a real menace. It is to be remembered that with a dog, either you or he will become the boss, and while it may be cute to some people to have a *small*, willful disobedient dog, very definitely it is not so in the case of a Rottweiler.

At the very least, your Rottweiler must understand and obey the commands "come," "down," "stay," "heel" and "sit." You can work with and teach him at home if you have the patience, and you will find available excellent books on the subject extremely helpful in teaching you how to proceed. Or, which is perhaps more fun, you can join a local obedience club. The American Kennel Club, the breeder from whom you purchased the dog, your veterinarian or a local pet supply shop can tell you where to find one if you do not know. It sometimes makes the task seem easier. Then, too, you can place your dog in the hands of a trainer who will do it for you. The latter method I would find the least satisfactory, as one then misses the opportunity of establishing a warmer, better relationship with the dog which develops through working together in obedience.

Ch. Graudstark's Irma La Deuce, CD, famous winner and great producing bitch owned by Bob and Lavinia Bolden and handled by Bert Halsey.

Opposite:
Ch. Grunberg Anker v.d. Adel, CD, owned and trained by Art and Ruth Twiss, Reading, MA.

Panamint Ideal Impression, CD, TDX, and working on CDX. Barbara Dillon owner.

Opposite:
Am., Can., Mex., Int. Ch. Rodsden's Goro v Sofienbusch, UDT, TDX, SchH 1, RO 76, going over the
Utility Bar in obedience competition. Goro is owned,
trained and handled by Jim Fowler.

Von Gailingen's Dark Delight, CD and Ch. Von Gailingen's Dassie Did It
taking breeder-owner Catherine Thompson for a ride.

If you are going to do it yourself, some basic rules are in order:
you remain calm and confident in attitude, never lose your
temper and punish the dog unjustly, never resort to cruelty, and
be quick and lavish with praise when your command is correctly
followed. Brutality in training will result in a resentful, cowed
dog—hardly a happy attitude. Remember that the Rottweiler is
devoted and anxious to please his master and this desire is the one
that should be encouraged in obedience training.

Formal obedience training can be followed by entering the dog
in obedience competition to work towards an obedience degree or
several. Obedience trials are held in conjunction with the majority of all-breed conformation dog shows and also frequently as
Specialty events. For a list, ask your dog's breeder or contact the
American Kennel Club.

In American Kennel Club recognized Obedience Trials, one
works to attain the following degrees: Companion Dog (C.D.),
Companion Dog Excellent (C.D.X.), Utility Dog (U.D.) and
Tracking Dog (T.D.), the latter fully covered in its own chapter.
These degrees are earned by receiving three "legs," or qualifying scores, at each level at A.K.C. Trials. All the dogs competing
at the same level perform the same exercises, some of which are

454

individual, others in a group. The degrees must be earned in order, with one completed prior to starting on the more advanced. The dogs are scored points on how well they perform each exercise, working for qualifying scores. There is a booklet available fully explaining the Rules and Regulations of American Kennel Obedience Trials which is available for the asking from 51 Madison Avenue, New York, NY 10010.

The ultimate title possible to attain for obedience work is that of Obedience Trial Champion (O.T.C.). To gain this one, dogs must receive the required number of points by placing first or second in Open or Utility after earning their U.D.

The exercises which must be performed for attainment of the title Companion Dog (C.D.) are heel on leash; heel free; stand for examination; recall; long sit and long stay. When this has been completed and the title earned, then one becomes eligible to compete for Companion Dog Excellent (C.D.X.), where the required exercises are heel free, drop on recall, retrieve over high jump, broad jump, long sit, long down. From there the dog graduates into the Utility Dog Classes (U.D.), where he must do scent discrimination (leather article), scent discrimination (metal article), signal exercise, directed retrieve, directed jumping, group stand for examination.

The American Kennel Club does not recognize Schutzhund training, nor does it issue titles for it. It is available in the United States through Schutzhund clubs, which probably your dog's breeder would know how to contact if you wish. It must be pointed out, however, that promiscuous or incorrectly done or partial Schutzhund training can be extremely dangerous, as a dog thus trained becomes comparable to a loaded gun and must be knowledgeably managed thereafter. A trained attack dog in irresponsible hands is something no one wishes to see. For all normal purposes it is my opinion that a Rottweiler, following his natural instincts of protection of his loved ones and their property, provides as well equipped a canine protector as one should need in a family pet, and Schutzhund training should be reserved for dogs that will be doing police work or other highly specialized guard dog duty. If you do decide to have a dog trained for Schutzhund work, make careful inquiry to ascertain that the person in whose hands you are placing it is really qualified to do a competent job and will return to you (or sell you) a completely trained reliable animal.

CHAPTER 24

Obedience: Top Ten Rottweilers 1973-1979

In 1973, the American Rottweiler Club embarked upon an effort to recognize the best working Rottweilers in the sport of obedience. But the system it devised did not appear to be operating with total equity and raw scores and class placements recorded in 1973 were not wholeheartedly endorsed by obedience enthusiasts. From 1974 through 1978, a different system was developed around a weighted score, but with this system it was found that dogs competing at higher levels were not being recognized. In 1979 a third system was put into use encompassing the higher skill levels as well as the lower. This system aimed at encouraging Rottweiler owners to continue in obedience beyond the Companion Dog degree and to give recognition to those dogs that scored well at the CDX and Utility levels as well.

For 1979 top obedience Rotties listed below, the "Average" column reflects the average of all qualifying scores earned from the number of events appearing in parenthesis in the "Class" column.

Level 1. Companion Dog, Companion Dog Excellent and Utility Dog Titles.
Level 2. Companion Dog, Companion Dog Excellent Titles Plus Utility Scores.
Level 3. Open and Utility Class Combined. 3 Open, 3 Utility Scores after U.D. Degree.
Level 4. C.D.X. and U.D. Titles.
Level 5. Utility Dog Title.
Level 6. C.D.X. Title plus Utility Scores.
Level 7. C.D. and C.D.X. Titles.
Level 8. C.D.X. Title.
Level 9. C.D. Title plus C.D.X. Scores.
Level 10. C.D. Title.

Ch. Kundri von Stolzenfels, CD, finished her championship with four majors and 17 points, owner-handled all the way by Michael Baker, Tucson, AZ. Kundri is pictured going Best of Breed from the classes under Judge Langdon Skarda.

Opposite:
With all those rosettes in the background, future champions Srigo's Eshenda v Lorac and Srigo's Elorac Missle Again give an example of the type of puppy at Srigo Kennels.

1979 TOP OBEDIENCE ROTTWEILERS

	Class	Average
# 1. Mondberg's Donnamira v Beier, U.D., G.L. Beck. Level 3	(4) Open (3) Utility	193.8 187.0
# 2. Lucene's Rhoda of Rajamul, U.D. J.A. Sudinski and J.G. Hendrick Level 5	(5) Utility	188.1
# 3. Autumn Von Steinig Bucht, C.D.X., S.K. Schaffer. Level 6	(3) Open (2) Utility	196.3 190.7
# 4. Gertase Kuchen, C.D.X., T.D., F. and D. Johnson. Level 7	(4) Novice (3) Open	193.6 192.8
# 5. Elsa von Arktos, C.D.X., L. Husith. Level 8	(10) Open	193.9
# 6. Cerberus Avatar v Kleinholz, C.D., J.R. and M.A. Adams.	(3) Novice (1) Open	189.8 188.5
# 7. Medeah's Shane De Michaele, C.D., C.M. Nunez and K.E. Twineham.	(6) Novice	197.2

Only seven places were awarded in 1979. C.D. (Companion Dog) titles were won by 120 Rottweilers in 1979; 25 Rotties won their C.D.X. (Companion Dog Excellent) titles; five won Utility Dog titles and 14 won Tracking Dog titles. A total of 164 obedience titles were awarded that year to Rottweilers by the American Kennel Club.

Obedience awards given from 1974 through 1978 were based on number of points earned. Points given during those years were distributed according to actual scores attained in obedience trials as follows:

170-173½— 1 Point		186-188½— 6 Points
174-176½— 2 Points		189-191½— 7 Points
177-179½— 3 Points		192-194½— 8 Points
180-182½— 4 Points		195-197½— 9 Points
183-185½— 5 Points		198-200 —10 Points

Above: Tracking for the TD title and for fun is Ch. Rodsden's Willa v d Harque, UDT, RO 321. Owned, trained and handled by Jane Wiedel. **Below:** Flying high over the Open 36 inch high jump is Am., Can. Ch. Rodsden's Elko Kastanienbaum CDX, TD, RO 1448.

1978 TOP TEN OBEDIENCE ROTTWEILERS

During 1978, 114 Rottweilers won their C.D. titles; ten won their C.D.X. while three were awarded their U.D. titles. Tracking Dog titles (T.D.) were awarded to 18.

	Class	Points
# 1. Merrymore's Jupiter, C.D. R.C. Mead.	(10) Novice	87
# 2. Mondberg's Donnamira v Beier, C.D.X. G.L. Beck.	(4) Novice (5) Open	70
# 3. Roc of Fedelis, C.D.X. V.F. Hart and C.A. Peterbaugh.	(3) Open (2) Utility	41
# 4. Ch. Welkerham's Rommel, U.D. R. Welker.	(3) Open (4) Utility	36
# 4. Tegelhagen's Cassandra, C.D. R. and R. Adams.	(4) Novice	36
# 5. Von Brukas Shasta, C.D. B. and K. Billings.	(5) Novice	35
# 6. Burpow's Titania Ekita, C.D.X. S.L. Powers.	(2) Novice (3) Open	33
# 7. Stablemate's Vasili Alexeen, C.D. A.L. Bassett.	(4) Novice	30
# 7. Ch. Northwind's Indigo, C.D., T.D. S.J. Suwinski.	(4) Novice	30
# 7. Ch. Rodsden's Bruin v Hungerbuhl, C.D., J. and G. Kittner.	(4) Novice	30
# 8. Germain's La Premiere, C.D. J.T. and K.M. Germain.	(2) Novice (2) Open	29
# 9. Rondar's April Dawn, C.D. R.M. Peterson.	(4) Novice	28

Am., Can. Ch. Rodsden's Kato v Donnaj at 2½ years going over the high jump. Owned and trained by Jan Marshall, Donnaj Kennels, who describes herself as ' willing slave to Kato.' **Below**: A stunning picture of a beautiful Rottweiler! "Star" or, more formally, Ch. Erdelied Astraea, CD, is owned by Ms. C.L. Rawlings, Coral Gables, FL. "Star" is a daughter of Ch. Donnaj Vt. Yankee of Paulus, CDX, ex Doroh's Erinys Von Eberle, CD, Am., Can. UD.

9. Georgian Court Excalibre, C.D.   (4) Novice   28
   J. and P. Uribarri.

#10. Nightshadow After The Storm,
   C.D.   (4) Novice   27
   R. and S. McMillan.

#10. Ch. Grandstarr's Pegasus, C.D.   (4) Novice   27
   K. MacLachlan.

1977 TOP TEN OBEDIENCE ROTTWEILERS

C.D. titles were awarded to 91 Rottweilers during 1977, C.D.X. titles to 17 with three dogs winning their U.D. titles and nine achieving T.D.

	Class	Points
# 1. Ch. Welkerhaus Rommel, U.D. R. Welker.	(7) Open (4) Utility	64
# 2. Elsa von Arktos, C.D., L. Huseth.	(6) Novice	48
# 3. Lyndhausen's Chancellor, C.D.X. L. Randall.	(3) Novice (3) Open	40
# 4. Ch. Mason von Odenwald, C.D. S. Oven and P. Hillmuth.	(4) Novice	37
# 5. Ch. Big Bo Jangles, C.D.X. L.E. and L.A. Powers.	(4) Open (1) Utility	34
# 5. Riegeles Caribe of Rosewood, C.D. R. and J. Rose.	(4) Novice	34
# 6. Max Von Sydow, C.D. P. and P. Wilson	(4) Novice	33
# 7. Judge Roy Bean v Morgen, C.D. J.E. Flores.	(4) Novice	32

Srigo's Johnny Come Lately, in El Salvador. This big boned, beautifully headed youngster took Best of Breed in Guatemala when six months old. Bred by Felicia Luburich, East Brunswick, NJ.

7. Ch. Julias Frans, C.D.   (5) Novice   32
    S. Hammarstrom.

8. Rodsden's Winterhawk, C.D.   (4) Novice   30
    D. Weninger.

9. Ch. Ebonstern Black Bart, C.D.   (4) Novice   29
    G. and S. Stiles and C. Wheeler.

9. Merrymoore's Fancy Fay, C.D.   (4) Novice   29
    Mrs. S. Carter.

9. Sir Duke of Rotwein, C.D.   (5) Novice   29
    T.W. Bailey.

#10. Merrymoore's Happy Hour, C.D.   (3) Novice   28
    R.E. Eisenhut.

#10. Ch. La Jon's Amos, C.D.   (5) Novice   28
    R.S. Wehling.

#10. Kyna Von Odenwald, C.D.   (5) Novice   28
    M. Schmidt and T. and
    C. Woodward.

1976 TOP TEN OBEDIENCE ROTTWEILERS

In 1976, 61 C.D. titles were awarded; ten Rotts won C.D.X. titles; three achieved their U.D. degrees while T.D.'s were awarded to five.

		Class	Points
# 1.	Ch. Welkerhaus Rommel, U.D. Mrs. R. Welker.	(11) Open (4) Utility	105
# 2.	Rodsden's Windsong Drava, C.D. R.M. Rose.	(5) Novice	43
# 3.	Rodsden's Chopper Du Trier, U.D. Mrs. L. Mathis.	(4) Open (2) Utility	39
# 4.	Adoram Hanz, C.D. D.W. Houchins.	(5) Novice	36
# 5.	Metzgerhund Blitz Aus Lamm, C.D., D.J. Kopec. Jr.	(4) Novice	35
# 6.	Ch. Northwind's Gino, C.D. E. Kneip.	(3) Novice (2) Open	34
# 6.	Panamint Sultan v Rheintal, C.D. D. and M. Teague.	(5) Novice	34
# 7.	Megan Von Der Insel, C.D. C. Neale.	(4) Novice	32
# 8.	Lucene's Rhoda of Kajamul, C.D. J.G. Hendrick and J.A. Sudinski	(4) Novice	31
# 8.	Merrymoore's Coco Moco, C.D. L. and J.C. Mauck.	(4) Novice	31
# 9.	Rodsden's Will V.D. Harque, U.D. H. Kane.	(20) Open (1) Utility	28
# 9.	Ch. Big Bo Jangles. L.E. and L.A. Powers.	(4) Open	28

On the job! Panamint Rottweilers bringing in the herd. Barbara Dillon, owner.

#10.	Doroh's Edrea v Eberle, C.D. J. and C. Epperly.	(3) Novice	25
#10.	Freeger's Lotta Gatstuberget, C.D.X., P.S. and C.H. Wood, Jr.	(4) Open	25
#10.	Grandstark's Ischia, C.D. R. Compton.	(4) Novice	25
#10.	Mondberg's Bulger v Breier, C.D. P.G. Pinsz.	(3) Novice	25
#10.	Panamint Saphir v Rheintal, C.D. L.E. Ang.	(4) Novice	25

1975 TOP TEN OBEDIENCE ROTTWEILERS

Points

# 1. Ch. Rodsden's Will V.D. Harque, C.D., H. Kane.	134
# 2. Rodsden's Chopper Du Trier, U.D. L.L. Mathis.	90
# 3. Jiggs v Gruenerwald, C.D. D. and A. Bottenfield.	57
# 4. Anni v Daralheim, C.D. D.V. and A.K. Wolf.	35

Ch. Dux v Hungerbuhl, RO 234, SchH I, imported by Dr. Eken and P.G. Rademacher left his distinct mark in the American show ring and was a top producer in the 1970's.

5. Rodsden's Scherge v Freiheit, C.D.
   W.P. Sloboda.

6. Ch. Welkerhaus Rommel, C.D.   32
   Mrs. R. Welker.

6. Rocky Ramon R., C.D.   32
   C.S. O'Leary.

6. Beck's Ebony Eva, C.D.   32
   J.C. Beck.

6. Arita v Buell, C.D.   32
   K.E. and S.R. Twineham.

7. Ch. Freeger's Nero, C.D.X.   29
   J.M. Wejrle.

8. Ch. Rodsden's Frolich Burga, C.D.   28
   J. and G. Kittner.

8. G.K.S. Madchen, C.D., J.C. Dean.   28

9. Kuhlwald's Yenta, C.D.   27
   A.P. Walsh.

#10. Dacco v Arktos, C.D.   26
   D. and C. Hammonds.

1974 TOP TEN OBEDIENCE ROTTWEILERS

Points

1. Ch. Rodsden's Helsa v Eberle,   422
   U.D., J.M. and C.S. Epperle.

2. Rodsden's Chopper Du Trier, U.D.   296
   Mrs. L. Mathis.

3. Rodsden's Will v.d. Harque, U.D.   170
   H. Kane.

Ch. Srigo's Zinger v Kurtz, CD, OFA, photographed May 2, 1976. Owned by Mary Stringer and Felicia Luburich.

Opposite:
See, Rottweilers do love water! Chivas von Meadow, a daughter of Ch. McCoy von Meadow, seven months old, doing her great Rottweiler dive. Donna Wormser, owner.

1973 TOP TEN OBEDIENCE ROTTWEILERS

Points

1. Rodsden's Chopper Du Trier,
C.D.X.,   2736½
Mrs. L. Mathis

2. Rodsden's Helsa v Eberle, C.D.X.   2306
J.M. and C.S. Epperle.

3. Rodsden's Will V.D. Harque,   1710
C.D.X., H. Kane.

4. Rodsden's Susse Poltergeist, C.D.T.   1291½
D. and F. Johnson.

5. Panamint Helmut v Rheintal   1026
F. and E. Shipper.

6. Ch. Rodsden's Willa V.D. Harque,   973
C.D.X., T.D. J.F. Wiedel.

7. Kavon Mr. Murphy, C.D.   928½
D.C. and C.H. Anderson.

8. De Riemer's Fritz   868½
E.D. and T. Wade.

9. Garm of Gertase, C.D.   793
H. and J. Mayorga.

#10. Rodsden's Hombre J. and D. Hedl.   769

For 1973 points were calculated on both scores and placement points. Only one Tracking Dog title was awarded in 1974 and one in 1973. In 1974, a T.D. certificate went to Tracydan's Brinka v Arba, T.D., owned by Ruth and Arthur Twiss. In 1973, the T.D. title was awarded to Ch. Rodsden's Kato v Donnaj, C.D.X. owned by Janet Marshall.

Opposite:
Ch. Rodsden's Tally v Hungerbuhl, CD (Ch. Dox v
Hungerbuhl ex Ch. Cora v Zimmerplatz), being
handled to a win by Sandy Taylor for herself and co-
owner Ron Taylor.

CHAPTER 25

Tracking With Your Rottweiler

THE PIONEERS THAT LED THE WAY

According to American Kennel Club records, the first Rottweiler to earn the AKC Tracking Dog Title was Gero v. Rabenhorst. He completed the requirements on August 8, 1941. For the next 28 years, no Rottweiler succeeded in earning an AKC TD title. Then on October 26, 1969, Russell's Herzchen became the second Rottweiler (first bitch) to add the "T" after her name. On September 27, 1970, Champion Axel v.d. Taverne, UDT, became the first Champion UDT Rottweiler of record. The very next weekend, on October 4, 1970, Grunberg Brummel v.d. Adel, Am., Can. TD, entered and passed his first of a continous string of 13 consecutive AKC Tracking Tests. In those days it was quite possible for dogs to gain entry into multiple tests after earning their titles. The best tracking dogs frequently built up long strings of successes. Brummel's perfect record of 13 AKC tests entered and 13 passed with never a failure stands unbroken and unapproached in his breed to this day. Brummel went on to earn his Canadian TD in preparation for attempting the Canadian Advanced Tracking routine. Unfortunately he died one week before he was to compete at that level for the first time. Brummel was listed in the December, '72, issue of *Front and Finish* as having passed more tracking tests in 1971 than any other dog of any breed.

At the starting flag. Am., Can. CD and Am., Can. TD Riegele's Berenger v Arba, with Arthur Twiss, handler, showing the first step in starting a track.

Opposite:
The great "super tracker" himself! Grunberg Brummel v.d. Adel, CD, owned, trained and handled by Ruth and Art Twiss. Note the beautiful head and expression of this dog, so definitely typical of the breed.

Riegele's Berenger v Arba, Am., Can. CD and TD, and Am., Can. Ch. Tracydan's Brinka v Arba, Am., Can. CD and TD, both owned by Ruth and Arthur Twiss, pictured in the process of earning their Canadian TD titles under judge, J. Charles Oliver at Montreal.

Not to be left out of the tracking history-making, West Coast fanciers found their own unique method of record-setting. On June 24, 1978, at the Emerald Dog Obedience Club Tracking Test in Eugene, Oregon, five of the ten dogs entered were Rottweilers from California. All were entered for the first time, and all five passed. They were: DeReimer's Roman Noble, CD; DeReimer's Mariken; Panamint Sultan v. Rheintal, CDX; Champion Panamint Anytime Anywhere, CD; and Champion Panamint Saphir v. Rheintal, CDX.

As tracking catches on with an increasing number of Rottweiler owners, the number of Rotties holding the title of Tracking Dog is expanding rapidly. Now with the AKC TDX Title available, there is an even greater challenge for tracking enthusiasts. Hopefully many Rottweiler-handler teams will continue on to the advanced level.

TRACKING WITH THE "AVERAGE" ROTTWEILER

In general Rottweilers appear to have at least average or above scenting and tracking ability. Their singleness of purpose and high threshold of tolerance for distraction add to their potential success in the tracking field. Since tracking, unlike other forms of training, puts the dog in a position of "Leader" rather than "Follower" in the dog-handler relationship, the Rottie's natural aggressiveness and "Top Dog" attitude usually make an enthusiastic tracking trainee.

Generally speaking there are no field conditions which will prove beyond the capacity of a reasonably healthy adult Rottweiler. However there are a number of small "hazards" to which the Rottweiler and his handler will be exposed—minor things which would be no problem with a smaller, less powerful or less aggressive breed.

The best tracking dogs work enthusiastically, pulling into their harnesses and travelling at a reasonably fast clip. Translated into Rottweiler terms, this can mean that the handler must cope with considerable forceful pulling and a rather impressive amount of speed. From the very beginning of the Rottweiler's training, he should not be allowed to run through his track at a speed greater than that which the handler can manage safely and with reasonable comfort for a distance of at least 500 yards. Fields frequently contain chuck holes, bumps, dips and other changes of terrain that could cause a bad fall or broken limb for either handler or dog. As there is no time limit in tracking, so long as the dog is working, there is no point to allowing the Rottweiler to turn a harmless tracking session into a dangerous endurance race. Remember, too, that a big dog with a long stride travelling at excessive speed can easily miss an article or overrun a turn in a matter of very few seconds.

Grunberg Brummel v.d. Adel, Am., Can. CD owned by Ruth and Arthur Twiss, doing an advanced track in practice. Owing to his owners' superstition, Brummel was never permitted to be photographed until after he was through working.

Downhill tracks can be especially hazardous with a big dog. It will prove very helpful to train your Rottweiler to respond to the command, "Slow Down!" In order to pass his test, the dog *must* complete the track with a handler attached to the other end of the lead! If you lose your balance, drop your lead and cannot retrieve it fast enough to finish the track with your dog, he will fail as surely as if he had taken a wrong turn.

While Rottweilers adapt quite well to all climates, they are happiest and most comfortable in cool weather. Their black coats and rather short forefaces make them a little more than normally susceptible to the heat. In a hot, dry field, under full midday sun, the tracking Rottie can suffer considerable discomfort and lose his customary enthusiasm. It is best to keep the dog as quiet and cool as possible until it is his turn to track. Offer a small drink of water—cool, not cold—just before taking him to his starting flag. Do not allow him to pull and tug all the way to the flag. Encourage him to work more slowly and to pull less than would normally be typical for him. Remember, a panting, gasping, overheated dog with a mouthful of swollen tongue isn't going to be able to smell much of anything.

Ideal tracking weather is also "ideal Rottweiler weather." Cool to cold temperatures, overcast skies and slightly damp ground constitute the "perfect tracking conditions." This is especially true when your tracking companion is a Rottweiler. Your dog will probably put forth his best and most impressive efforts in early spring and late fall tests.

PREPARING YOUR ROTTWEILER FOR THE FIELD

Since the Rottweiler is a big dog, finding the best equipment to use with him is not easy. The harness must be sturdy, but not cumbersome. A plain harness of leather or nylon webbing will work best. Avoid the temptation to select a heavy, padded working harness with rings on the sides. Such a piece of equipment is an impediment in the field. The best style for a tracking harness is one which comes to a "v" at the forechest and passes between the front legs, then up over the back. It forms sort of a modified figure 8. A conventional harness will work well, too. Just be sure the front piece fits so that it does not interfere with the front legs or ride so high that it cuts into the lower part of the dog's throat

Above: "On the Track." Here Brinka has found the scent and is under way. **Below:** Ch. Panamint Anytime Anywhere, CD, TD. A fantastic worker belonging to Panamint Kennels, Baring, WA.

when he is pulling into it. Pressure at that point will affect the dog's breathing, rendering him unwilling or unable to pull properly, as well as causing him great discomfort.

Rules require that a lead is used that is at least 20' long. Most handlers prefer 30 to 40 feet of lead, with a knot tied at 20' to remind us of our minimum. With Rottweilers, we find that the green nylon webbing about ½ to ¾" wide works best. Obviously anything too light will snap under the pulling pressure of such a powerful dog. Rope or thin braided nylon, while generally strong enough, will tear the handler's hands unmercifully. We feel that anything wider or heavier than the ¾" nylon web is simply too heavy and awkward to handle. Now properly outfitted, the Rottweiler and his handler are ready to tackle the tracking exercise.

HINTS FOR THE TRAINING SESSION

Training can be started at any time—before or after conformation or obedience, or in conjunction with either or both. As with all training, the younger the dog is when he starts, the better, generally speaking. All precautions which would apply to any other young puppy will apply to Rottweiler pups also. The only healthy Rottweiler puppy we would hesitate to start at a very young age would be a puppy with a weak or questionable front. Pulling against the harness may not be harmful, but it certainly is not helpful either to the weak front, considering the desired tracking position with head lowered between the front feet, nose to ground and center of gravity extremely low and forward. We feel this position might exaggerate and encourage the puppy's tendency to wing his elbows and paddle with his front feet.

Advanced age of the dog should not prevent the handler from giving tracking a try, as long as the dog is in generally good health. On the whole, tracking is neither fatiguing nor violent. We have worked with beginner trainees (of other breeds) up to the age of 12 years, and some have been outstanding students. None have suffered any harm from their hours in the field. In fact the older, retired dog will often revel in the attention and thoroughly enjoy his new-found outlet for mental and physical energy.

Any of the various training methods outlined in books and articles about tracking or used widely by fanciers in the different geographic sections of the country will work as well for the Rottweiler as for any other breed. The choice is entirely up to the individual handler. In making your selection, some consideration should be given to choosing a program with which you can receive help, if needed, from more experienced tracking enthusiasts in your particular region.

Rottweilers catch on easily to what they are being taught, so in most cases you should have little difficulty getting your point across to your dog regardless of the method you have chosen. If you do have a pupil who seems a little less motivated than average, food incentives will go a long way toward remedying the situation. We always use a food treat (usually boiled liver) under the article in the beginning stages of training. Right up until test day, we offer the dog a liver treat from hand at the end of the track. It is given to the dog as soon as the handler reaches the article. In a real test it should be withheld until the dog is out of the field. Just be sure to be very lavish with your praise.

In selecting your articles, be sure to use a leather or leather-like glove or wallet, as this is what will be used at the test. Also be absolutely sure that the article used does actually belong to the tracklayer. *Do not* allow the tracklayer to use an article belonging to any other person.

It is not required for the tracking dog to pick up or retrieve the article. He is required simply to stop and clearly indicate it, at which point the handler must pick it up. If your dog likes to retrieve or can be taught to do so easily, wonderful! But if retrieving is not his strong point, don't push the issue. There is nothing to be gained by forcing an unwilling and often stubborn student to retrieve. It is more important that your Rottweiler performs happily and enthusiastically in the field.

Tracking is a sport in which the handler, tracklayers and judges should all be striving to build the dog's confidence in his natural ability by encouraging him with success in the field. *Never* should the human element set up a situation designed to defeat the dog by making it impossible for him to follow the track or find the aritcle. In all training sessions, the dog must reach a successful conclusion by finding a legitimate article at the end of the track. The tracklayer should always carry an extra article which can be used if, for any reason, the dog is unable to find the original drop. This may occur because the dog loses the scent and goes off the track; because the tracklayer forgets where the track goes; because either the handler or tracklayer inadvertently causes the dog to be pulled off the correct track; or because an intruder—human or otherwise—fouls the track and/or removes the article. When it becomes apparent that the dog is not going to be able to complete the track successfully, the tracklayer should walk a short distance from a point near where the dog is believed to have lost the track and drop the spare article while the handler diverts the dog's attention. Then the dog should be put on this new extension of his track so that he can find the article quickly and easily. He should be praised, given his treat and led to believe that he has successfully completed the task set for him. Under *no* circumstances should the dog ever be allowed to leave the field without finding an article.

As far as working conditions go, remember that while it is necessary to train at all times of day, under all weather conditions and in all sorts of field cover, on the whole the physical conditions of the session should be matched to the experience level and capacity of the dog. Beginners should be worked under the best possible conditions. Experienced dogs should be introduced to all possible extremes, but these should be treated as exceptions and not be allowed to become a daily routine.

The most important single factor for the handler in tracking is to learn to "read your dog." Here the Rottweiler's size, strength and enthusiasm are very much an advantage. There is nothing very subtle about a working Rottweiler! Usually when on the track, he will throw himself into his harness, lower his center of gravity and dig in with all four feet using such force that it is virtually impossible not to recognize the signal that he is on the track. If you should happen to miss his cue, you may well find yourself pulled off your feet. Rottweilers can be very stubborn. If they are sure of what they are doing and are not fatigued, they will not take "no" for an answer. If you are slow to respond or refuse to follow your dog, he will ask you to follow just so often. Getting no response, he will finally tell you where to go with one lusty, unrestrainable lunge!

However, a word of caution: when making your dog prove his corners, be careful not to over play your part of "hard-to-move." This can be especially important if you plan to continue into advanced tracking. Keep your lead taut at all times. Follow only when the dog is clearly tracking. But don't make him prove himself to the point of exhaustion. While your Rottweiler is strong enough to pull you quite easily through the 440-500 yards of a regular TD Track, when the length is extended to 800 or more

"The End of the Track." Brinka has reached the destination.

Left to right are pictured Judge Peggy Mellon, Panamint Ideal Impression at seven months with handler, and Judge Benjamin Harris at the Orange Empire Dog Club tracking test, Jan. 27, 1979. This lovely Rottweiler gained her Tracking Dog title in one day at this event and at so early an age! Barbara Dillon, owner.

yards even the strongest Rottie is going to be hard pressed to drag a resistant handler the entire distance. If he is allowed to tire early in the track, he may give up entirely before he reaches the end. As the Rottweiler progresses into the TDX routine, there will be a number of changes in his working pattern. On the positive side, when working the older tracks which are harder to follow, he will have to slow down to a pace probably more comfortable for his handler. On the negative side, he will be much more cautious, reducing the force with which he pulls to a degree which may make it harder to read him. Be prepared to change your handling habits a bit. Keep your lead tight but give more readily, especially on changes of direction that might indicate corners.

It is the persistence and enthusiasm of the Rottweiler that make tracking behind him one of the greatest thrills of our doggy sport.

AN ALTERNATE SYSTEM FOR TRAINING THE VERY YOUNG PUPPY OR THE ADULT DOG WITH "PSYCHOLOGICAL HANG-UPS"

A very young puppy will often not be terribly highly motivated to track and locate a glove or wallet, whether there is a piece of freshly cooked liver under it or not. Likewise, a highly trained obedience dog or a dog with deeply rooted insecurities may prove unwilling to leave his handler's side to step forward into a position of leadership. In such cases when conventional methods fail, you may find the procedure outlined below helpful. We have found that it works very well with any dog who is extremely owner-oriented.

You will need an assistant who is not a member of the dog's human family. Select a training area which offers trees, bushes or rises in the ground behind which you can hide. Have your assistant hold the dog on lead. Let the dog watch you place the flag in the ground and tramp down the area. Then while the assistant blocks the dog's view, proceed in a straight line to the nearest hiding place. Take with you a treat and an article. As soon as you are concealed, your assistant will allow the dog to sniff the ground around the starting flag. If necessary the assistant will guide the dog along the track until the dog finds you. In most cases, the dog's compulsion to find you should be strong enough for him to step out willingly in front of the strange handler, thus taking the lead in following your path. When the dog finds you, immediately take him from the assistant, praise and pet him, and offer him the treat, which you will appear to be carrying in the article. The assistant should remain purely passive and offer no praise once the dog finds you. *You* walk the dog back to the starting point. Repeat this procedure several times. Use the method until the dog clearly understands that the object of the activity is to lead the way to the location of an object by using his nose to follow the ground scent of his quarry. This may take one session or several outings, depending on the dog. As soon as the dog is responding consistently, you can begin to use the more conventional method of your choice. If the dog reverts, go back to the hiding game. Most dogs don't revert once they know what is expected of them.

The length of time it will take to prepare your dog for Tracking Test entry will vary with the individual dog and the training prosess of the handler. However it is reasonable to expect that most Rottweilers can accomplish their goal within one year's time.

SPECIAL BENEFITS FROM TRACKING

In addition to being a fine sport, tracking training can also be of considerable therapeutic value for the Rottweiler with a problem. We have seen evidence in several instances of its effectiveness in diminishing or overcoming a variety of difficulties. For instance, there was:

ANKER: A finished champion and CD titlist whose general attitude in the ring ranged from passive at best to bored and sluggish at worst. Although he was not a particularly talented tracking candidate, he greatly enjoyed the position of authority he discovered at the end of his tracking lead. After a year of training, we noticed a great deal of renewed interest and animation in his breed ring showmanship.

EBONY: A dear little bitch, very cruelly treated as a puppy and eventually placed in the loving home of a kind and understanding breeder. She loved and trusted her owner, but would retreat to the darkest corner of her kennel in the presence of any outsider. Her fear of men was especially strong. When she was several years old, she joined us with her owner for one tracking session. We began this session in one part of the field and with Ebby and her owner far enough away for her to feel unthreatened. She had considerable talent for tracking and after two or three tracks was able to follow a stranger's scent. We both laid tracks for her, each time becoming more and more visible and staying closer to her. By the end of the afternoon, she posed for pictures with her half-brother, Brummel. When we left the field, we all left together—we with our two males and Ebby's owner with Ebby walking beside us and accepting gentle petting.

BRUMMEL: The holder of the 13-string record. Totally disjointed from severe hip dysplasia and suffering from osteochondritis dessicans in one shoulder, he was declared a cripple at the age of 6 months. We were advised to put him down. Since we felt he could adjust, we elected to give him the chance to live. At six months he could not run the length of his 100' backyard. Yet as an adult, after a brief period of tracking training, he was able to run his 13 very impressive tracks of 440-500 yards in times that averaged three to eight minutes.

Whether your Rottweiler is a finished champion, obedience hopeful or is enjoyed simply as a much loved pet, he and you can find great joy and a whole new dimension to your companionship by taking to the fields for an exhilarating day of tracking.

Grunberg Brummel v.d. Adel, Am., Can. TD, never failed an AKC/Tracking Dog Test, and amassed a consecutive string of 13 entered and passed. A record for the breed that remains unbroken. In 1971 he passed more tracking tests than any other dog of any breed. Arthur and Ruth Twiss, owners.

Below: Five California Rottweilers that earned their Tracking Dog Degrees at tests in Eugene OR, given by the Emerald Dog Obedience Club. From left: Panamint Sultan v Rheintal, CDX, trainer-handler, Margaret Teague; Ch. Panamint Anytime Anywhere, CD, trainer-handler, Dennis Teague; De Reimer's Mariken, trainer-handler, Rocky Rothrock; De Reimer's Roman Noble, CD, trainer-handler, Mid Rothrock; Panamint Saphir v Rheintal, CD, trainer-handler, Lucy Ang.

CHAPTER 26

The Veterinarian's Corner

Joseph P. Sayres, DVM
Buffalo, New York

By way of introduction to this chapter concerning the medical aspects of the care of your Rottweiler, I think we should spend a few minutes discussing how to choose your veterinarian.

Up until recent years, there has been a lot of misunderstanding and even animosity between veterinarians and breeders. Some distrust arose on the breeders' part because most veterinarians were not familiar with or not even interested in learning about purebred dogs. Some of the problems were peculiar to certain breeds and some of them would crop up at inconvenient times. Veterinarians were then beset by breeders who thought that they knew more about the medical problems of their dogs than did the vets. The veterinarians very often were called only for emergency work or when it was too late to save a sick dog that had been treated too long by lay people in the kennel. There also was the problem that many breeders had never figured veterinary fees in their budgets and consequently were slow in paying their bills, if indeed they paid them at all.

These problems have been to a large extent solved. Education and better communication between breeders and veterinarians have eliminated most areas of friction.

Today veterinary education and training have advanced to a point paralleling that of human standards. This has resulted in advances in the field of Veterinary Science in the last two decades. Sophisticated diagnostic procedures, new and advanced surgical techniques and modern well-equipped hospitals all make for improved medical care for our dogs.

Luna von Stolzenfels, CD, at six months. Linda Griswold, owner.
Opposite:
Frank Aube looks proudly at his future winners, two
of the six young puppies from Ch. Pfeffer von
Gruenerwald.

Educated breeders now realize that, while they may know more about the general husbandry of their dogs and the unique traits of the Rottweiler, they should not attempt to diagnose and treat their ailments.

In choosing your veterinarian you can afford to be selective. He or she should be outgoing and friendly, should be interested in your dogs and, in the case of breeders, interested in your breeding programs. Veterinarians should always be willing to talk freely with you. Such things as fees, availability for emergencies, what services are and are not available, should be talked about and understood before a good, lasting and rewarding relationship with your veterinarian can be established.

You can expect your veterinarian's office, clinic or hospital to be spotlessly clean, free from undesirable odors, be well equipped and to be staffed by sincere, friendly personnel who act willingly to serve you at all times. All employees there should be clean, neat in their appearance and be conversant with whatever services that you require. You may also expect that your dog will be treated carefully and kindly at all times by the doctor and his staff.

Your veterinarian should be competent and participate in continuing education programs in order to keep up with changes and new improvements in his field. He should also, however, be aware of his limitations. If he doesn't feel confident in doing certain procedures, then he should say so and refer you to qualified individuals to take care of the problem. Seeking second opinions and consulting with specialists on difficult cases are more the rule than the exception nowadays. That is as it should be.

You will know that if your veterinarian is a member of the American Animal Hospital Association he and his facility have had to measure up to very high standards of quality and are subjected to inspections every two years to keep it that way.

Many excellent veterinarians and veterinary hospitals by choice do not belong to the American Animal Hospital Association. You can satisfy your curiosity about these places by taking guided tours of the facilities and by learning by word of mouth about the quality of medicine being practiced at these hospitals.

So far we have discussed only what you should expect from your veterinarian. Now, let's discuss what the veterinarian expects from his clients.

Most of all, I think that he expects his clients to be open and frank in their relations with him. He doesn't like to be double-checked and "second guessed" behind his back. He also likes for you to be able to handle your pet so that he in turn can examine him. It is also expected that you can restrain your dog and keep him from bothering other pets that he may come in contact with. He expects to be paid a fair fee, and promptly, for the services rendered. Fees in an area tend to be consistent and variations are due only to complications or unforeseen problems. Medicine is not an exact science so therefore things can happen that may be unpredictable.

If you are dissatisfied in any way with the services rendered or fees that were charged, then ask to discuss these things in a friendly manner with the doctor. If his explanations are not satisfactory or he refuses to talk to you about the problem, then you are justified in seeking another doctor.

The veterinarian expects to provide his services for your animals during regular hours whenever possible. He also realizes that in a kennel or breeding operation emergencies can occur at any time, and his services will be needed at off hours. You should find out how these emergencies will be handled and be satisfied with the procedures.

No veterinarian can be on duty 24 hours of every day. Today cooperative veterinarians group together to take turns covering each other's emergency calls. Some cities have emergency clinics that operate solely to take care of those catastrophes that usually happen in the middle of the night or on weekends.

My conclusion, after thirty years of practice, is that most disagreements and hard feelings between clients and veterinarians are the result of a breakdown in communication. Find a veterinarian that you can talk to and can be comfortable with, and you'll make a valuable friend.

In using veterinary services to their best advantage, I believe that you will find that prevention of diseases and problems is more valuable than trying to cure these things after they occur. In other words, an ounce of prevention is worth a pound of cure.

Rottweilers as a breed remain remarkably free from congenital defects. From the publication "Congenital Defects in Dogs" published by Ralston Purina Company, we notice that diabetes mellitus (sugar diabetes) is the only congenital defect listed for the breed.

In addition, a recent listing of breed defects with a probable genetic base published in the American Kennel Club *Gazette* mentions deafness as the only defect pertaining to Rottweilers.

Breeding programs should be set up to eliminate those defects that are thought to be congenital or inherited. In Rottweilers, the aforementioned problems of deafness and diabetes, as well as hip and elbow dysplasias, can be eliminated by selective breeding.

By proper and vigilant vaccination programs, the following contagious diseases can be eliminated: distemper, hepatitis, leptospirosis, rabies, parainfluenza and parvovirus enteritis.

With proper sanitation and the guided use of insecticides and vermifuges, the following conditions can become extinct or of only minor importance: round worm infestation, hook worm infestation, whip worm infestation, coccidiosis, tape worm infestation, fleas, ticks and lice.

These problems will be dealt with individually as our chapter progresses.

The following schedule of inoculations should be set up and followed religiously to prevent infectious diseases:

Disease	Age to Vaccinate
Distemper	6 to 8 weeks old. Second inoculation to be given at 12 to 16 weeks of age. Re-vaccinate annually.
Hepatitis (Adenovirus)	Same as distemper.
Parainfluenza (Kennel Cough)	Same as distemper.
Leptospirosis	Give first vaccine at 9 weeks old. Re-vaccinate with second DHP injection at 12 to 16 weeks of age. Re-vaccinate annually.
Parvovirus	Give first vaccine at 6 to 8 weeks old. Second vaccine 2 to 4 weeks later. Duration of immunity from 2 injections established at only 4 months at the time of this writing. Re-vaccinate annually. Re-vaccinate before dog shows or going to boarding kennels if more than 6 months have elapsed since the last shot.

| Rabies | First inoculation at 3 to 4 months old, then re-vaccinate when 1 year old and at least every 3 years after that. If dog is over 4 months old at the time of the first vaccination, then re-vaccinate in one year and then once every 3 years after that. |

Vaccines used are all modified live virus vaccines except for leptospirosis which is a killed bacterium and parvovirus vaccine which is a killed virus vaccine for feline distemper.

Other communicable diseases for which no vaccine has been perfected as yet are: canine brucellosis, canine coronavirus, canine rotavirus.

A brief description of the more common of our infectious diseases follows.

Distemper

This disease is caused by a highly contagious, airborne virus. The symptoms are varied and may involve all of the dog's systems. A pneumonic form is common with heavy eye and nose discharges, coughing and lung congestion. The digestive system may be involved as evidenced by vomiting, diarrhea and weight loss. The skin may show a pustular type rash on the abdomen. Nervous system involvement is common with convulsions, chorea, paralysis as persistent symptoms. This virus may have an affinity for nerve tissue and cause encephalitis and degeneration of the spinal cord. These changes for the most part are irreversible and death or severe crippling ensues.

There is no specific remedy or cure for distemper, and recoveries when they occur can only be attributed to the natural resistance of the patient, good nursing care and control of secondary infections with antibiotics.

That's the bad news about distemper. The good news is that we rarely see a case of distemper in most areas in this day and age because of the efficiency of the vaccination program. This situation is proof that prevention by vaccination has been very effective in almost eradicating this dreaded disease.

Hepatitis

Another contagious viral disease affecting the liver of its victims. This is not an airborne virus and can be spread only be contact. Although rarely seen today because of good prevention by vaccination programs, this virus is capable of producing a very acute, fulminating, severe infection and can cause death in a very short time. Symptoms of high temperature, lethargy, anorexia and vomiting are the same as for other diseases. Careful evaluation by a veterinarian is necessary to confirm the diagnosis of this disease.

The old canine infectious hepatitis vaccine has been replaced by a canine adenovirus type 2 strain vaccine which is safer and superior. The new vaccine seems to be free of post-vaccination complications such as blue eye, shedding of the virus in the urine and some kidney problems.

Leptospirosis

This is a disease that seriously affects the kidneys of dogs, most domestic animals and man. For this reason, it can become a public health hazard. In urban and slum areas, the disease is carried by rats and mice in their urine. It is caused by a spirochete organism which is very resistant to treatment. Symptoms include fever, depression, dehydration, excess thirst, persistent vomiting, occasional diarrhea and jaundice in the latter stages. Again, it is not always easy to diagnose so your veterinarian will have to do some laboratory work to confirm it.

We see very few cases of leptospirosis in dogs and then only in the unvaccinated ones. The vaccine is generally given concurrently with the distemper and hepatitis vaccinations. Preventive inoculations have resulted in the almost complete demise of this dreaded disease.

Parainfluenza

This describes any one of a number of upper respiratory conditions, a common one of which is kennel cough. It is caused by a throat-inhabiting virus that causes an inflammation of the trachea (wind pipe) and larynx (voice box). Coughing is the main symptom and fortunately it rarely causes any other systemic problems. The virus is airborne, highly contagious and is the scourge of boarding kennels. A vaccine is available that will protect against this contagious respiratory disease and should be given as part of your vaccination program, along with the distemper, hepatitis, parvovirus and leptospirosis shots. Pregnant bitches should not be vaccinated against parainfluenza because of the possibility of infecting the unborn puppies. As there may be more than one infectious agent involved in contagious upper respiratory disease of dogs, vaccination against parainfluenza is not a complete guarantee to protect against all of them.

Rabies

This is a well known virus-caused disease that is almost always fatal and is transmissible to man and other warm blooded animals. The virus causes very severe brain damage. Sources of the infection include foxes, skunks, raccoons, as well as domesticated dogs and cats. Transmission is by introduction of the virus by saliva into bite wounds. Incubation in certain animals may be from three to eight weeks. In a dog, clinical signs will appear within five days. Symptoms fall into two categories depending on what stage the disease is in when seen. There is the dumb form and the furious form. A change of personality takes place and in the furious form, individuals become hypersensitive and overreact to noise and stimuli. They will bite any object that moves. In dumb rabies, the typical picture of the loosely hanging jaw and tongue presents itself. Diagnosis is only confirmed by finding the virus and characteristic lesions in the brain by a laboratory. All tissues and fluids from rabid animals should be considered infectious and you should be careful not to come in contact with them. Prevention by vaccination is a must because there is no treatment for rabid dogs.

Contagious Canine Viral Diarrheas

Canine Coronavirus (CCV)

This is a highly contagious virus that spreads rapidly to susceptible dogs. The source of infection is through infectious bowel movements. The incubation period is one to four days, and the virus will be found in feces for as long as two weeks. It is hard to tell the difference sometimes between cases of diarrhea caused by coronavirus and parvovirus. Coronavirus generally is less severe and causes a more chronic or sporadic type of diarrhea. The fecal material may be orange in color and have a very bad odor. Occasionally it will also contain blood. Vomiting sometimes precedes the diarrhea, but loss of appetite and listlessness are consistent signs of the disease. Fever may or may not be present. Recovery is the rule after eight to ten days, but treatment with fluids, antibiotics, intestinal protectants and good nursing care

are necessary in the more severe watery diarrhea cases. Dogs that survive these infections become immune but for an unknown length of time.

To control an outbreak of this virus in a kennel, very stringent hygienic measures must be taken. Proper and quick disposal of feces, isolation of affected animals and disinfection with a one to thirty dilution of Clorox are all effective means of controlling an outbreak in the kennel.

There is no vaccine yet available for prevention of canine coronavirus. Human infections by this virus have not been reported.

Canine Parvovirus (CPV)

This is the newest and most highly publicized member of the intestinal virus family. Cat distemper virus is a member of the same family but differs from canine parvovirus biologically, and it has been impossible to produce this disease in dogs using cat virus as the inducing agent and conversely canine parvovirus will not produce the disease in a cat. However, vaccines for both species will produce immunity in the dog. The origin of CPV is still unknown.

Canine parvovirus is very contagious and acts rapidly. The main source of infection is contaminated bowel movements. Direct contact between dogs is not necessary, and carriers such as people, fleas, instruments, etc., may carry and transmit the virus.

The incubation period is five to fourteen days. The symptoms are fever, severe vomiting and diarrhea, often with blood, depression and dehydration. Feces may appear yellowish grey streaked with blood. Young animals are more severely affected and a shock-like death may occur in two days. In animals less than six weeks old, the virus will cause an inflammation of the heart muscle, causing heart failure and death. These pups do not have diarrhea. A reduction in the number of white blood cells is a common finding early in the disease.

The virus is passed in the feces for one to two weeks and may possibly be shed in the saliva and urine also. This virus has also been found in the coats of dogs. The mortality rate at time of writing is unknown.

Dogs that recover from the disease develop an immunity to it. Again, the duration of this immunity is unknown. Control measures include disinfection of the kennels, animals and equipment and isolation of sick individuals.

Treatment is very similar to that for coronavirus, namely intravenous fluid therapy, administration of broad spectrum antibiotics, intestinal protectants and good nursing care.

Transmission to humans has not been proven.

Clinical studies have proven that vaccination with two injections of the approved canine vaccine given two to four weeks apart will provide good immunity for at least four months and possibly longer as future studies may show. At present, puppies should be vaccinated when six to eight weeks old, followed with a second injection two to four weeks later. Full protection does not develop until one week following the second injection. The present recommendations are for annual re-vaccinations with an additional injection recommended before dog shows or boarding in kennels if a shot has not been given within six months.

Canine Rotavirus (CRV)

This virus has been demonstrated in dogs with a mild diarrhea but again with more severe cases in very young puppies. Very little is known about this virus.

A milder type of diarrhea is present for eight to ten days. The puppies do not run a temperature and continue to eat. Dogs usually recover naturally from this infection. There is no vaccine available for this virus.

Canine Brucellosis

This is a disease of dogs that causes both abortions and sterility. It is caused by a small bacterium closely related to the agent that causes undulant fever in man and abortion in cows. It occurs worldwide.

Symptoms of brucellosis sometimes are difficult to determine, and some individuals with the disease may appear healthy. Vague symptoms such as lethargy, swollen glands, poor hair coat and stiffness in the back legs may be present. This organism does not cause death and may stay in the dog's system for months and even years. The latter animals have breeding problems and infect other dogs.

Poor results in your breeding program may be the only indication that brucellosis is in your kennel. Apparently normal bitches abort without warning. This usually occurs forty-five to fifty-five days after mating. Successive litters will also be aborted. In males, signs of the disease are inflammation of the skin of the scrotum, shrunken testicles and swollen tender testicles. Fertility declines and chronically infected males become sterile. The disease in both sexes is transmitted at the time of mating.

Other sources of infection are aborted puppies and birth membranes and discharge from the womb at the time of abortions. Humans can be infected, but such infections are rare and mild. Unlike in the dog, the disease in humans responds readily to antibiotics.

Diagnosis is done by blood testing which should be done carefully. None of the present tests are infallible and false positives may occur. The only certain way that canine brucellosis can be diagnosed is by isolating the *B. canis* organism from blood or aborted material for which special techniques are required.

Treatment of infected individuals has proven ineffective in most cases. Sterility in males is permanent. Spaying or castrating infected pets should be considered as this will halt the spread of the disease and is an alternative to euthanasia.

At present, there is no vaccine against this important disease.

Our best hope in dealing with canine brucellosis is prevention. The following suggestions are made in order to prevent the occurrence of this malady in your dogs:

1. Test breed stock annually and by all means breed only uninfected animals.
2. Test bitches several weeks before their heat periods.
3. Do not bring any new dogs into your kennel unless they have two negative tests taken a month apart.
4. If a bitch aborts, isolate her, wear gloves when handling soiled bedding, disinfect the premises with Roccal.
5. If a male loses interest in breeding or fails to produce after several matings, have him checked.
6. Consult your veterinarian for further information about this disease, alert other breeders and support the research that is going on at the John A. Baker Institute for Animal Health at Cornell University.

This concludes the section on important contagious and infectious diseases of dogs. A discussion on external parasites that affect dogs is now in order.

External Parasites

The control and eradication of external parasites depends on the repeated use of good quality insecticide sprays or powders during the warm months. Make a routine practice of using these products at seven day intervals throughout the season. It is also imperative that sleeping quarters be treated also.

Fleas

They are brown, wingless insects with laterally compressed bodies and strong legs, and are blood suckers. Their life cycle comprises eighteen to twenty-one days from egg to adult flea. They can live without food for one year in high humidity but die in a few days in low humidity. They multiply rapidly and are more prevalent in the warm months. They can cause a severe skin inflammation in those individuals that are allergic or sensitive to the flea bite or saliva of the flea. They can act as a vector for many diseases and do carry tapeworms. Control measures must include persistent, continual use of flea collars or flea medallions, or sprays or powders. The dog's bedding and premises must also be treated because the eggs are there. Foggers, vacuuming or the use of professional exterminators may have to be used. All dogs and cats in the same household must be treated at the same time.

Ticks

There are hard and soft species of ticks. Both species are blood suckers and cause severe skin inflammations at times on their host. They act as a vector for Rocky Mountain spotted fever, as well as other diseases. Hibernation through an entire winter is not uncommon. The female tick lays as many as 1000 to 5000 eggs in crevices and cracks in walls. These eggs will hatch in about three weeks and then a month later become adult ticks. Ticks generally locate around the host's neck, ears and between the toes. They can cause anemia and serious blood loss if allowed to grow and multiply. It is not a good idea to pick ticks off the dogs because of the danger of a reaction in the skin. Just apply the tick spray directly on the ticks who then die and fall off eventually. Affected dogs should be dipped every two weeks. The premises, kennels and yards should be treated every two weeks during the summer months, being sure to apply the insecticide to walls and in all cracks and crevices.

Lice

There are two kinds of lice, namely the sucking louse and the biting louse. They spend their entire life on their host but can be spread by direct contact or through contaminated combs and brushes. Their life cycle is 21 days, and their eggs, known as nits, attach to the hairs of the dog. The neck and shoulder region, as well as the ear flaps, are the most common areas to be inhabited by these pesky parasites. They cause itchiness, some blood loss, and inflammation of the skin. Eradication will result from the dipping or dusting with methyl carbonate or Thuron once a week for three to four weeks. It is a good idea to fine comb the dogs after each dip to remove the dead lice and nits.

Ask your veterinarian to provide the insecticides and advice or control measures for all of these external parasites.

Internal Parasites

The eradication and control of internal parasites in dogs will occupy a good deal of your time and energy. These pests will be considered next.

Puppies should be tested for worms at four weeks of age and then six weeks later. It is also wise to test them again six weeks following their last worm treatment to be sure the treatments have been successful. Annual fecal tests are advisable throughout your dog's life. All worming should be done only under the supervision of your veterinarian.

The most common internal parasites encountered will be the following:

Ascarids

This includes round worms, puppy worms, stomach worms, milk worms. Puppies become infested shortly after birth and occasionally even before birth. Ascarids can be difficult to eradicate. When passed in the stool or thrown up, they look somewhat like cooked spaghetti when fresh or like rubber bands when they are dried up. Two treatments at least two weeks apart will eliminate ascarids from most puppies. An occasional individual may need more wormings according to the status of the life cycle of the worm in its system at the time of worming. Good sanitary conditions must prevail and immediate picking up of bowel movements is necessary to keep this worms' populations down.

Hook worms

This is another troublesome internal parasite that we find in dogs. They are blood suckers and also cause bleeding from the site of their attachment to the lining of the intestine when they move from one site to another. They can cause a blood loss type of anemia and serious consequences, particularly in young puppies.

Their life cycle is direct and their eggs may be ingested or pass through the skin of its host. Treatment of yards and runs where the dogs defecate with 5% sodium borate solution is said to kill the eggs in the soil. Two or three worm treatments three to four weeks apart may be necessary to get rid of hook worms. New injectable products administered by your veterinarian have proven more effective than remedies used in the past. Repeated fecal examinations may be necessary to detect the eggs in the feces. These eggs pass out of the body only sporadically or in showers, so that it is easy to miss finding them unless repeated stool testing is done. As with any parasite, good sanitary conditions in the kennel and outside runs will help eradicate this worm.

Whip worms

These are a prevalent parasite in some kennels and in some individual dogs. They cause an intermittent mucous type diarrhea. As they live only in the dog's appendix, it is extremely difficult to reach them with any worm medicine given by mouth. Injections seem to be the most effective treatment, and to be effective these have to be repeated several times over a long period of time. Here again, repeated fresh stool samples must be examined by your veterinarian to be sure that this pest has been eradicated. Appendectomies are indicated in only the most severe chronic cases. Needless to repeat again is the fact that cleanliness is next to Godliness and most important in getting rid of this parasite.

Tapeworms

They are another common internal parasite of dogs. They differ in their mode of transmission as they have an indirect life cycle. This means part of it must be spent in an intermediate host. Fleas, fish, rabbits and field mice all may act as an intermediate host for the tapeworm. Fleas are the most common source of tapeworms for dogs, although dogs that live near water may eat raw fish and get them and hunting dogs that eat the entrails of rabbits may get them from that source. Another distinguishing feature of the tapeworm is the suction apparatus which is part of the head. This enables the tapeworm to attach itself to the lining of the intestine. If after worming just the head remains, it has the capability of regenerating into another worm. This is one reason why they are so difficult to get rid of. It will require several treatments to get all of the entire tapeworms out of a dog's system. These worms are easily recognized by the appearance of their segments which break off and appear on top of a dog's bowel movement or stuck to the hair around the rectal area. These segments may appear alive and mobile at times, but most often are dead and dried up when found. They look like flat pieces of rice and may be white or brown when detected. Elimination of the intermediate host is an integral part of any plan to rid our dogs of this worm. Repeated wormings may be necessary to kill all the adult tapeworms in the intestine.

Other Parasites

Less commonly occurring parasitic diseases such as demodectic and sarcoptic mange should be diagnosed and treated only by your veterinarian. You are wise to consult your doctor whenever any unusual condition occurs and persists in your dog's coat and skin. These conditions are difficult to diagnose and treat at best, so that the earlier a diagnosis is obtained, the better the chances are for successful treatment. Other skin conditions such as ringworm, flea bite allergy, bacterial infections, eczemas, hormonal problems, etc. all have to be considered.

Before leaving the topic of internal parasites, it should be stressed that all worming procedures be done carefully and only with the advice and supervision of your veterinarian. The medicants used to kill the parasites are, to a certain extent, toxic so they should be used with care.

We have all been alerted to the dangers of heartworm disease in most sections of our country. This chapter would not be complete without a comprehensive report on this serious parasitic disease.

Heartworm Disease

Just as the name implies, this disease is caused by an actual worm that goes through its life cycle in the blood stream of its victims. It ultimately makes its home in the right chambers of the heart and in the large vessels that transport the blood to the lungs. They vary in size from 2.3 inches to 16 inches. Adult worms can survive up to five years in the heart.

By its nature, this is a very serious disease and can cause irreversible damage to the lungs and heart of its host.

The disease is transmitted and carried by female mosquitoes that have infected themselves after biting an infected dog, passing it on to the next dog they come in contact with.

The disease has been reported wherever mosquitoes are found, and now cases have been reported over most of the United States. Rare cases have been reported in man and cats. It is most prevalent in warmer climates where the mosquito population is the greatest, but hot beds of infection exist in the more temperate parts of the United States and Canada also.

Concerted efforts and vigorous measures must be taken to control and prevent this very serious threat to our dog population. The most effective means of eradication, I believe, shall come through annual blood testing for early detection, by the use of preventive medicine during mosquito exposure times and also by ridding our dog's environment of mosquitoes.

Annual blood testing is necessary to detect cases that haven't started to show symptoms yet and thus can be treated effectively. It also enables your veterinarian to prescribe the preventive medicine safely to those individuals that test negative. There is a ten to 15 percent margin of error in the test, which may lead to some false negative tests. Individuals that test negative but are showing classical symptoms of the disease such as loss of stamina, coughing, loss of weight and heart failure should be further evaluated with chest X-rays, blood counts and electrocardiograms.

Serious consequences may result when the preventive medication is given to a dog that has heartworm already in his system. That is why it is so important to have your dog tested annually before starting the preventive medicine.

In order to be most effective, the preventive drug diethylcarbamazine should be given in daily doses of 2.5 mg. per lb. of body weight or five mg. per kilogram of body weight of your dog. This routine should be started 15 days prior to exposure to mosquitoes and be continued until 60 days after exposure. Common and trade names for this drug are: Caricide, Styrid-Caricide and D.E.C. It comes in liquid and tablet forms.

This drug has come under criticism by some breeders and individuals that claim that it affects fertility and causes some serious reactions. Controlled studies have shown no evidence that this drug produces sterility or abnormal sperm count or quality. Long term studies on reproduction when the drug was given at the rate of 4.9 mg. per lb. of body weight for two years showed no signs of toxic effects on: body weight maintenance, growth rate of pups, feed consumption, conception rate, numbers of healthy pups whelped, ratio of male to female pups, blood counts and liver function tests. It is reported as a well tolerated medication, and many thousands of dogs have benefited from its use. From personal experience, I find just an occasional dog who will vomit the medicine or get an upset stomach from it. The new enteric coated pills have eliminated this small problem.

However if you still don't want to give the preventive, especially to your breeding stock, an alternative procedure would be to test your dogs every six months for early detection of the disease, so that it can be treated as soon as possible.

Heartworm infestation can be treated successfully. There is a one to five percent mortality rate from the treatment. It can be expected that treatment may be completed without side effects if the disease hasn't already caused irreversible problems in the heart, lungs, liver, kidneys, etc. Careful testing, monitoring and supervision are essential to success in treatment. Treatment is far from hopeless these days and if the disease is detected early enough a successful outcome is more the rule than the exception. In conclusion, remember that one case of heartworm disease in your area is one too many, especially if that one case is your dog. By following the steps mentioned in this article, we can go a long way in ridding ourselves of this serious threat to our dogs.

HOME REMEDIES

You have repeatedly read here of my instructions to call your veterinarian when your animals are sick. This is the best advice I can give you. There are a few home remedies, however, that may get you over some rough spots while trying to get professional help.

I think it is a good idea to keep some medical supplies or a first aid kit on hand. The kit should contain the following items: roll of cotton, gauze bandages, hydrogen peroxide, tincture of metaphen, cotton applicator swabs, BFI powder, rectal thermometer, adhesive tape, boric acid crystals, tweezers and Vaseline.

A word here on how to take a dog's temperature may be in order. Always lubricate the thermometer with Vaseline and insert it carefully into the rectum about two inches. Hold it there for two to three minutes, then read it.

My favorite home remedies follow:

For vomiting: Mix one tablespoon of table salt to one pint of water and dissolve the salt thoroughly. Then give one tablespoonful of the mixture to the patient. After waiting one hour repeat the procedure and skip the next meal. The dog may vomit a little after the first dose but the second dose works to settle the stomach. This mixture not only provides chlorides but acts as a mild astringent and many times in mild digestive upsets will work to stop the vomiting.

While on the subject of liquid remedies, I should mention how to administer liquid medicines to dogs. Simply pull the lips away from the side of the mouth, making a pocket to deposit the liquid in. Slightly tilt the dog's head and he will be able to swallow it properly. Giving liquids by opening the mouth and pouring them directly on the tongue is an invitation to disaster because inhalation pneumonia can result. Putting it in the side of the mouth gives the dog time to have it in his mouth and then swallow it properly.

Tablets are best administered by forcing the dog's mouth open and pushing the pill down over the middle of the tongue in the back of his mouth. If put in the right place, a reflex tongue reaction will force the pill down the throat to be swallowed. There also is no objection to giving the pills in favorite foods as long as you carefully determine that the medicine is surely swallowed with the food.

For diarrhea: In the case of large breeds, give three or four tablespoons of Kaopectate or milk of bismuth every four hours. Skip the next meal, and if the bowels persist in being loose, then start a bland diet of boiled ground lean beef and boiled rice in the proportions of half and half. Three or four doses of this medicine should suffice. If the diarrhea persists and particularly is accompanied by depression, lethargy and loss of appetite, your veterinarian should be consulted immediately. With all these new viral-caused diarrheas floating around, time is of the essence in securing treatment.

Mild stimulant: Dilute brandy half and half with water, add a little sugar and give a tablespoonful of the mixture every four to five hours.

Mild sedative: Dilute brandy half and half with water, add a little sugar and give a tablespoon of the mixture every 20 to 30 minutes until the desired effect is attained.

Using brandy for both sedation and stimulation is possible by varying the time interval between doses. Given every four to five hours, it's a stimulant but given every 20 to 30 minutes it acts as a sedative.

Treatment of minor cuts and wounds: Cleanse them first with soap and water, preferably tincture of green soap. Apply a mild antiseptic two or three times daily until healed. If the cut is deep and fairly long and bleeding, then a bandage should be applied until professional help can be obtained.

Whenever attempting to bandage wounds, first apply a layer or two of gauze over the cleaned and treated wound. Then apply a layer of cotton and then another layer or two of gauze. The bandage must be snug enough to stay on but not so tight as to impair the circulation to the part. Adhesive tape should be applied over the second layer of gauze to keep the bandage as clean and dry as possible until you can get the dog to the doctor.

Tourniquets should be applied only in cases of profusely bleeding wounds. They are applied tightly between the wound and the heart in addition to the pressure bandage that should be applied directly to the wound. The tourniquets must be released and reapplied at 15 minute intervals.

Burns: The application of ice or very cold water and compresses is the way to treat a skin burn. Apply the cold packs as soon as possible and take the dog immediately to your vet.

Frost bite: A rarely occurring problem but the secret in treating this condition is to restore normal body temperature gradually to the affected parts. In other words, use cold water then tepid water to thaw out the area slowly and restore circulation. In cases of severe freezing or shock due to bitter cold temperature, take the individual to the veterinarian as soon as possible.

Abscesses and infected cysts: Obvious abscesses and infected cysts that occur between the toes may be encouraged to drain by using hot boric acid packs and saturated dressings every few hours until professional aid can be secured. The boric acid solution is made by dissolving one tablespoon of crystals to one cup of hot water. Apply frequently to the swollen area. Further treatment by a veterinarian may involve lancing and thoroughly draining and cleaning out the abscess cavity. As most abscesses are badly infected, systemic antibiotics are generally indicated.

Heat stroke or heat exhaustion: A word about the serious affects of heat on a dog. It never ceases to amaze me how many people have to be warned and advised not to leave their dogs in cars or vans with the windows closed on a warm day at dog shows.

A dog's heat regulating mechanism is not nearly as good as ours. Consequently, they feel the heat more than we do. Keep them as cool and as well ventilated as possible in the hot weather.

Another opportunity for shock is taking your dog out of a cool air-conditioned vehicle and exposing him immediately to the hot outdoors. Make the change as gradual as you can because a rapid change like that can cause a shock-like reaction.

In cases of suspected heat stroke which manifests itself with very high body temperatures (as high as 106-107-108° sometimes), severe panting, weakness, shaking and collapse, act quickly in getting him into a cold bath or shower or by putting ice cold compresses on his head. Then, again without delay, rush him to the nearest veterinarian for further treatment. Prevention is the key here and with a little common sense, heat stroke and exhaustion can be avoided.

Poisons: Many dogs are poisoned annually by unscrupulous people who hate dogs. Many others are the victims of poisoning just due to the careless use of rat and ant poisons, insecticides, herbicides, anti-freeze solutions, drugs and so forth. Dogs also insist on eating poisonous plants either in the house or outdoors which can lead to serious consequences. Common sources of these toxic products include: daffodils, oleanders, poinsettias, mistletoe, philodendron, delphiniums, monkshood, foxglove, iris, lilies of the valley, rhubarb, spinach, tomato vines, rhododendron, cherry, peach, oak, elderberry and black locust, jack in the pulpit, dutchman's breeches, water hemlock, mushrooms, buttercups, poison hemlock, nightshade, jimson weed, marijuana, locoweed and lupine.

Things like grain contaminants can exist in dog food. The most common ones are ergot and corn cockle.

Chemicals comprise perhaps the largest and most common source of poisoning in our environment. These are things that our dogs may be exposed to every day. Careful handling and storage of these products are essential.

Toxic materials are found in all of the following groups of materials:

Arts and crafts supplies, photographic supplies, automotive and machinery products such as antifreeze and de-icers, rust inhibitors, brake fluids, engine and carburetor cleaners, lubricants, gasoline, kerosene, radiator cleaners and windshield washers. Cleaners, bleaches and polishes, disinfectants, sanitizers all contain products that are potentially dangerous.

Even health and beauty aids such as some bath oils, perfumes, corn removers, deodorants, anti-perspirants, athlete's foot remedies, eye makeup, hair dyes and preparations, diet pills, headache remedies, laxatives, liniments, fingernail polish removers, sleeping pills, suntan lotions, amphetamines, shaving lotions, colognes, shampoos and certain ointments may contain materials toxic if ingested in large enough quantities.

Paints and related products also can be dangerous: caulking compounds, driers, thinners, paints, paint brush cleaners, paint and varnish removers, preservatives, floor and wood cleaners all fit into the category.

Pest poisons for birds, fungi, insects, weeds, rats and mice, ants and snails all can be toxic and sometimes fatal to dogs.

Miscellaneous things like fire extinguishers and non-skid products for slippery floors can be unsafe. Most all solvents such as carbon tetrachloride, benzene, toluene, acetone, mineral spirits, kerosene and turpentine are dangerous.

The previous paragraphs serve to illustrate how many products in our everyday environment can be hazardous or fatal to our dogs.

In cases of suspected poisoning, one should be aware of what to do until professional help can be obtained. Keep the animal protected, quiet and warm. If contact is on the skin, eye or body surface, cleanse and flush the area with copious amounts of water. Protect him from further exposure.

Inducing vomiting may be dangerous and should be done only on the advice of a veterinarian. Giving peroxide may induce vomiting in some cases. It is better to allow the animal to drink as much water as it wants. This will dilute the poison. Giving milk or raw egg whites is helpful many times to delay absorption of the toxic products.

Do not attempt to give anything by mouth if the patient is convulsing, depressed or unconscious.

Do not waste time getting veterinary service as quickly as possible. Take any vomited material or suspected material and its container with you to the vet. If the suspected product is known, valuable time can be saved in administering specific treatment. The suspected specimens should be uncontaminated and be put in clean containers.

A word to the wise should be sufficient. Keep all products that in any way can harm your dog away from him.

Bloat: One of the most serious and difficult problems and real emergency situation that can occur is that of bloat. Other names for this condition are torsion and acute indigestion. This condition generally occurs in larger breeds after the consumption of a large meal (usually dry feed) and then the drinking of a lot of water immediately after eating. Follow this performance with a vigorous exercise period and the stage is set for bloat to set in. The stomach, being pendulous and overloaded at this point, can become twisted or rotated. This of course cuts off the circulation to the stomach and spleen and may also interfere with the large blood vessels coming to and from the liver. A shock-like syndrome follows and death may ensue shortly if heroic measures are not undertaken to save the stricken animal. If ever there was an emergency, this is truly one. Dry heaves, painful loud crying and abdominal enlargement take place in a very short time.

Relief of the torsion requires immediate surgery to right the stomach to its normal position and to keep it there. Circulation may then return to normal. In cases of acute indigestion without torsion, the distress and bloat may be relieved by passing a stomach tube to allow the gas to escape. At the risk of being redundant, it must be said that this condition is very acute and requires immediate and heroic deeds to save the victim.

Preventive measures include dividing these dogs' normal diet into three or four meals a day. Water should not be given for one hour before and one hour after each meal, and no exercise is advisable for an hour or two after eating.

With breeders and veterinarians becoming more aware of the bloat syndrome, I feel that more of these cases will be saved than in the past.

Whelping: We cannot leave the subject of emergencies without considering the subject of whelping. Most bitches whelp without any problems. It is wise, however, to watch them closely during this time. I feel that no bitch should go more than two hours in actual labor without producing a puppy. This includes the time before the first one as well as between puppies. If more than two hours elapse, then the dam should be examined by a veterinarian. It will then be determined if she is indeed in trouble or is just a slow whelper. This rule of thumb gives us time to find out if there is a problem, what it may be and have time to save both dam and puppies in most cases.

It is good practice to have your bitches examined for pregnancy 3½ to four weeks after mating, as well as at term around day 58 or 59. These procedures will enable the veterinarian to discover any troubles that can occur during pregnancy, as well as alert him to when the whelping is going to take place. Knowing this, he can plan to provide service if needed during off hours.

Bitches that are difficult to breed, miss pregnancies or have irregular reproductive cycles should have physical exams including laboratory tests to determine the cause of the trouble. These tests may be expensive but a lot of breeding and sterility problems due to sub-par physical condition, hormonal imbalances or hypo-thyroidism can be corrected. If a valuable bitch is restored to her normal reproductive capacity, the reward more than offsets the medical costs.

Another important thing to remember about whelping and raising puppies is to keep them warm enough. This means at room temperature of 75° to 80° for the first ten days to two weeks until the puppies are able to generate their own body heat. Be sure the dam keeps them close and leave a light burning at night for the first week so she won't lose track of any of them or accidentally lie on one of them. Chilling remains the biggest cause of death of newborn puppies. Other causes are malnutrition, toxic milk, hemorrhage, viral and bacterial infections. Blood type incompatibilities have been introduced lately as causes of trouble.

Consultation with your veterinarian concerning these and any other breeding problems you've had in the past may result in the solution of these problems. This may result in larger litters with a higher survival rate.

Providing medical services from cradle to grave is the slogan of many veterinarians, and rightly so these days.

The average life expectancy for our dogs these days is about 13 years. Sad to say, this is a short time compared to our life span. Larger breeds historically do not live as long as the medium sized or smaller breeds. However, I think that with proper care the Rottweiler should be expected to reach this age.

Approaching Old Age: This is a good time to speak about approaching old age and some of the problems we can expect during that time. Arthritis, kidney disease, heart failure and cataracts are probably the most common ailments in older dogs. When our pet has trouble getting up in the morning or jumping up or going upstairs, you can bet that some form of a joint problem is starting. Giving two enteric coated aspirin tablets three times a day for five days very often will help these individuals. This dosage is for a Rottweiler but dosages adjusted downward for smaller breeds can also be helpful. This is relatively free of side effects and as long as nothing else is wrong, your dog will get a bit of relief.

Signs of kidney weakness are excessive drinking, inability to hold urine through the night, loss of weight, inappetence, more than occasional bouts of vomiting and diarrhea. If any of these signs present themselves, it would be worthwhile to have a checkup. Very often corrective measures in diet and administering some medicine will result in prolonging your dog's life.

Some form and degree of heart failure exists in a lot of older animals. Symptoms of chronic congestive heart failure consist of a chronic cough, especially after exercise, lack of stamina, lethargy, abdominal enlargement and labored breathing at times. If diagnosed and treated early in the disease, many heart patients live to a ripe old age.

Cataracts form in the lenses of most, if not all, old dogs. They are a part of the normal aging process. Total blindness from cataracts is generally not produced for a long time. Distant and peripheral vision remain satisfactory for the expected life span of the dog. Rarely is total blindness produced by these aging cataracts before the dog's life expectancy is reached. There is no effective treatment for cataracts other than their surgical removal, which is contraindicated in the older patient that has any vision at all left.

Hip Dysplasia: It is becoming more evident that most of the arthritis in older dogs in large breeds is the result of problems in bone growth and development when the individual was very young. Problems such as panosteitis, hip dysplasia, elbow dysplasia and osteochondrosis dessicans all are often precursors of arthritis. In Rottweilers, according to information from the Orthopedic Foundation for Animals, these joint and bone problems are quite prevalent.

At any rate, hip dysplasia seems to be a developmental condition and not a congenital anomaly. It is thought to be an inherited defect, with many genes being responsible for its development. Environmental factors also enter into the severity of the pathology in the hip joints. Nutrition during the growth period has been an important factor. Over-feeding and over-supplementation of diets have caused an abnormal growth rate with overweight puppies. These individuals, if they were susceptible to hip dysplasia in the first place, show more severe lesions of hip dysplasia. Restricted feeding of growing dogs is necessary for normal bone growth and development.

Signs of hip dysplasia vary from one dog to another but some of the more common ones are: difficulty in getting up after laying for awhile, rabbit-like gait with both rear legs moving forward at the same time when running, lethargy, walking with a swaying gait in the rear legs. In a lot of cases, a period of pain and discomfort at nine months to one year old will resolve itself and even though the dysplasia is still there, most of the symptoms may disappear.

It is recommended that dysplastic individuals not be bred, that they not be allowed to get overweight and that they should have moderate exercise.

The selection of dysplastic-free individuals for breeding stock eventually will result in the production of sounder hip joints in affected breeds. This factor, of course, is only one consideration in the breeding and production of an overall better Rottweiler.

Ch. Srigo's Xclusive v Kurtz taking five points from the Puppy Bitch Class by going Best of Opposite Sex over "specials." Felicia Luburich, breeder, owner, handler.

GLOSSARY

To the uninitiated it must seem that fanciers of purebred dogs speak a special language all their own. In a way, we do. To help make this book more comprehensive to our readers, following is a list of terms, abbreviations and titles which you will run across through our pages which may be unfamiliar to you. We hope they will lead to fuller understanding.

Ahnentafel: Pedigree issued in Germany by the ADRK Stud Book Office, furnished to the breeder of a litter to be transferred to the owners of each of the individual puppies. A very comprehensive and detailed paper which includes information such as a critique of the beauty and quality of the parents and grandparents based on the examination required for breeding approval at a Club test, condition of the hip structure, training and beauty titles, plus registration numbers. For the third and fourth generation the critique is omitted, but the registration number and titles earned are included.

Allegemeiner Deutscher Rottweiler Klub (ADRK): The Rottweiler Club of Germany.

American Kennel Club (AKC): The official registry for purebred dogs in the United States. Publishes and maintains the Stud Book. Handles all litter and individual registrations, transfers of ownership, etc. Keeps all United States show award records, issues championships and other titles as earned, approves and licenses dog show and obedience judges, licenses or issues approval to all point dog shows or recognized match shows. Creates and enforces the rules and regulations by which the breeding, raising, exhibiting, handling and judging of purebred dogs in this country is governed.

Almond Eye: The shape of the tissue surrounding the eye creating an almond shaped appearance.

Angulation: The angles formed by the meeting of the bones, generally referring to the shoulder and upper arm in the forequarters and the stifle and hock in the hindquarters.

Bad Bite: One in which the teeth do not meet correctly according to the specifications of the Breed Standard.

Bad Mouth: Can refer to a wryness or malformation of the jaw or to incorrect dentition.

A dog to guard you and your possessions, and to offer faithful family membership, is the Rottweiler. Ch. Graudstark's Luger is a typical member of the breed. A show winner and family dog, he is a source of much pleasure to his owners, Mark and Pat Schwartz of Noblehaus Rottweilers.

Opposite:
Ch. Radio Ranch's Hombre v Axel, owner-handled by
Pamela Weller, Radio Ranch Rottweilers.

Balance: Symmetry and proportion. A well-balanced dog is one in which all the parts appear in correct ratio to one another. Height to length. Head to body. Neck to head and body. Skull to foreface.

Beefy: Refers to an overly muscular condition or overdevelopment of the shoulders or hindquarters or both.

Best of Breed: The dog or bitch that has been adjudged as being the individual most closely conforming to the Standard in competition with others of its breed.

Best of Opposite Sex: The dog or bitch adjudged Best of Opposite Sex to the one adjudged Best of Breed. If the Best of Breed is a dog, then the Best of Opposite Sex will be the bitch adjudged best of all of that sex in competition. If the Best of Breed is a bitch, then the same holds true conversely.

Best of Winners: The dog or bitch selected as the better of the two between the Winners Dog and the Winners Bitch.

Best in Show: The dog or bitch chosen as the best representative of any dog in any breed at a particular dog show.

Bitch: The correct term for a female dog.

Bite: The manner in which the dog's upper and lower teeth meet.

Blocky: Squareness or cube-like formation of the head.

Bloom: A word used to describe coat in good condition.

Blue Ribbon Winner: Dog that wins first prize at an A.K.C. Point Show.

Brace: Two dogs, or a dog and a bitch, similar in appearance and moving together in unison.

Breed: Purebred dogs descended from mutual ancestors refined and developed by man.

Breeder: A person who breeds dogs.

Breeding Particulars: Name of the breeder, names of the sire and dam, date of birth, sex.

Brisket: The forepart of the body between the forelegs and beneath the chest.

Brood Bitch: A bitch used primarily for breeding.

Bull Neck: A muscular, short and heavy neck.

Bundesseiger (BS): A German title for a dog selected as champion at an individual club's show at one show each year.

CACIB: A Challenge Certificate offered by the Federation Cynologique Internationale towards a dog's championship.

Canine: Dogs, jackals, wolves or foxes as a group.

Canines: The four sharp pointed teeth at the front of the jaws, two upper and two lower, flanking the incisors, often referred to as fangs.

Carpals: Pastern joint bones.

516

Castrate: To neuter a dog by removal of the testicles.

Cat-foot: The short-toed, round, tight foot similar to that of a cat.

Champion (CH): A dog or bitch that has won a total of fifteen points including two "majors," the total under not less than three judges, two of which must have awarded the "majors," at A.K.C. member or licensed dog shows.

Character: Appearance, behavior and temperament considered correct in an individual breed of dog.

Cheeky: Cheeks which bulge or are rounded in appearance.

Chest: The part of the body enclosed by the ribs.

Chiseled: Clean cut below the eyes.

Choke Collar: A chain or leather collar that gives maximum control over the dog. Tightened or relaxed by the pressure on the lead caused by either pulling of the dog or tautness with which held by the handler.

Chops: Pendulous, loose skin creating jowls.

Cloddy: Thickset or overly heavy or low in build.

Close-coupled: Compact in appearance. Short in the loin.

Coarse: Lacking in refinement and elegance.

Coat: The hair which covers the dog.

Condition: A dog said to be in good condition is one carrying exactly the right amount of weight, whose coat looks live and glossy, and that exhibits a general appearance and demeanor of well being.

Conformation: The framework of the dog, its form and structure in terms of its compliance to the breed standard.

Coupling: The section of the body known as the loin. A short-coupled dog is one in which the loin is short.

Cow-hocked: When the hocks turn inward at the joint, causing the hock joints to approach one another with the result that the feet toe outward instead of straight ahead.

Crabbing: A dog moving with his body at an angle rather than coming straight on. Otherwise referred to as sidewheeling or sidewinding.

Crest: The arched portion of the back of the neck.

Cropping: The cutting of the ear leather, usually performed to cause the ear to stand erect.

Crossing Action: A fault in the forequarters caused by loose or poorly knit shoulders.

Croup: The portion of the back directly above the hind legs.

Cryptorchid: An adult dog with testicles not normally descended. A disqualification as dogs with this condition cannot be shown.

Dam: Female parent of a dog or bitch.

Ch. Bergluft's Centa (Ch. Axel vom Schwanenschlag ex Ch. Drossel vom
Molzberg) finishing title at Mahoning Shenango Kennel Club, 1975, under
Judge, Council Parker. Mrs. Dorit S. Rogers, owner.

Opposite:
Ch. Centurion's Che Von Der Barr, born Jan. 24, 1974,
by Ch. Northwind's Barras ex Ch. Rodsden's Ericka
Diedre Dahl. Breeder, Leslie Fulcher. Che finished
his championship at 14 months of age, owner-
handled, undefeated in his class, gaining his final
points at the Colonial Rottweiler Club Specialty,
Trenton Kennel Club, 1975. His career included 132
Bests of Breed and 26 Group placements, including
five Working Group firsts. Among his Best of Breed
wins was the Medallion Rottweiler Club second Independent Specialty, 1977, with an entry of 100. Bred
very selectively Che has 10 finished champion progeny to date, with at least four more pointed and
many more too young to have been shown at this
time. Che belongs to Josef and Donna Hedl, Chicago, IL.

519

Deadgrass: A dull tan color.

Dentition: Arrangement of the teeth.

Dewclaws: Extra claws on the inside of the legs. Should generally be removed several days following the puppy's birth. Required in some breeds. Unimportant in others. Sometimes a disqualification. All according to the individual breed Standard.

Dewlap: Excess loose and pendulous skin at the throat.

Diagonals: The right front and left rear leg make up the right diagonal. The left front and right rear the left diagonal. These diagonals move in unison as the dog trots.

Dish Faced: The condition existing when the tip of the nose is placed higher than the stop.

Disqualification: A fault or condition so designated by the Standard of the breed. Judges must withhold awards at dog shows from dogs having disqualifying faults, noting the reason for having done so in the Judges Book. The owner may appeal this decision, but a disqualified dog cannot again be shown until it has been officially re-instated by the American Kennel Club.

Distemper Teeth: A condition so called due to its early association with dogs having suffered from this disease. It refers to discolored, badly stained or pitted teeth.

Divergent Hocks: Frequently referred to as bandy legs or barrel hocks as well. The condition in which the hocks turn outward, thus the exact opposite of cowhocks.

Dock: Shortening a tail by cutting it.

Dog: A male of the species. Also used to collectively describe male and female canines.

Dog Show: A competition in which dogs have been entered for the purpose of receiving the opinion of a judge based on their conformation to individual breed standards.

Dog Show, All Breeds: A dog show in which classification may be provided, and usually is, for every breed of dog recognized by the American Kennel Club.

Dog Show, Specialty: A dog show featuring one breed only. Specialty Shows are generally considered to be the showcases of a breed, and to win at one is an especially coveted honor and achievement as competition at them is particularly keen.

Domed: A condition of the top-skull by which it is rounded rather than flat.

Double Coat: A coat that consists of a harsh, weather resistant protective outer coat, with a short, soft undercoat providing warmth.

Downfaced: A downward inclination of the muzzle towards the tip of the nose.

Down in Pastern: A softness or weakness of the pastern causing a pronounced variation from the vertical.

Drag: A trail having been prepared by dragging a bag, generally bearing the strong scent of an animal, along the ground.

Drawing: The selection of dogs by lot that decides in which pairs they will be run at a specific field trial.

Drive: The powerful action of the hindquarters which should equal the degree of reach of the forequarters.

Drop Ear: Ears carried drooping or folded forward.

Dry Head: One exhibiting no excess wrinkle.

Dry Neck: A clean, firm neckline free of throatiness or excess skin.

Dudley Nose: Flesh colored nose.

Elbow: The joint of the forearm and upper arm.

Elbow, Out at: The condition by which the elbow points out from the body rather than being held close.

Even Bite: Exact meeting of the front teeth, tip to tip with no overlap of the upper or lower jaw. Generally considered to be less serviceable than a scissors bite, although equally permissible or preferred in some breeds.

Ewe Neck: An unattractive concave curvature of the top area of the neckline.

Expression: The typical appearance of the breed as one studies the head from the front. Should be alert and interested.

Eyeteeth: The upper canines.

Faking: The artificial altering of the natural appearance of a dog. A highly frowed upon and unethical practice which should lead, upon discovery by the judge, to instant dismissal from competition in the show ring.

Fallow: Pale cream, fawn or yellowish red coloring.

Fancier: A person actively involved in the sport of purebred dogs.

Fancy: Dog breeders and others actively involved with purebred dogs comprise the Dog Fancy.

Fangs: The canine teeth.

Fawn: A brownish or reddish color.

Federation Cynologique Internationale (F.C.I.): A canine authority representing numerous countries, principally European, all of which consent to certain practices and breed identification.

Feet East and West: An expression describing toes on the forefeet turning outward rather than pointing straight ahead.

Fiddle Front: Caused by elbows protruding from the desired closeness to the body, resulting in pasterns which approach one another too closely and feet turning outward, the whole resembling the shape of a violin.

Ch. Srigo's Madchen v Kurtz doesn't at all object to winning in the rain!
Here she is taking Best of Opposite Sex, Felicia Luburich, handling.

Opposite:
Above left: Ch. Nick vom Silahopp, the sire of 12
champions, imported from Germany and owned by
Bill and Dorothea Gruenerwald, Colorado Springs,
CO. **Above right:** What is more fun than a baby Rott-
weiler? Maybe *two* of them! From the family of
Karen and Alan Kruse. **Below:** This is one of the
many outstanding Rottweilers bred by Jack and Dr.
Evelyn Ellman of von Stolzenfels fame. Ch. Heiko
von Ammerberg, CD, belongs to von Ammerberg
Kennels, by whom he was purchased from the
Ellmans. Sired by Ch. Centurion's Che von der Barr
out of Ellmans' famed Ch. Cosi von Steigstrassle.

Finishing a Dog: Refers to completing a dog's conformation championship or its obedience title.

Flank: The side of the body through the loin area.

Flat Bone: Bones of the leg which are not round.

Flat-sided: Ribs that are flat down the sides rather than slightly rounded.

Flews: A pendulous condition of the inner corners of the upper lips.

Flying Ears: Ears correctly carried dropped or folded that stand up or tend to "fly" upon occasion.

Flyer: An especially promising or exciting young dog.

Flying Trot: The pace at which you should never move your show dog in the ring. All four feet leave the ground briefly during each half stride, making correct evaluation of the dog's normal gait virtually impossible.

Forearm: The front leg from elbow to pastern.

Foreface: The muzzle of the dog.

Front: The forepart of the body viewed head on, including the head, forelegs and shoulders, chest and feet.

Futurity: A competition for dogs less than twelve months of age for which puppies are nominated at or prior to birth. Usually highly competitive among breeders.

Gait: The manner in which a dog travels.

Gallop: The fastest gait. Never to be used in the show ring.

Gay Tail: Tail carried high.

Goose Rump: Too sloping (steep) in croup.

Groom: To bathe, brush, comb and trim your dog.

Gun Shy: Fear of the sight or sound of a gun.

Hackles: Hair on the back and neck that rises when the dog is aroused.

Hackney Action: High lifting of the front feet, in the manner of a hackney pony.

Ham: Muscular development of the upper hind leg.

Handler: A person who shows dogs in bench competition or in obedience, either as an amateur (without pay) or a professional (who is paid for the service).

Harefoot: An elongated paw, like the foot of a hare.

Harness: A leather strap worn around the chest and shoulders with a ring at the top above the withers.

Haw: A third eyelid or excess membrane.

Heat: The period during which a bitch can be bred.

Heel: A command ordering the dog to follow close to the handler.

Hindquarters: Rear assemblage of the legs.

Hock: The joint between the second thigh and the metatarsus.

Hocks Well Let Down: Expression denoting that the hock joint should be placed low towards the ground.

Honorable Scars: Those incurred as a result of working injuries.

International Champion: A dog awarded four CACIB cards at F.C.I. Dog Shows.

Incisors: The front teeth between the canines.

Jowls: Flesh of lips and jaws.

Judge: Person making the decisions at a dog show, obedience trial or field trial. Must be approved and licensed by A.K.C. in order to officiate at events where points towards championship titles are awarded.

Kennel: The building in which dogs are housed. Or used in reference to a person's collection of dogs.

Knee Joint: Stifle joint.

Knitting and Purling: Crossing and throwing of forefeet as dog moves.

Knuckling Over: A double jointed wrist, sometimes accompanied by enlarged bone development in the area, causing the joint to double over from the dog's weight.

Layback: Used in two different ways. A) As descriptin of well angulated shoulders. B) As description of a short-faced dog where pushed-in nose placement is accompanied by undershot jaw.

Leather: The ear flap.

Leistungssieger (LS): A German title awarded to a Working Champion. The top obedience title in Germany, awarded only at one show during each year.

Level Bite: The teeth of both jaws meeting exactly even, tip to tip. Also referred to as pincer bite.

Level Gait: A dog moving smoothly carrying topline level.

Lippy: Lips that are pendulous or do not fit tightly.

Loaded Shoulder: Those overburdened with excessive muscular development.

Loin: Area of the sides between the lower ribs and hindquarters.

Lumber: Superfluous flesh.

Lumbering: A clumsy, awkward gait.

Major: A Winners Dog or Winners Bitch award carrying with it three, four or five championship points in accordance with the number of dogs or bitches defeated.

Match Show: An informal dog show where no championship points are awarded and entries can be made upon arrival. Excellent practice area for future show dogs and for the inexperienced exhibitor as the entire atmosphere is relaxed and congenial.

This is the third Rottweiler Brace to win Best Brace in Show in the United States, and the first in an area other than the West Coast. Am., Can. Ch. Donnaj Vt. Yankee of Paulus CDX (left), and Ch. Donnaj Crusader, owner-handled by Mrs. Donald S. Marshall at the Eastern Dog Club event, December 1979.

Opposite:
Ch. Panamint Fancy Viking, one of the outstanding Rottweilers for which Barbara Dillon's Panamint Kennel is so respected and admired.

Mate: To breed a dog and a bitch together.

Milk Teeth: The first baby teeth.

Miscellaneous Class: A class provided at A.K.C. Point Shows in which specific breeds may compete in the absence of their own breed classification.

Molars: Four premolars are located on each side of the upper and lower jaws. Two molars exist on each side of the upper jaw. Three on either side below. Lower molars have two roots. Upper molars have three roots.

Molera: Abnormal ossification of the skull.

Monorchid: A dog with only one properly descended testicle. This condition is a disqualification for competition at A.K.C. dog shows.

Nick: A successful breeding that results in puppies of excellent quality is said to "nick."

Nose: Describes the organ of smell, but also refers to a dog's talent at scenting.

Obedience Trial: A licensed Obedience Trial is one held under A.K.C. rules at which it is possible to gain a "leg" towards a dog's Obedience Title.

Obedience Trial Champion (O.T.CH.): Denotes that a dog has attained Obedience Trial Championship under A.K.C. regulations, having gained a specified number of points and first place awards.

Oblique Shoulders: Shoulders angulated to be well laid back.

Occiput: Upper back point of skull.

Orthopedic Foundation for Animals (OFA): This organization reads the hip radiographs of dogs and certifies the existence of or freedom from hip dysplasia. Board Certified Radiologists read vast numbers of these films each year.

Out at Shoulder: A loose assemblage of the shoulder blades.

Oval Chest: Deep with only moderate width.

Overshot: Upper incisors considerably overlap the lower incisors.

Pacing: A gait in which both right legs and both left legs move concurrently, causing a rolling action.

Paddling: Faulty gait in which the front legs swing forward in a stiff upward motion.

Pads: Thick protective covering of the bottom of the foot. Serves as shock absorber.

Paper Foot: Thin pads accompanying a flat foot.

Pastern: The area of the foreleg between the wrist and the foot.

Perro (Companion) Dog (P.C.): Mexican Companion Dog.

Pigeon Chest: A dog with a protruding, short breastbone.

Pigeon-Toed: Toes which point inward, as do those of pigeons.

Police Dog: Any dog that has been trained to do police work; generally members of certain Working Breeds.

Put Down: To prepare a dog for the show ring.

Quality: Excellence of type and conformation.

Racy: Lightly built, appearing overly long in leg and lacking substance.

Rangy: Excessive length of body combined with lack of depth through the ribs and chest.

Reach: The length with which the forelegs reach out in gaiting, which should correspond with the strength and drive of the hindquarters.

Register: To record your dog with the American Kennel Club.

Registration Certificate: The paper you receive denoting your dog's registration has been recorded with A.K.C., giving the breed, assigned name, names of sire and dam, date of birth, breeder and owner along with the assigned Stud Book number of the dog.

Reserve Winners Dog or Reserve Winners Bitch: After the judging of Winners Dog and Winners Bitch, the remaining first prize dogs or bitches remain in the ring where they are joined by the dog or bitch that was second in the class to the one awarded Winners Dog or Winners Bitch, provided he or she was defeated by only that one dog or bitch during the previous course of that day's judging. From these a Reserve Winner is selected. Should the Winners Dog or Winners Bitch award subsequently be disallowed owing to any technicality, the Reserve Winner is then automatically moved up to Winners in the A.K.C. records, and the points awarded to the Winners Dog or Bitch then transfer to the Reserve Winners Dog or Bitch. This is a safeguard award, for although it happens infrequently, should the winner of the championship points be found to have been ineligible to receive them, if there were not a Reserve Winner they would then be wasted points.

RO: Followed by numbers and placed after the name of a dog or bitch, signifies that the animal has been tested for hip dysplasia and found to be clear.

Roach Back: A convex curvature in the top line of the dog.

Rocking Horse: An expression used to describe a dog that has been overly extended in forequarters and hindquarters by the handler, i.e., forefeet placed too far forward, hind feet pulled overly far behind, making the dog resemble a child's rocking horse. To be avoided in presenting your dog for judging.

Rolling gait: An aimless, ambling type of action correct in some breeds but a fault in others.

Saddle Back: Of excessive length with a dip behind the withers.

Srigo's Incredible Is the Word had to be content with a second to his litter brother in the Colonial Rottweiler Club Specialty.

Opposite:
Am., Can. Ch. Erich Von Paulus, by Ch. Lyn-Mar Acres Arras von Kinta ex Ch. Amsel Von Andan, CD, is the magnificent Rottweiler discovered in the New Haven dog pound by Barbara Baris and Thomas Condon.

531

Schweizer Sieger (SS): A champion in Switzerland.

Scissors Bite: In which the outer side of the lower incisors touches the inner side of the upper incisors. Generally considered to be the most serviceable type of jaw formation.

Second Thigh: The area of the hindquarters between the hock and the stifle.

Septum: The vertical line between the nostrils.

Set Up: To pose your dog in position for examination by the judge. Sometimes referred to as stacking.

Shelly: A body lacking in substance.

Shoulder Height: The dog's height from the ground to the withers.

Sire: The male parent.

Skully: An expression referring to a coarse or overly massive skull.

Slab Sides: Flat sides with little spring of rib.

Soundness: Mental and physical well being.

Spay: To neuter a bitch by surgery.

Specialty Club: An organization devoted to sponsoring an individual breed.

Stance: The natural position a dog assumes in standing.

Standard: The official description of the ideal specimen of a breed. The Standard of Perfection is drawn up by the Parent Specialty Club, approved by its membership and by the American Kennel Club, and serves as a guide to breeders and to judges in decisions regarding the merit or lack of it in individual dogs.

Stifle: The joint of the hind leg corresponding to a person's knee cap.

Stilted: Refers to the somewhat choppy gait of a dog lacking rear angulation.

Stop: The step-up from nose to skull. An indentation at the juncture of skull and nasal bone.

Straight Behind: Lacking angulation at the hock joint.

Straight Shouldered: Lacking angulation of the shoulder blades.

Stud Book: In which the breeding records of all recognized breeds are recorded.

Stud Dog: A male dog that is a proven sire.

Substance: Degree of bone size.

Swayback: Weakness in the topline between the withers and the hipbones.

Tail Set: Placement of the tail at its base.

Tracking Dog (T.D.): A title awarded to a dog that has passed an A.K.C. Licensed or Member Club Tracking Test.

Tracking Dog Excellent (T.D.X.): An advanced Tracking Degree.

Team: Generally four dogs.

Throatiness: Excessive loose skin at the throat.

Topline: The dog's back from withers to tailset.

Trail: Hunting by following a ground scent.

Trot: The gait in which the dog moves in a rhythmic two beat action, right front and left hind foot and left front and right hind foot each striking the ground together.

Tuck Up: A noticeable shallowness of the body at the loin, creating a small-waisted appearance.

Type: The combination of features which make a breed unique, distinguishing it from all others.

Utility Dog (U.D.): Advanced level of Obedience Degree.

Utility Dog Tracking (U.D.T.): Indicates that the dog has gained both Utility Dog and Tracking Dog Degrees.

Undershot: The front teeth of the lower jaw overlap the front teeth of the upper jaw.

Upper Arm: The foreleg between the forearm and the shoulder blade.

Walk: Gait in which three legs support the body, each foot lifting in regular sequence one at a time off the ground.

Walleye: A blue eye, fish eye or pearl eye, caused by a whitish appearance of the iris.

Weedy: Lacking in sufficient bone and substance.

Well Let Down: Short hocks, hock joint low to the ground.

Weltsieger (WS): World Champion. One show a year in Germany is designated as being the show at which this World Championship will be awarded.

Wet Neck: Dewlap or superfluous skin.

Wheaten: Fawn or pale yellow color.

Wheel Back: Roached back, with topline considerably arched over the loin.

Winners Dog or Winners Bitch: The awards which are accompanied by championship points, based on the number of dogs defeated.

Withers: The highest point of the shoulders, right behind the neck.

Wry Mouth: When the lower jaw is twisted and does not correctly align with the upper jaw.

The lovely Rottweiler bitch, Tobar's Ruffian, with eight points including both majors at two years old, belongs to Barbara Baris and Thomas Condon. Handled by Marty Silver.

Opposite:
Ch. Lyn-Mar Acres Cassie v Amri, by Ch. Lyn-mar Acres Arras v Kinta from the English bitch, Plaissance Irma. Mrs. Margaret Walton, owner, Lyn-Mar Acres Kennels, Mt. Holly, NJ.

BEST OF
WINNERS
PHOTO
BY *Graham*

535

Index

Names of the dogs listed herein are those of only the earliest German dogs that formed the foundation of the breed in the United States, or those of the very first winners in conformation or obedience competition in the earliest years of Rottweiler exhibition in this country.

Ch. Bethel Farms Apollo winning Best of Breed at the Greater Fredericksburg Kennel Club, 1980, from Judge Herman Fellton, handled by Bert Halsey. Apollo is head man at Bethel Farms, owned by Bob and Lavinia Bolden, co-owned with Radio Ranch.

Opposite:
Ehrenwache's Andernach winning under Maurice Baker, handled by Joy Brewster. Andernach is a member of the Medallion Rottweiler Club's Hall of Fame and was dam of six champions, including Am., Bda. Ch. Adler von Andan, CD. Owned by Anna Tilghman, Centreville, MD.

BEST OF
OPPOSITE

GILBERT PHOTO

540